CALIFORNIA CENTRAL COAST RAILWAYS

RICK HAMMAN

Otter B Books

California Central Coaast Railways

copyright 1980 By Rick Hamman

Revised and updated, 2002

Otter B Books
1891 Sixteenth Avenue
Santa Cruz, CA 95062

ISBN 1-890625-00-0

Manufactured in the United States of America

Originally published in 1980 by Pruett Publishing.

Library of Congress Cataloging in Publication Data

Hamman, Rick, 1944-
California central coast railways.

Bibliography: p.
Includes index.
1.   Railroads-California—Santa Cruz Co.—History.
2.   Lumber trade—California-Santa Cruz Co.—History.
3.   Santa Cruz Co., Calif.—Industries—History.
I.   Title.

HE277I.C2H35   385'.09794'71   80-14664

Cover captions: Front: The Molino Timber Company's Shay #1 is seen crossing the "Lone Tree" trestle in Aptos Creek Canyon.

Back (black & white): Southern Pacific Consolidated steam locomotive #2706 in 1951. It subsequently spent over 40 years in the playground at Watsonville's Ramsey Park, and is now being restored for active duty.

Back (color): Recently, Roaring Camp & Big Trees Narrow Gauge Railroad's "Dixiana" Shay #1 (older than the Shay on the front cover) crosses Dear Creek Trestle under full power.

Acknowledgments

Although an Author is given the credit for writing a book, most who have done so realize they are only a small part of the whole. Therefore, in recognition of same, I would personally like to thank all of the following individuals and organizations to which I am indebted:

Jean Andrus
Mrs. Alberta Aram
Ted Benson
Muriel Bently
Gerald M. Best
Rita Bottom
Alfred Brumit
Ben Cahill
Elizabeth Castro
Francis J. Carney
Pat Crowley
George Cress
William Connell
Lawrence W. Coffee
Carol Champion
Chapin A. Day
Maxine Freeman
Basil N. Frykland
H.W. Fabing
Shirley Gleason
Mr. Gaffney
George Garrety
Dan Glass
Bob Gray
Malcolm Gaddis
Barbara Giffen
Howard Griffths
H.W. Gove
Barbara Hartman
John Humphrey
William Harry
Mrs. W.P. Hendricks
John Holm
Jimmy Hartman
Paul Johnston
Henry Johnson
Blair Kough
Anne Locatelli
Vince Locatelli

Mrs. George Ley
Warren "Skip" Littlefield
Ray Larsen
Mrs. Leask
Jan Magruder
Jerry McCabe
Father Mickevitt
Rita Mattei
Sue Meschi
Mrs. Betty Mudd
J.E. O'Lague
Mrs. Alverda Orlando
Ralph Peterson
Arlene Pike
Mary Peckham
Ed Pohle
Stan Stevens
Jack Sinnott
Harold Soper
Mr. & Mrs. Albert Snyder
Lena Sonognini
Al Schadel
Louis Stein Jr.
Anne Schaefer
Doug Sarmento
Vernon Sappers
Ted Toft
Mrs. Carl Tyree
Valarie Tobitt
Karm West
Bill Wulf
Bob Willey
Ted Wurm
Tom Wilson
Mrs. Ruth Wilson
John A. Wood
B.H. Ward
Donald Younger
W. Zinsmaster

Granite Rock Company
Society of California Pioneers
San Jose Historical Museum
Lone Star Industries
Santa Cruz Lumber Company
San Francisco Zoological Society
Santa Clara County Dept. of Public Works
Roaring Camp & Big Trees Narrow Gauge RR
California State Dept. of Parks & Recreation
United States Geological Survey, Menlo Park
California State Library, Sacramento
The Redwood Keg
Boulder Creek Historical Society
The Tumbleweed
Southern Lumber Company
Charles Ford Company
Southern Pacific Company
National Association of Retired Railroad
    Employees, Santa Cruz Chapter
Colt Industries LTD.
San Benito County Clerks Office
Santa Cruz County Clerks Office
Santa Clara County Clerks Office
San Mateo County Clerks Office
Santa Cruz County Octagon Museum
Pajaro Valley Historical Association
Palo Alto Historical Society
Santa Cruz City Museum
University of Santa Clara
De Anza College, Historical Collection
Stanford University Library
University of Calif. Santa Cruz, Special
    Collections
University of Calif. Berkeley, Bancroft
    Library
California State Public Utilities Commission
Seaside Company

In addition to the above, I would also especially like to thank Vic Itani for all his priceless maps; Santa Cruz County Historian Extraordinaire, Harold Van Gorder for the loan of his memories and photographs; Woods Mattingley for the gracious use of his notes and photographs on Aptos Creek covering over 1500 hours of research; the late Fred Stoes for being in the right place at the right time with a camera; Bruce MacGregor for his friendship, sharing of photographic wealth, and commitment to the preservation of Santa Cruz County history (a subject which has consumed much of our joint time); and finally, my family: daughters Laurel, Julie and Karen and their mother, Carol, for their unending patience and understanding of this time consuming project.

— Rick Hamman

This book is dedicated to the Memory of the late Fred C. Stoes: A Craftsman, A Fireman, A Rail Historian, A Photographer, and most of all, A Friend. Without his help, his guidance, and his kindness, this book would have never happened ...

Contents

List of Maps

Introduction

Some fifty miles south of the Golden Gate entrance to San Francisco Bay and forty miles north of the City of Monterey lies a small strip of unique California Central Coast land, 15-miles in width and 34-miles in length, known as Santa Cruz County. It is unique because it is one of the smallest counties in the state and because it has some of the most diverse geographic conditions found in California. This diversity divides itself into four very different geographical areas: the North Coast, the San Lorenzo River Basin, the Central County, and the Pajaro (Pa'ha'ro) Valley.

The North Coast is an area stretching from the southern city of Santa Cruz to a northern point on Ano Nuevo Bay, which is bounded on the west by the Pacific Ocean and on the east, two to three miles inland, by the 2,000 to 2,500 foot Ben Lomond Mountain Range. Because of the somewhat cool and moist weather conditions brought on by the proximity of the ocean and because most of this land is bottom land from the mountain, the area has always been good for farming such things as artichokes, Brussels sprouts, lettuce, spinach and other similar crops. Because of previous ocean history the area is rich in sandstone-limestone type deposits with some of the finest Portland Cement coming out of the Davenport locality and sand from the Wilder Creek.

To the east of the North Coast is the very different San Lorenzo River Basin. Here one finds a densely forested watershed area where monsterous Redwood Trees, large Ponderosa and Fir Pine Trees, and stately Tanbark Oak and twisted Madrone trees abound in numbers too many to count. The area, known as the San Lorenzo Valley, is bounded on the west by the Ben Lomond Mountain Range and, twelve miles further inland, by the 3,000 foot Santa Cruz Mountain range, which extends all along the eastern boundary of the County. It is here that because of these two

ranges and the effect they have on storms coming in off the sea that 60-80 inches of rain falls in the average year. All of this water, once used, is funneled out of the Valley through a narrow seven mile granite gorge known as the San Lorenzo Canyon and is returned to the sea at the City of Santa Cruz. Also here, because of previous ocean history, are large sandstone-limestone type deposits from which, among other things, comes some of the finest glass sand on the west coast.

The Central County is an area of rolling mountains which extend from the Santa Cruz Range to the Monterey Bay. It is the land of the Soquel, much like the San Lorenzo, but more open. Here not only are dense forests found, but also large tracts of fertile hills well suited to the growing of apples, cherries, plums, apricots and grapes. It is also the land of the Aptos and the Valencia where the density of forested mountain areas extend deep into hidden canyons some of which are 1,200 feet in depth and only three-eighths of a mile across. Closer to the ocean and Monterey Bay the Central County is similar to the North Coast with rich farmlands, many of which until recently produced sugar beets.

The southern portion of the County is perhaps in its own way the most interesting of all. Just eight miles from the dense forests is a lush, flat, fertile, garden known as the Pajaro Valley through which the river of the same name brings its precious water from the lower Santa Clara and San Juan Valleys to the Monterey Bay. From this land comes a major portion of the Country's strawberries and the world famous Watsonville Apples. It, like most of the coastal land, has a moderate climate and is well suited to the fruit tree and the plow.

It was in 1791 when the Franciscan Monks first tried to bring their brand of Spanish civility to this area. On a hill overlooking Monterey Bay and the mouth of the San Lorenzo river they founded the

Mission of Santa Cruz (Holy Cross). In 1846 the United States flag went up over the area and it soon became part of the County of Santa Cruz and the State of California. With the beginning of westward expansion and the burgeoning of the nearby City of San Francisco and surrounding Bay Area the hidden mineral, agricultural and board-foot lumber wealth of Santa Cruz County soon came into demand. In short order, settlers, squatters and homesteaders moved in and papermills, powdermills, small lumbering operations and farms were started. By 1865 business and commerce had become established and local entrepreneurs began to see a need for a railroad connection with the outside world to help generate larger profits from product and produce.

By 1870 the dream of a rail connection had become a reality with the arrival of the Southern Pacific at Pajaro near Watsonville. Now that a railroad was established the development — some would later call it desecration — of the County could begin. For the next fifty years hundreds of millions of board-feet of lumber would leave the canyons of the North Coast, the San Lorenzo River Basin, the Aptos and Valencia Creeks, and the upper Soquel to help build the west. Limestone operations and Cement plants would be established, powdermills would be expanded, and the farming areas of the County would develop to feed the increasing western population; new crops like the sugar beet would be started to compete with the Cuban cane sugar which was then supplying most of the country's needs, and the County because of the endless miles of beautiful seashores and green forests would become a major tourist attraction for the nearby San Francisco Bay Area population.

Of course, to do all this work a network of railroads would be developed throughout the County, extending into every little gulch and canyon, small mountain town, and rich agricultural valley. The first railroads would be what the local citizenry called the Narrow Gauge (three feet from rail to rail). As the trains became larger and the demand for more capacity increased, the Standard Gauge of today (four feet eight and one half inches between the rails) or what the locals called the "Broad Gauge" came into being. Before it would all be over almost every corner of the County would see some type of a railroad operation.

With the coming of the 1930's and 1940's, the automobile, the bus, and the truck would play a more dominant role in the movement of goods and people. The logging of the first growth trees in the Santa Cruz Mountains would come to an end and the many small railroads and unnecessary branch lines would be abandoned. While freight railroading would continue within the County, passenger service would be a thing of the past. By the end of the 1970's, the once large railroad network would be reduced to a single freight train per day operation from the Southern Pacific Coast mainline at Watsonville Junction (Pajaro) to the City of Santa Cruz.

Today life and the development, good or bad, of Santa Cruz County continues. The population is now some 200,000 persons with more coming. Major portions of the County which at one time were vast logging and lumbering operations are now devoted to State Parks. Logging does continue however, although in a much saner, ecological manner, with over 15,000,000 board-feet of lumber produced each year; sand and gravel leaves the County by the truckload; and, farming is still a very dominant industry within the County.

To look at the future of Santa Cruz County, of course, is to look at its past. Because this is a railroad book we will confine its boundaries to include only those things which pertain to the history of railroading within the County and the Industries which supported it. Rather than give a spike and tie account of each of the many miles of abandoned lines it is hoped that this book will be an anthology of all lines, written from the point of view of the life and times of those who lived it. In that vein there will be much use of personal experiences including those of this writer. It is my hope that as you read this you can come away with some of the, while not necessarily important at least, interesting history of the county. May you find as much enjoyment in reading this book and looking at its pictures as I did in writing the text and discovering each print.

Sincerely,
Rick Hamman, 1980

Twenty-two years have come and gone since this book was first written and published, and a lot of tonnage has rolled over the rails in that time. During the early 1970's this book was primarily a research project done out of love for the subject. In the interim, your author has gone from detached observer to active participant in railroad affairs. This involved helping formulate the San Lorenzo Valley General Plan — Transportation; being a past member of the Santa Cruz County Transportation Policies Committee; a member of RAIL, a joint counties (Santa Clara and Santa Cruz) political action group to Revive Alternative Inter-county Lines; consultant and crew person for the Santa Cruz, Big Trees & Pacific Railway; and, President of the Eccles & Eastern Railroad. Thus, the discerning reader may notice a more impassioned tone in the new Chapter 7 written for this revised and updated edition. Joyfully, railroading and railroad history continues to be a viable and intersting arena.

Again sincerely,
Rick Hamman, 2002

S.C.V.M.L. Co. abandoned right-of-way north of Boulder Creek. — Rick Hamman

We linger on the threshold of the past
Longing our footsteps to retrace,
And since our thoughts go where our feet cannot,
How oft we live in some remembered spot,
Or speak again to some beloved face ...

M.B. Hoffman — 1872

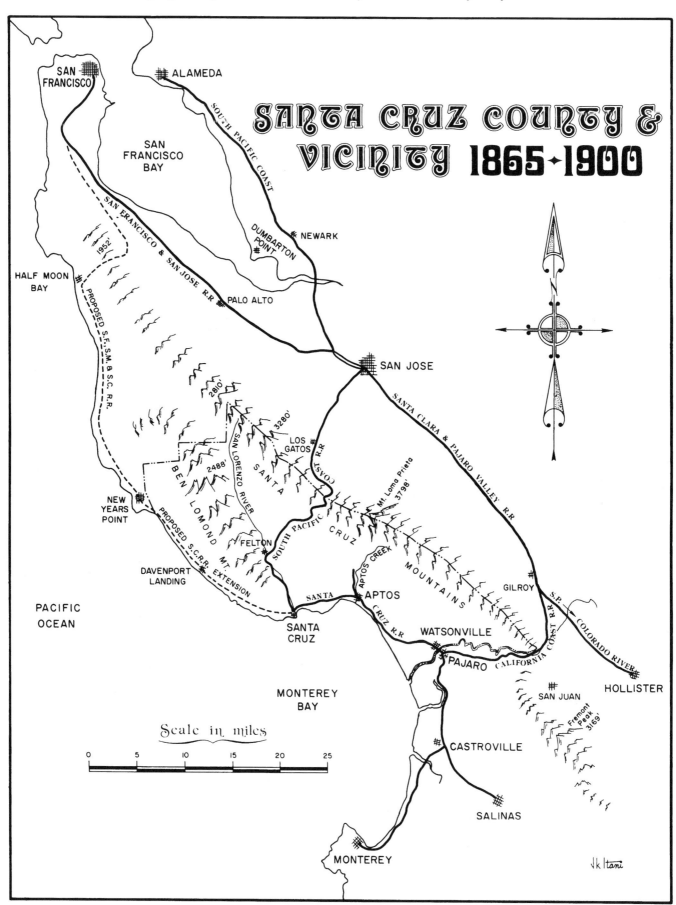

SANTA CRUZ COUNTY & VICINITY 1865-1900

1

The Expanding Dream: Rails to Santa Cruz

The pioneer has completed his mission, let us of this generation, achieve ours. The pioneer started from Eden westward, with the rising sun. His long and weary journey across the seas and continents, with famine and fame now ended, has halted before the shores of the Pacific. He has pitched his tent, to behold the sun go down beyond the western main. His mission accomplished, he now heralds the crossing of empire; he beholds it moving majestically along its mighty pathway by the procession of nations with their arms and arts following on where he has trod, to subdue nature, spread the agencies of civilization over the plains and the mountains; he beholds each yielding to an irresistible attraction, and becoming a part of the mighty whole. One by one, he sees them grow to become servants to man, until the railway and the telegraph, weary of the slow movement that time begets, speed on in their mission to do the errands of progress, and reach the goal of linking the continents and the seas with lightning and steam; he hails their arrival on the golden shores of California. For he knows that the all-conquering army of civilization, moving like a mighty ocean tide, will soon follow to bear him company; cities begin to rise, and arts and industry engage to subdue the wilderness; until nature and civilization unite to consummate the purposes of man in harmony with Providence ...

L.U. Reavis Esq.
November, 1872
Inland Monthly

The California Coast Railroad Company

Santa Cruz, June 23rd, 1867: Yesterday, a joint stock company was formed by some of our local men of means to build a railroad from Gilroy to Watsonville. The name of said road is to be the California Coast Railroad Company. Its capital stock, to be sold to the general public at large, is listed at $400,000. Directors of the Company are N.W. Chittenden, Charles Ford, A.L. Sanborn, A.W. Blair, T.D. Alexander, and F.A. Hihn. As most of you are aware, the management of the San Francisco and San Jose Railroad Company, which recently began service between the same named cities, has also incorporated the Santa Clara and Pajaro Valley Railroad Company to extend their road to Gilroy. Once this line and the California Coast Railroad are completed, and they most assuredly will be, we will have our first rail connection to San Jose and San Francisco. Soon, that long awaited dream of local development and economic prosperity will be just around the corner for all of us ...

Ever since the passage of the Homestead Act in 1862, the local citizens had dreamed of the day when the vast and varied untapped resources of Santa Cruz County could be shipped in quantity to the expanding humanity that was moving west. Already, over 300,000 settlers had crossed the nation to California and Oregon to lay claim to their 160-acres of FREE land, and many more thousands were coming. Soon, there would be untold quantities of lime, lumber, powder, and farm produce needed to feed this hungering expansion. For Santa Cruz County, this would mean hundreds of millions of board feet of timber to be harvested, mountains to be gouged for their mineral deposits, fields to be cultivated, and orchards to be grown. Once the California Coast railroad was completed to Gilroy, freight would no longer have to be shipped via slow steamer to San Francisco or even smaller, and slower, freight wagon over the Santa Cruz Mountains. Now a mainline railway, providing unlimited capacity service, would be available to ship any and all quantities of freight to any point that was served by rail in the state.

By February of 1868, construction had begun on the Santa Clara and Pajaro Valley Railroad. It was predicted that the line would be completed and in

Thought to be one of the earliest photos of Santa Cruz, this view depicts the city as it looked in 1856. — Courtesy: Santa Cruz City Museum Collection

operation to Gilroy by April of the following year. At the same time, the California Coast Railroad was well on its way to selling the necessary stock subscriptions which would legally allow its construction to begin.

In March of 1868, the San Francisco and San Jose Railroad and the Santa Clara and Pajaro Valley Railroad were reorganized under the name of the "Southern Pacific Railroad Company." Previously, on July 27th, 1866, the 39th Congress had passed an Act approving the construction of the Atlantic and Pacific Railroad from St. Louis, Missouri to San Francisco. A significant clause in the Act provided that:

> The Southern Pacific Railroad Company incorporated under the laws of the State of California on December 2, 1865, is hereby authorized to connect with said Atlantic and Pacific Railroad formed under this Act, at such a point near the boundary line of the State of California, as they shall deem most suitable for a railroad line to San Francisco.

It was the Southern Pacific's plan, once it reached Gilroy, to build south to Hollister and Tres Pinos, through the San Benito Valley, across the Diablo range of Coastal Mountains, and into the San Joaquin Valley. Upon entering the San Joaquin Valley, the line

would continue on to Bakersfield, cross over the Tehachapi Mountains to Mohave and traverse the desert to the Atlantic and Pacific Railroad at the Colorado River. Thus, the stage was set. Once the California Coast was completed to Gilroy from Watsonville and the S.P. extended from San Jose, Santa Cruz County would have its first rail line to San Francisco. In addition, once the Southern Pacific connected with the Atlantic and Pacific at the California border, the county would also have the capability of nation-wide distribution for all of its products and produce.

Sometime in mid-1868, the BIG FOUR of Central Pacific fame began to take a keen interest in the proposed operation of the Southern Pacific. If it was ever to connect with the Atlantic and Pacific as planned, the Central Pacific would have an unfriendly rival road into San Francisco. This, the powerful gentlemen concluded, would just not be in the best interests of the Central Pacific and its stockholders. As a result, Hopkins, Crocker, Stanford, and Huntington, through some shrewd stock manipulations and backroom politics with the city fathers of San Francisco — who owned a large chunk of the S.P. — acquired a controlling interest in the road. It wasn't long before the Southern Pacific was tucked neatly in the fold of the Central Pacific portfolio and the Atlantic and Pacific would have to look elsewhere for a connection into California. With this change, came the prospect for Santa Cruz County that, while they would still have a San Francisco connection once the California Coast railroad was completed, they would no longer have a transcontinental link.

On March 13th, 1869, the Southern Pacific Railroad began operations between San Jose and Gilroy. The local people of Watsonville knew that, with any luck at all, it would only be a matter of time before they too would hear the sounds of the steel wheel on the route of the iron compass. But, what about Santa Cruz? Surely a line should also be built between the two cities. After all, most of the prime timber canyons and agricultural belts would intersect at such a road, not to mention the lime and powder industries which were already well underway. To that end, a meeting was called, a committee was formed to study all possibilities, and the findings were to be presented as soon as possible.

On Saturday evening, October 30th, 1869, the second meeting of the now official Railroad Committee took place in the Court House in Santa Cruz. In attendance were all of the committee members and interested men of means of the area. After hours of debate over the findings presented, some of which included building a railroad over the Santa Cruz Mountains to San Jose rather than around them through Watsonville, conclusions were drawn. Most present agreed that a railroad to Watsonville was the only practical route at present, and that such a road should commence as soon as possible. In addition, it was recommended that the county issue bonds and loan its credit to the amount of $12,000 per mile to promote such a road. Also, it was asked of and agreed to by the committee that that portion of the California Coast Railroad which would operate in said County also receive the same financial assistance from the County.

The year is 1857. The steamship Santa Cruz, belonging to Davis & Jordan is seen underway in an artist's rendering. Before the railroads came ship was the way you traveled from the Central Coast. A typical trip to San Francisco left the Davis & Jordan Santa Cruz wharf at 10:00PM. By 6:00AM the next morning you were in the City by the bay. A full day's business could be conducted in San Francisco with the ship returning to Santa Cruz at 2:00PM, arriving shortly before midnight. Round trip fare: $5.00. — Courtesy: UCSC Special Collections

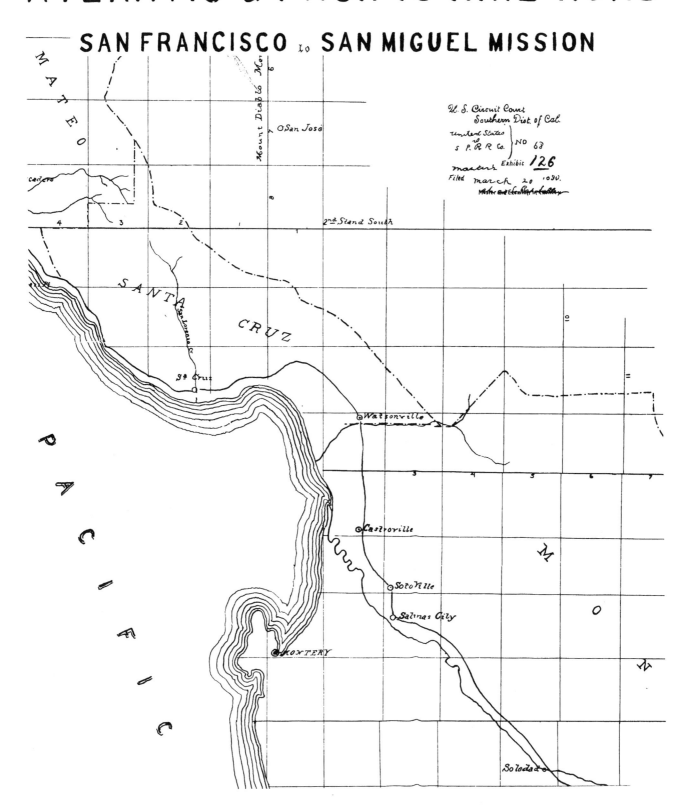

MAP
of
ATLANTIC & PACIFIC RAIL ROAD
SAN FRANCISCO to SAN MIGUEL MISSION

MATEO

Mount Diablo Mer.

O San José

Cadero

2nd Stand South

U. S. Circuit Court
Southern Dist. of Cal.
United States
S. P. R R Co.) NO 68
masters   Exhibit 126
Filed March 20 1890.

SANTA

CRUZ

S.to Lorenzo C.

S.t Cruz

PACIFIC

Watsonville

Castroville

Soto Ville

Salinas City

MONTERY

Soledad

The original Atlantic & Pacific Railroad line as surveyed through Santa Cruz County. — Courtesy: Stanford University Library

In early January of 1870, F.A. Hihn, a member of the Railroad Committee, a wealthy Santa Cruz man of ability, and a current State Assemblyman, introduced a railroad bill to authorize the County of Santa Cruz to aid in the construction of railroads and other roads in said county. Included in the bill was a rail line from the eastern county line to the town of Santa Cruz and two branch lines, one up Soquel Creek into the Hylands and the other up the San Lorenzo River to Felton. Interestingly enough, Hihn had heavy financial interests in both the areas which would be served by such branch lines. Another interesting point was that Hihn made no mention in the bill of the California Coast Railroad Company in which he also held a heavy financial interest. Could he perhaps have known something he wasn't revealing?

The California Southern Railroad Company/Southern Pacific

On January 22, 1870, the management of the Southern Pacific, realizing the potential for profit in Santa Cruz and Monterey Counties, incorporated under the name of the California Southern Railroad Company to build a 45-mile line from Gilroy via Watsonville to Salinas. Shortly thereafter, on March 5th, Hihn changed the railroad bill to include the California Southern, and the California Coast Railroad disappeared into eternity.

April 9th, 1870; Sacramento News Release: The bill (A.B. 264) authorizing Santa Cruz County to vote on a proposition to aid a railroad from the Pajaro River to the town of Santa Cruz in the amount of $210,000 total was defeated in the legislature.

The news was shattering to the local people in Santa Cruz. "Where do those fancy-pants gentlemen of politics get off deciding what we will and won't do locally!" Some of the local press blamed Hihn because of his financial interests in the outcome of the bill. Others felt it was the pressure of the big counties competing for funding that caused the failure of the bill. One fact was certain: the economic resources of the county still lay nurturing in the womb of the future and many of the local citizens were beginning to wonder if, and when, the baby was ever going to be born.

With the defeat of the railroad bill, the possibility of any financial assistance from the county to help pay for a railroad from Gilroy to Watsonville had all but disappeared. As a result, the Southern Pacific shelved its plans to build to Salinas until such time as financial conditions would warrant said construction. At first, the S.P. had decided to go ahead and construct the line out of their own pocket, but after evaluating their financial condition and their current legal problems with the United States

Congress, they decided against it.

Sometime during the Summer of 1870, at the insistence of the Atlantic and Pacific management, Congress asked the Southern Pacific to declare its intentions with regard to its previous commitments to build to the California border. Was the S.P. now in fact controlled by a rival operation, namely the Central Pacific, or was the railroad still as it had originally been incorporated? In answer to this question, on October 12th, 1870, under the direction of the Big Four, the San Francisco and San Jose Railroad, the Santa Clara and Pajaro Valley Railroad, and the California Southern Railroad were officially consolidated under the new corporate banner of the "Southern Pacific Railroad Company." It was also officially recorded that the management of the Central Pacific and the management of the Southern Pacific were one and the same. So much for the Atlantic and Pacific connection into California.

Shortly after the ink had dried on the consolidation documents, it became public knowledge that the Southern Pacific had been planning all along to use its right-of-way to the Colorado River to connect with the proposed Texas & Pacific Railroad at Fort Yuma. Thus, on January 2, 1871, the S.P. began construction from Gilroy toward Hollister. By March 3rd, the date when Congress formally approved the Texas & Pacific Railroad Act, the construction of the line had begun in earnest.

It was about this time that the people in Watsonville, spurred by the local newspaper the "Pajaronian," began to grumble the same old chant, "If Watsonville is ever to make it, we must have a railroad to Gilroy." The immediate future for such a line, however, looked bleak. The Southern Pacific had all of its money and manpower tied up in construction to Bakersfield, and they weren't about to slow down for a branch line to Watsonville. At least that seemed to be the expressed sentiment. On June I st, undaunted by previous communications with the railroad, a group of prominent Watsonville citizens went to the S.P. to plead their case. Unaware of the Southern Pacific's plans, they were startled beyond comprehension when the railroad management informed them that just as soon as the line to Bakersfield had reached Hollister, a branch line would be built from Gilroy to Salinas via Watsonville and Castroville. Could this be true? Was Santa Cruz County to finally be blessed with its first real connection to the outside world?

On July 17th, 1871, all doubt was removed. Ground-breaking ceremonies were held at Gilroy for the beginning of the first railroad to Salinas via Watsonville. It was predicted by the S.P. that in just a short four months Santa Cruz County would be provided with through broad gauge freight and

Fred A. Hihn. — Courtesy: California State Library Collection

passenger trains to San Francisco.

About the only obstacle to stand in the way of the completion of the line was the crossing of the Pajaro River at the southeastern boundary of Santa Cruz County near the Chittenden Ranch. Here, a bridge 432 feet in length and 50 feet high, comprised of 82 feet of approach and four 87 1/2 foot Howe Truss sections, would be constructed to span the canyon which the Pajaro River had gouged out aeons ago. Considering that it was the largest bridge the Southern Pacific had ever constructed up to that time, it was quite a piece of engineering for such a short branch line.

Once the actual engineering and construction of the right-of-way started, the local people of Watsonville began to watch the placement of survey markers with great interest. Something was going wrong! The survey markers didn't come back across the Pajaro River such that the line would be able to pass through town on its way to Castroville and Salinas. Instead, they stayed on the south side of the river, traversing a narrow ridge near Aromas and then passing on through to Pajaro, a small community about a mile out of Watsonville. As a result, the "Pajaronian" was soon writing editorials on the woes of not having a railroad through town. Obviously, it

No number or railroad name along with similar mechanical features suggests that this locomotive, shown here at Pajaro shortly after the Southern Pacific began in 1871, is one of the original San Francisco & San Jose engines. — Courtesy: Roy Graves Collection, U.C. Berkeley, Bancroft Library

was the fault of the town fathers for not convincing the S.P. of the financial benefits available once the line was built through Watsonville. In truth, however, the Southern Pacific saw such action as a way to eliminate the necessity of two additional bridges across the Pajaro River and at the same time provide a central shipping area for the whole Pajaro Valley.

By the beginning of November, the Pajaro River bridge had been completed, the short tunnel was through at Aromas, the grading had been finished as far as Watsonville, and ties and rail were going down at an unprecedented rate. Already, Henry C. Pratt, a local boy, had been hired as the first freight agent for the new station at Pajaro. In addition, the freight warehouse adjoining the station wasn't even completed yet, and even now merchants and farmers were eagerly storing their products and produce to await shipment to an expected market.

The Santa Cruz & Watsonville Railroad Co.

Along with the local anticipation of a completed rail line by the citizens of Watsonville also came a new realization for the people in Santa Cruz. Once the Southern Pacific began operations out of the Pajaro Valley — "The Valley of the Birds" — the businessmen of Santa Cruz would no longer be able to compete with their counterparts in Watsonville. This would be especially true in the lumber and produce markets. Because of this insight, it wasn't long before the local populace of Santa Cruz, with F.A. Hihn leading the cause, began clamoring for a new railroad to Pajaro. In a short time, much to the objection of the Watsonville citizenry, the Santa Cruzans managed to ramrod a county ballot measure through, calling for a special election to vote on just such an issue.

Up until recently, such a county procedure would not have been possible. However, shortly after the State Legislature had defeated F.A. Hihn's previous railroad bill in 1870, it passed another bill, making it no longer necessary for any county in California to have prior approval before such a vote could be taken. This was done to induce the expansion of railroads throughout the state. Thus, the citizens of Santa Cruz had new leverage, and they, too, were going to have a connection with the Southern Pacific.

Already, the resentment was beginning to build between the two towns. Facts and figures, depending on whose side of the fence you were on, were being blown way out of proportion. The local people of Santa Cruz, among other things, were asking for a county subsidy of $ 100,000 to aid in the construction of the railroad. The viewpoint of the people in Watsonville on the matter was obvious. "Why should we authorize the expenditure of our hard-earned tax dollars to fund some fly-by-night railroad to Santa Cruz which won't benefit us one iota. We soon will have our own rail connection at no expense to the good tax-paying residents of Watsonville. It's clear that if Santa Cruz had anything to offer in the way of inducements to secure a railroad to its boundaries, the Southern Pacific would have certainly extended the line to there."

On November 26th, 1871, the first broad gauge train arrived in Pajaro for the return trip to San Francisco. A short two weeks later, the County of Santa Cruz voted on the issue of whether a broad gauge rail line should be established between the Southern Pacific Railroad Company at Pajaro and the City of Santa Cruz. As had been anticipated, the railroad measure won by a heavy margin in all of the precincts except those around Watsonville. Had the bill depended on the Watsonville precincts, it never would have passed.

Soon, a mad scurry was on by the local businessmen to incorporate a railroad that would meet all of the terms and conditions of the measure which had just been passed by the electorate. On January 18th, 1872, the Santa Cruz and Watsonville Railroad Company filed formal Articles of Incorporation with the Secretary of States Office in Sacramento to build a 20-mile broad gauge rail line from the town of Pajaro in Monterey County to the town of Santa Cruz in Santa Cruz County. Its capital was listed at $500,000. Its officers and directors were F.A. Hihn, President; D. Tuthill, Secretary; Anthony Elihu, W.F. Peabody, Titus Hale, and Samuel A. Bartlett.

On the same day, the Santa Cruz County Board of Supervisors awarded the contract and the $ 100,000 subsidy to the Santa Cruz and Watsonville Railroad Company to build said road. The only conditions in the contract of any significance were that the construction would start within six months and be completed within two years. Also, in order to show good faith, five miles of right-of-way would have to be completed before the first portion of the $5,000 per mile subsidy would be awarded.

Finally, after a false start and some disagreeable politics, Santa Cruz County was going to have its long awaited rail connection with the Southern Pacific at Pajaro. Soon, the necessary stock would be subscribed to, and construction could begin. At least that's the way everybody in the County of Santa Cruz saw it.

The Atlantic and Pacific Railroad/ The San Francisco & Atlantic Railroad

All during the months of February and March, while the Santa Cruz and Watsonville management were busily trying to secure the necessary stock subscriptions, the S.P. was continuing construction toward the newly created Texas & Pacific. At the same time, the Atlantic and Pacific Railroad, now that it was no longer to connect with the Southern Pacific, was again trying to regain a foothold into California.

On April 26th, 1872, a delegation of St. Louis, Missouri citizens, representing the Atlantic and Pacific Railroad Company, went to San Francisco to devise ways and means for building a railroad between the two cities. The visitors consulted with the San Francisco Committee of One Hundred, a well-known commercial club of that city. The negotiations seemed to progress favorably. On May 6th, at a public conference, the Committee of One Hundred resolved to ally themselves with the Atlantic and Pacific for the purposes of building such a road. They further agreed that after three selected members of the group had completed a thorough inspection of the Atlantic and Pacific, and found it to be satisfactory, a contract would be signed, formalizing negotiations.

Sometime toward the end of May, the three members from Missouri telegraphed back to San Francisco and confirmed that everything was substantially correct as presented. They recommended that proceedings commence at once to begin the railroad between the two cities.

"We're gonna be on the mainline of a transcontinental railway between St. Louis and San Francisco." This was the elated cry of the local populace when the news spread that on June 1st, 1872, the San Francisco and Atlantic Railroad Company had filed articles of incorporation to construct a railroad from San Francisco via Santa Cruz and the Coast to the Atlantic and Pacific Railroad at the California border. So much for raising funds to help build the miniscule Santa Cruz and Watsonville Railroad, now that a mainline railway would be passing through both Watsonville and Santa Cruz.

In a few short years, if all went according to schedule, the Atlantic and Pacific and the San Francisco and Atlantic Railroads would bridge the East with the West, and Santa Cruz County would find itself on the mainline of a transcontinental railroad. Already, the local residents had seen the A&P surveyors at work within the county, and most were looking forward with great anticipation to the coming event. Unfortunately for the local folks, their railroad future was once again resting at the mercy of outside interests. To think that the Central Pacific and the Southern Pacific directorate were going to sit idly by while a rival railroad built a competing line into San Francisco was pure folly.

By the end of July, the San Francisco and Atlantic Railroad had already obtained subscriptions in the amount of $3,900,000. Likewise, many more millions had been committed. It was at this point that the Central

Pacific management decided it was about time to stop this severe threat by exerting all the financial and political influence they could muster among the Committee of One Hundred. Before they were through, the Committee's personal loyalties were so badly divided on the issue of financial support for the A & P Railroad that the entire project looked hopeless.

In order to salvage its interest in obtaining a route into California, and at the same time deal with the problems generated by the Committee of One Hundred, the Atlantic and Pacific management abandoned all ideas of coming into San Francisco and instead turned its eyes toward San Diego. As history would later tell it, in 1884 the Atlantic and Pacific (Atchison, Topeka & Santa Fe) would finally complete its transcontinental link to San Diego and later to Los Angeles. In addition, another line would be built up the San Joaquin Valley into Oakland with adjoining ferry service to San Francisco. So much for the dream of a transcontinental railroad through Santa Cruz County.

The Santa Cruz Railroad

To the Committee on Railroads:
The Atlantic and Pacific R.R. Co. having changed their route, and the owners of the Southern Pacific Railroad Co. not complying with their promises to build a wide gauge railroad, from Santa Cruz to Watsonville, we are forced to conclude that if we want a railroad we must build it ourselves. A wide gauge railroad from Santa Cruz connecting with the Southern Pacific Railroad near Watsonville cannot be built for less than $25,000 per mile, or say $500,000. In addition to the subsidy granted for this purpose, amounting to $100,000, the further sum of $400,000 would have to be raised by private subscription and loans. This is impossible.

We must therefore build a cheaper road. A narrow gauge 3 foot wide Railroad can be built from the Pajaro depot to Santa Cruz, for $12,500 per mile with equipment, or, say $250,000, and can be continued further along the coast to the northern line of our county, without equipment, at a cost of $12,500 per mile, or say $250,000 more ... It is therefore proposed that a company be organized to build a Narrow Gauge Railroad, commencing on the line of the Southern Pacific Railroad, near the Pajaro River, and running thence along or near the survey of the Atlantic and Pacific Railroad, along or near the coast to the northern Boundary Line of our county, a distance of about 40 miles. That county aid be solicited to the amount of $6,000 per mile, such aid to be in lieu of the subsidy already granted ...

F.A. Hihn
Santa Cruz, Sept. 4th, 1872

Thus, the prospects of a railroad between Santa Cruz and Pajaro were once again left to the fate of the local citizens. For years they had dreamed of that day when finally a railroad would put Santa Cruz County on the map. Up to now, it had not come to pass. Once again, F.A. Hihn, as he had done so many times in the past, was championing the cause for such a railroad. Would it turn out to be a reality this time? Only the future tide of events would tell.

On October 14th, 1872, a group of prominent citizens, representing the now famous Railroad Committee of Santa Cruz, set out to do their own survey over the old Atlantic and Pacific course. It was their intention to try to determine the necessary facts for a new bond election. By October 25th, the survey was completed. On November 5th, the plan as presented by Hihn was approved by a two-to-one majority in a general election. On November 8th, the Board of Supervisors voted unanimously in favor of the immediate construction and subsidy of said railroad.

Now, all that was left to fulfill the long-standing dream was for a railroad company to step forward and sign on the dotted line. Once again a mad scurry was on among the local men of means to meet the necessary requirements for filing articles of incorporation for such a railroad company. Soon, Santa Cruz County would, once and for all, have its very own railroad.

By the first of the new year, 1873, all was in readiness for F.A. Hihn and Associates to step forward and sign the contract to start construction. The year looked bright with promise. Everywhere, the local gentry were taking a good long look toward the County's economic future. All that could be seen and predicted was prosperity, prosperity, and more prosperity; perhaps, too much prosperity.

One early winter's day in late January, an unsuspecting visit was paid to the city of Santa Cruz by none other than Leland Stanford himself. It seemed that he, too, along with some of his railroad friends, sensed the prosperity in the air. So much so, in fact, that he announced to the local press that the Southern Pacific Railroad Company would very shortly be building a broad gauge branch line to the city of Santa Cruz from Pajaro. So much for the narrow gauge railroad of Fred Hihn. Once again an outside interest was laying greater opportunity at the doorstep of the County, and perhaps this time it would come to something. Unlike many of the previously unsuccessful attempts, the local residents had more faith in the Southern Pacific. History had already proven that when they and their corporate management set out to do something, it usually came to pass.

In early February, the Southern Pacific brought in their best surveying and engineering crews to ascertain all of the pertinent data so necessary for the

This is the only known view of the Monterey & Salinas Valley Railroad. It depicts the early yards and depot as they appeared in 1875 at Monterey. Had plans and dreams worked out, the M. & S.V. would have been part of a San Francisco to Los Angeles narrow gauge system.
— Courtesy: Fred Stoes Collection

Henry Clark Peckham poses in his baggage-expressman Santa Cruz Railroad uniform along with his brother. — Courtesy: Marjorie Peckham Collection

construction of the line. Toward the end of the month, after the initial surveying and engineering had been completed, Leland Stanford returned to announce that just as soon as sufficient capital had been raised, both from independent investors and County subsidy, construction would begin.

In the spring of 1873, an event was to take place across the nation that would, more or less, decide the immediate future of railroading in Santa Cruz County. For years the country had been suffering under the heavy financial burden incurred during the Civil War. In addition, railway construction fever had taken the nation's conscience by storm. Every little hamlet in every state, including Santa Cruz, wanted to be on the mainline of a railroad. As a result, many railroads would be built without any thought to their financial soundness. Also, overtrading on the stock market, inflated credit, and fluctuating currency were dealing severe blows to the nation's money market. Likewise,

vast new farm lands had been opened in the Midwest that required great expenditures of capital to make the operations successful. With the opening of these new lands would also come an economic change in the agricultural centers of trade between the farmers in the East and their new competitors in the Midwest. Finally, the economics of the nation could take no more. All of these monetary woes came together at the same point in time and created one of the worst financial panics this nation was ever to see.

Shortly after the Panic began, the local residents of Santa Cruz County received the ominous news that, due to the financial conditions of the time, Leland Stanford had been unable to obtain the necessary credit to construct the branch line; in addition, the word was received that construction of the Southern Pacific's mainline via Hollister would be discontinued until such time as the railroad was in a better financial position.

By the first of April, it had become obvious that if there was ever to be a railroad between Santa Cruz and Pajaro, or anywhere else in the county for that matter, the local residents were going to have to pay for it. Because times were hard and because Santa Cruz County was deep in an economic depression, once again a narrow gauge rather than a broad gauge railroad was proposed to meet the demands of the local citizens. On May 24th, 1873, a prospectus for the Santa Cruz Railroad Company was offered to the local residents by F.A. Hihn and "Associates." In a short two months, $100,000 had been subscribed to, and the railroad had met all of the requirements to become a legal entity with which the county could conduct business.

It must have been a very somber and yet anxious time for Fred A. Hihn on that early August 4th, 1873, Monday morning shortly before he and the Board of Supervisors were to meet in session to sign contractual agreements between the Santa Cruz Railroad Company and the County of Santa Cruz. In reflection, he probably pondered the not too successful events of the past which had led him to this particular point in history.

In 1861, he had organized a group of men to build a railroad up the San Lorenzo River into the rich timberlands of the San Lorenzo Valley. After finally getting construction underway in 1868, the line was only to be halted by a lawsuit involving the property of Henry Cowell. In 1869, he had tried to organize the California Coast Railroad between Gilroy and Watsonville. Later, when its successor, the Southern Pacific, came along, he threw all of his legislative weight behind its proposed operation only to have his efforts defeated in Sacramento. In 1871, he again brought together a group of Santa Cruz businessmen to construct the Santa Cruz and Watsonville Railroad. It was his hope that, once built, the S.P. would take it over. He never got that chance. This time, the Atlantic and Pacific got in the way of his plans. Now, after one slight pause while the Southern Pacific finally tried to do some fancy footwork, he once again was before the people representing a new railroad company. Would this one make it? Would rails ever be laid down and a train run between Santa Cruz and Pajaro? Was this finally the moment which he had worked so hard for or was there to be yet another?

The time had come. It was now 10:00 a.m., and the Santa Cruz County Board of Supervisors had been called to order. After a rather lengthy public hearing had been completed, the Board voted unanimously to enter into a contract with the Santa Cruz Railroad Company to build the 40-mile road from Pajaro, through the City of Santa Cruz, to a point in the southeast corner of the New Years Rancho on the northern boundary of the county. Included in the

contract were the following conditions: First, the roadbed shall consist of ties of redwood well ballasted; second, the rails shall be of at least 30-lb. iron on the average and shall be appropriately spliced with fishplates of adequate strength. Lastly, a subsidy of $6,000 per mile, or $240,000 total shall be granted by the County of Santa Cruz to the Santa Cruz Railroad to aid this construction. The only condition placed on the subsidy was that five miles of rail must be laid from the San Lorenzo River and a construction train run over them before an initial grant of $30,000 would be issued.

The beginnings of the Santa Cruz Railroad were now a reality. Ten days after the signing of the contract, Mr. Binney and his crew of surveyors and engineers were hard at work on the first portion of the right-of-way, charting its final location between Santa Cruz and Pajaro. It had been decided by management that the second portion of the right-of-way between Santa Cruz and New Years Point would not be undertaken until such time as the first portion had been completed.

It was estimated that because the final alignment of the right-of-way would depend on just where the route would cross the 20 some odd creeks, rivers, and sloughs found between Santa Cruz and Pajaro, the survey would take over two months to complete. Unfortunately for the railroad, Santa Cruz County's many streams and tributaries descended to the coastline in such a fashion as to give the land the complexion of an old washboard. Thus, the problem which confronted Mr. Binney was to try to survey a right-of-way as level as possible through this washboard and still stay within the financial means of the railroad. Previously, in February, when the Southern Pacific had initially surveyed their broad gauge route, they had decided to go inland along the stage road to avoid this washboard problem. When Mr. Binney first started the survey for the Santa Cruz Railroad, he also considered this route as the best alignment for the right-of-way to take. After thoroughly examining the topography of the area, however, and taking into consideration the fact that he was building a narrow gauge rather than a broad gauge railroad, he abandoned this plan in favor of a route which hugged the Monterey Bay coastline. While this coastline alignment would require much more compensation for the washboard effect, in the long run it would prove to be an economically wiser choice. Unlike the S.P.'s survey whose final inland alignment would have crested at a point 440 feet above sea level, the route chosen by Mr. Binney reached a maximum elevation of only 160 feet. In addition, by choosing this alignment, he would save the railroad over two and a half miles of unnecessary right-of-way.

By the 1st of November, the final alignment had

been selected and grading and construction were ready to begin. All in all, the right-of-way would be 21.36 miles in length when finished. It would have a ruling grade of no more than 2% except for a few short distances where a grade of 2.5% would be encountered. While there would be no requirements for tunnels along the line, eight rather substantial bridges would have to be erected before the route could be opened for business.

Toward the end of November, events were starting to happen which were causing people's cynicism to give way to guarded anticipation. For the first time, the local folks were beginning to believe that, once and for all, there really was going to be a railroad in Santa Cruz County. Already, the Santa Cruz Railroad had awarded a contract to a mill in the East for most of the necessary rails, switch frogs, spikes, nails, and iron. In addition, some of the local lumbering concerns had been awarded contracts to supply the square timber and planking needed for the trestles and culverts along the right-of-way. Also, redwood ties were beginning to be stockpiled for construction use. The new year of 1874 was fast approaching, and most people knew it wouldn't be long before the sights and sounds of a construction train would be bestowed upon the county.

The Santa Cruz Sentinel
Friday, December 29th, 1873
(S.C.R.R. No. 1)

The first rail was laid today and the first car was placed upon the track at Wood's Lagoon ... Built by the Santa Cruz Foundry, it is painted dark red on the side and on the side is inscribed S.C.R.R. No. I ...

Interestingly enough, there were those in the county who did not share the local enthusiasm found in Santa Cruz, Soquel, and Aptos. When the residents of Watsonville found out that the Santa Cruz Railroad - a railroad which they as a voting group had not initially wanted, and now one on which they were required to spend all of their hard-earned county tax dollars - was not going to pass through town, public sentiment was anything but enthusiastic. It seems that the Watsonville City Council had voted against giving the S.C.R.R. a street franchise through town to the Pajaro River. As a result, the railroad had decided the final alignment of the right-of-way into Pajaro would be through the San Andreas Gulch and across the Pajaro River about a half-mile west of Watsonville. This meant that the line of the railroad would be along the right bank of the Pajaro River and not near or through Watsonville on its way to the interchange point with the Southern Pacific.

The explanation offered by the railroad's management concerning this change in plans was that it would allow for the possibility of future expansion into a three-county narrow gauge system. It was their stated intention that the line, once into Monterey County, could be extended to Moss Landing and the Monterey and Salinas Valley Railroad as soon as the financial means to do so became available. Thus, by crossing the Pajaro River closer to the coast, the railroad would be able to establish such a connection. As of now, it looked like nothing would change this projected plan. The final alignment of the right-of-way had been selected, and Watsonville was to be circumvented.

With the coming of the Summer of 1874, construction of the S.C.R.R. was well underway. Four miles of used "T" rail had been purchased from the Sutro Tunnel Company Railroad in San Francisco, and it was now being spiked down from the San Lorenzo River to Camp Capitola. Bridge-builder Tom Carter had begun construction of the many trestles, and construction superintendent Whelferling had his Chinese track crews hard at work on the grading of the line. All was in readiness for the first major shipment of rail to arrive from the East. Unfortunately for the Santa Cruz Railroad, such was not to be their good fortune.

Shortly after the heavily laden ship *The John Bright* had left the Eastern Seaboard with its cargo of rail bound for Santa Cruz, it sailed into a fierce summer storm off the coast of Brazil. Unable to cope with the pounding waves and the hurricane-force winds, it broke up and sank. As could be guessed, its cargo was a total loss. While the accident would most certainly delay the construction of the railroad, management was relieved that the loss had not imposed any additional financial burden on the company. As a practical course of business, the rail had been insured for plus ten percent. Therefore, it was simply a matter of getting a duplicate order of rail dispatched from the East as soon as possible.

Within three to four months, a second ship, *The Whittier* set sail for Santa Cruz with a duplicate order of rail. Everything was going fine until somewhere off the coast of Brazil, *The Whittier* caught fire. Fortunately, the ship's crew was able to extinguish the fire and get the ship into the port of Montevideo with its cargo intact. Unfortunately for the S.C.R.R., the ship would have to be tied up for almost four months while the necessary repairs could be made to those areas that had been severely damaged by the fire.

This was a crushing blow to the company, for it meant that the construction of the line, with the exception of the grading and bridge building, would have to be halted until late in the summer of 1875. Also, because they had not yet laid five miles of track,

15

it meant the Company would receive no financial assistance from the County to help pay for the work already completed. In order to alleviate the company's cash-flow problems and at the same time continue construction, management was compelled to place a third order for rail with the more expensive San Francisco Rolling Mills. It was expected that, with any luck at all, the rail would arrive by the following February.

Meanwhile, in mid-October, the S.C.R.R. was to receive its first locomotive. It was a dinkey little five-ton 0-4-0 puffer belly, appropriately named "The Betsy Jane." It had been designed by Mr. Becker of Santa Cruz and built in the shops at San Francisco. While it was small in comparison to the S.P. broad gauge locomotives that had brought it to Pajaro, it was large in the minds of the local folks who first saw it placed on the tracks at Wood's Lagoon. Here, after so many anxious years of waiting, sat the first real sign of progress and productivity for Santa Cruz County. Surprisingly, there was really no pomp and circumstance involved with its arrival, as most people had seen bigger steam donkeys pass through town; once, however, it began to shuttle its little construction train back and forth along its narrow gauge right-of-way, it soon became the local topic of conversation.

It should be noted at this point that while most of the people of Watsonville had resigned themselves to not being on the mainline of the Santa Cruz Railroad, there was still a lot of back-door grumbling and politicking going on about the issue. Increased pressure was being put on the Board of Supervisors concerning the matter, and many of the town's residents felt that they had a good chance of persuading the railroad to change its route with regard to Watsonville.

On December 9th, 1874, the Santa Cruz Railroad, anxious to win public approval and at the same time interested in acquiring the initial portion of the county's bonds, operated its first construction train over five miles of completed right-of-way. The run consisted of "The Betsy Jane" pulling some makeshift work cars, loaded with local dignitaries and representatives of the press, over the route from the San Lorenzo River to the other side of Camp Capitola and back. With the conclusion of the round-trip, the operation was deemed a success, and the completion of the line looked forward to at the earliest possible date.

Now that the first five miles of track had been completed and a construction train run over them, the railroad requested that the county deliver the first $30,000 in bonds. It was at this point that the local businessmen of Watsonville made their first calculated move. In two separate actions, one by Charles Ford and one by William Patterson, taxpayers suits were filed in Superior Court. One contended

that the Santa Cruz Railroad had not lived up to the stated terms and conditions of the August 4th, 1873, contract with the county. It charged that the contract stated the railroad was to pass "near" the town of Watsonville. The suit alleged that half a mile was not "near." The second suit claimed that since the Act of April 4th, 1870, empowering local boards of Supervisors to issue bonds for the development of railroads within their respective counties, had recently been rescinded by the Legislature, the contract was no longer valid. As a result, the suits jointly requested that the bonds be withheld until such time as they were resolved. The Courts, pending final deliberations, agreed with the requests and issued an injunction withholding the bonds.

Without the first and subsequent bonds from the county, the Santa Cruz Railroad would be financially against the wall. Realizing this, Hihn, Spreckels, and others, meeting in private sessions with the local politicos of Watsonville, agreed to reroute the railroad near town. Since that time when the first street franchise had been turned down, the local folks of Watsonville had had a change of heart. Now they realized the railroad could be very beneficial to their future. Thus, when a second request for a street franchise was filed with the City Council, it was unanimously approved. With the City of Watsonville now on the narrow gauge line, the suit involving proximity to town was dropped. The other suit however, involving the county tax subsidy was not such an easy matter.

Ever since the incorporation of the S.C.R.R., there had been those people in the Watsonville area who were dead set against any County subsidy for said railroad, no matter what. This situation, of course, generated much ill will between communities. As a result, it would be almost a year before the litigation, brought on by the change in state law concerning county railroad subsidy, would be ruled on in favor of the railroad. Not knowing this ahead of time, Hihn, Spreckels, and other stockholders would have to pony up the rest of the monies to complete the line out of their own pockets. This, while uncomfortable, was done.

In early February of 1875, the rail necessary to complete the line to Pajaro arrived from San Francisco. From then on, it was only a matter of how fast the track could be laid down and the right-of-way completed. By February 25th, six miles of track had been laid down from Santa Cruz to the Valencia Creek bridge; on March 20th, "The Betsy Jane" crossed Aptos Creek for the first time and pulled into Aptos; on April 17th, the bridge over the San Lorenzo River was completed, and connections were made on both sides. By April 24th, grading had been completed on Rincon Street, and track had been laid to the Cherry Street Depot.

All during the early months of 1875, while the S.C.R.R. was feverishly spiking down rail as fast as it could be spotted, another company, the Santa Cruz and Felton Railroad, was hard at work building a narrow gauge line up the San Lorenzo River to Felton. Once completed, the Santa Cruz and Felton would connect with the Santa Cruz Railroad at Santa Cruz and thus offer a shipping outlet for all of the timber up the San Lorenzo Canyon. As the time and the tide of events were continuing, somewhat of a competitive mood had been established between the two roads. It got to the point where each company was one-upping the other for the news headlines of the day. Finally, in a move to pacify some anxious stockholders and at the same time put the S.C.R.R. in the position of number one, management announced that on May 22nd, 1875, the grand opening of the line would be celebrated. It didn't make any difference that only eight miles of railroad, from the Cherry Street Depot in Santa Cruz to the Valencia Creek bridge at Aptos, had been finished and that the line to Pajaro would not be completed until at least January of the following year. The railroad would begin operations (of some type), and that's all there was to it. Thus, after two Grand Balls were held to celebrate the opening of the railroad, one at Claus Spreckels' fine Aptos Hotel and one a week later at the Pacific Ocean House in Santa Cruz, fifty-cent excursion service began on the weekends between town and end of track.

By the beginning of summer, work on the railroad was progressing rapidly. Unlike flat-land railroads, the construction of the Santa Cruz line was a very slow and a very arduous task. Many cuts and fills were required to get the line from one small gulch to another. At each large gulch, a trestle or bridge was required. As each gulch was encountered, progress would be slowed until it was crossed. Altogether, there would be almost a mile of trestles and bridges necessary to cross these many gulches, gullies, creeks, and rivers caused by the washboard effect of the coastline.

With the coming of August, track-laying had reached the 160-foot summit at the San Andreas Ranch. From this point on, the only obstacles between end of track and Watsonville were a short 2.5% downhill grade out of the San Andreas Gulch and a large fill required across the Watsonville Slough. As a result, it was estimated that as much as 1,800 feet of track per day would be spiked into place and that the line would be through to Watsonville by Christmas. From Watsonville, it was just a hoot and a holler across the Pajaro River to Pajaro. Already, the forms and frames for the bridge had been put in place, and with a little fair weather, it was expected that the line could be opened by January of 1876.

Santa Cruz Railroad May 1880 timetable as it appeared in the *Santa Cruz Courier Item* newspaper.

A little fair weather was something that the railroad didn't get. With the coming of the Winter rains, came some devastating torrential downpours that wiped out fill after fill and dumped tons of earth along the right-of-way and in the many cuts. From this repeated bombardment, it would take the railroad almost five more months to replace, repair, and sufficiently strengthen its right-of-way before it could finally open for business. . .

It was still rather cold for a Spring morning in May. The fog was creeping back to sea out of the Pajaro Valley, leaving portions of itself to hover over the marshy areas of the Watsonville Slough. The sun was just about to show itself over the horizon, and all over the Valley of the Birds, a new dawn was approaching. It wasn't just another day about to take place, but rather a day of importance and significance to the enduring history of the area. It was May 7th, 1876. At last, the long-awaited day had come. For the first time in the history of Santa Cruz County, a passenger train was about to run from Pajaro via Watsonville, Aptos, and Camp Capitola to Santa Cruz.

The Pacific, a brand new narrow gauge 4-4-0 steam product of Baldwin, had recently been delivered to the S.C.R.R. at Pajaro. In addition, the railroad's first coach, "the Teresa," named after F.A.

Hihn's wife, had just arrived from the Carter Brothers shops in Newark. The two sat coupled to each other on the ready track at Pajaro waiting for the day's events.

It was no coincidence that the Druids had scheduled their annual picnic at Aptos to fall on this historic day. Unlike previous years, this year's celebration was to be special. Not only was Santa Cruz County celebrating the coming of the railroad, but, also it was celebrating the first one hundred years since the birth of the Nation. Together, these two events would make this particular Sunday a day to remember for a long time to come.

By 8:30 a.m., over two hundred picnickers had lined the station platform at the Cherry Street Depot in Santa Cruz to await the departure of the first of two trains that would take them to the Druid's celebration in Aptos. There she sat, that perky little modified pot belly stove that some people called a locomotive. "The Betsy Jane" by name, with her five colorful makeshift cars, all decorated in red, white, and blue ribbons and banners, with an abundance of flowers and flags, was about ready to make the first scheduled passenger run from Santa Cruz to Aptos. Excitement was in the air. Soon it would be 9:00 a.m., and the event of the year would begin.

An early S.P. "Daisy Train" with locomotive #40 poses at Monterey about to leave for Pajaro, and finally, San Francisco. — Courtesy: Guy Dunscomb Collection

18

Passengers await the San Francisco to Salinas Southern Pacific train at Pajaro, circa 1888. — Courtesy: Roy Graves Collection, U.C. Berkeley, Bancroft Library

At the same time that "The Pacific" in Watsonville and "The Betsy Jane" in Santa Cruz were about to get underway, the local folks in Aptos were busily taking care of the last-minute details concerning the celebration that was about to follow.

At 9:30 a.m., one of the ladies who was spreading a checkered tablecloth in the picnic grounds stood still for a moment and cocked an ear toward Santa Cruz. "Here she comes," screamed the high-pitched female voice, shuddering with excitement. The wail of the whistle and the chattering of the stack could be heard as The Betsy Jane approached Aptos at the breakneck speed of 15 miles per hour. "Ah, look! There she is on the Aptos Creek Bridge," cried a small child. All dropped what they were doing and rushed to trackside to greet the happy throng of picnickers who were about to arrive. Oh, what a day this would be, what a gala day, what a festive day! Excitement was growing. Everyone disembarked from the train, and the Betsy Jane and her five-car special returned to Santa Cruz for its second trip. Soon, it was 11:30 a.m. and the Betsy Jane had again arrived in Aptos to the same onrush of enthusiasm.

By noon all of the day's planned activites were well along. Many hundreds of picnickers were enjoying the wide variety of goodies that had been carefully prepared and packed in their festive baskets, while speaker after speaker toasted the many items that needed toasting. The Betsy Jane and her five-car train sat unattended while its crew was off partaking of some mouth-watering delights.

Suddenly, someone shouted! "I heard a whistle; I heard a whistle!" Everyone paused. Could it be one of the many steamers out in the Bay? No, the whistle was heard again, this time by more. All at once a distant thunder began to fill the warm afternoon air. It was getting closer and closer and louder and louder. This was it, the occasion that everyone had come for was about to happen. Bill Holser, fireman, made a mad dash for the Betsy Jane. He grabbed the whistle cord and commenced to blow long continuous blasts. In return, the same long continuous blasts were heard in the distance. Soon, all of the people were gathered trackside. Bells were ringing, whistles blowing, crowds were cheering. The air was shattering with mighty explosions from the cylinders of some monstrous steam locomotive approaching from the East. In an instant, as if no time had passed at all, a plume of dark smoke was seen filtering through the trees in the direction of the Valencia Creek bridge. People were shouting, little children were crying, tears of joy streamed the faces of many onlookers. And then, all at once, there it was. The most beautiful 22-ton piece of steam power ever to be seen in Santa Cruz County, with its equally lavish coach, came charging out of the trees and across the bridge toward the crowd at Aptos. Oh, what a sight to behold as the gallant Pacific, its boiler panting in unison to the geometrical sounds that were being emitted from its drivers, gently slowed to a stop among the crowd. Inch by inch it worked its way forward, until at last it touched noses with the prideful little Betsy Jane; all at once, the Santa Cruz Railroad was a reality. Hats flew, guns went off, the air was filled with the ear-shattering sounds of bells and steam whistles and screaming voices. It was as if the completion of the transcontinental railroad, rather than a little 2 1 -mile narrow gauge operation, was being celebrated for the very first time.

Thus, Sunday, the 7th of May, 1876, came and went; all who had been present on that day knew in the bottom of the hearts that Santa Cruz County had come of age. . .

While many of the local citizens of the county viewed the completion of the Santa Cruz Railroad as merely a connection with the broad gauge Southern Pacific at Pajaro, there were many others with much bigger goals in mind. All up and down the California coastline, a plan had been initiated to connect the city of San Francisco with Los Angeles via a network of narrow gauge railroads. To that end, several local companies along the projected route were at various stages of incorporation and construction. The San Francisco, San Mateo and Santa Cruz Railroad had incorporated at a capital cost of $2,000,000 to build a line from the city of San Francisco down the coast to the San Mateo-Santa Cruz County border. Already, over $185,000 of stock had been subscribed to and approximately 35 miles of right-of-way in San Mateo County had been purchased. From Santa Cruz to the San Mateo-Santa Cruz County border, the Santa Cruz Railroad would soon be starting the second leg of their operation up the coast. In San Benito County and Monterey County, the San Benito Railroad, under the careful guidance of Senator Thomas Flint, had recently been incorporated to build a fine from Hollister via San Juan (Bautista) to Millard's Landing on the Monterey Bay. From Millard's Landing, connections were to be made north to the Santa Cruz Railroad and south to the Monterey and Salinas Valley Railroad. The Monterey and Salinas Valley, already having completed the line between the cities of the same names, was to build south down the Salinas Valley

to a point where it would connect with the San Luis Obispo and Santa Maria Railroad building north.

As of early 1876, the narrow gauge plan looked most feasible. Money was continuing to be raised, right-of-way purchases were being pursued, and interest among investors in the project was increasing. Barring any future disasters, financial turn-arounds, or interference by outside interests, many believed that a narrow gauge railroad connecting San Francisco with Los Angeles would soon be a reality.

About the time the Santa Cruz Railroad began its long anticipated operations between Santa Cruz and Pajaro, another railroad company, the Santa Clara Valley Railroad, had begun constructing a narrow gauge line from San Jose to Dumbarton Point near Alviso. Included in its Articles of Incorporation were the statements that the railroad, when completed, would extend to Saratoga, Alameda, and Santa Cruz. If this line was ever completed, the Santa Cruz Railroad would face some stiff competition out of the county. A preliminary survey confirming this competition had already been accomplished by the Santa Clara Valley Railroad, and local Santa Cruz Railroad investors were becoming uncertain as to the profitable future of their own railroad.

Fortunately for the Santa Cruz investors, while the Santa Clara Valley Railroad had sound financial backing and much local enthusiasm, this competing line would never materialize. The disastrous Winter of 1875-1876, which had done so much damage to the S.C.R.R., also befell the Santa Clara Valley Railroad. After the rains had ceased and the rivers subsided, all that was left of the line were five miles of graded mud between Alviso and Dumbarton Point, some disarrayed survey markers, a few muddy ties, and a packet full of abandoned real estate vouchers. Had it not been for this untimely Act of God, the Santa Cruz Railroad might have soon seen its first real competition out of the county.

By the 30th of June, the Santa Cruz Railroad had become an established fact in the community. Each day would see the "Pacific" pulling a mixed train of freight and passengers between Santa Cruz and Pajaro. Engineer Garcelon was at the throttle while the always courteous Conductor B.C. Toll looked after the needs of the passengers. H.C. Peckham was in charge of all of the onboard baggage and U.S. mail, and G.S. Mordune and F. Ely were the responsible brakemen. While the trip was anything but fast, the passengers gladly accepted the hour and 45 minutes of riding in relative comfort as compared to the bone-jarring ride of the old stage line which used to make the same trip.

With the coming of the Summer of 1877, the Santa Cruz Railroad had completed its first year of successful operations. All told, after expenses and accrued interest, the company had managed to eke out

Above: The construction engine the "Betsy Jane" relaxes near Aptos. — Courtesy: Roy Graves Collection, U.C. Berkeley, Bancroft Library

Below: The "Jupiter" poses in Santa Cruz, 1878. — Courtesy: Fred Stoes Collection

Broad gauge locomotive #1312 with the Santa Cruz passenger train crosses Capitola Trestle. — Courtesy: U.C. Santa Cruz Special Collections

a $5,201.86 profit. Not bad for the first year. To do this, the company had acquired a second 4-4-0 locomotive, "The Jupiter," five additional passenger cars, one express car, three gondolas, two boxcars, and 21 flatcars. By the end of the first year, the railroad had gone from one to two mixed trains a day and extra excursion trains on the weekends. The Santa Cruz and Felton Railroad was shipping hundreds of thousands of board feet of timber from Felton via the Santa Cruz Railroad to Pajaro, and the Southern Pacific had worked up connecting service for

weekend excursions into Santa Cruz. Barring any unforeseen circumstances, the future of the railroad looked nothing but bright.

About this time when all seemed to be going to well, one James G. Fair, a Nevada comstock millionaire, had been ordered by his doctors to retire to San Francisco for a little rest and relaxation. Being a very active man all his life, he soon grew restless with having no involvement in financial dealings. In addition, he had quite a large sum of capital on hand that was not seeing any investment. After several months of inactivity, he decided it was about time to get back in the ball game of life. It wasn't long before he had hit upon an investment that would bring him both personal accomplishment and financial opportunity.

Unlike many other California-Nevada capitalist counterparts, Fair had never become involved in the building of a railroad. As it was the fashionable thing to do at the time and because he had no personal liking for the "Big Four," he decided that this would be his next financial endeavor. But which one, and to where? After a false start, he concluded that the building of a railroad much along the survey of the abandoned Santa Clara Valley Railroad would be just the ticket. To join him in the venture he convinced James Flood to invest heavily in its capitalization. To run the

railroad he brought in an old friend, Alfred E. (Hog) Davis. Together they set out to build the South Pacific Coast Railroad from Alameda around the San Francisco Bay to Los Gatos and then over the mountains to Santa Cruz.

All of a sudden, the fate of the Santa Cruz Railroad became a picture of doom. Once the impending news hit that the South Pacific Coast Railroad had purchased most of the necessary right-of-way and had begun construction, the bright future of the Santa Cruz Railroad came to an abrupt end. With the projected loss of the freight from the Santa Cruz and Felton Railroad to the South Pacific Coast, and the loss of a large portion of passenger revenue due to a shorter route over the mountains, the Santa Cruz

F.A. Hihn's Capitola Hotel, shown here around 1900, was a prime weekend and summer resort which saw many visitors arriving and departing by train from the San Francisco Bay Area. — Courtesy: U.C. Santa Cruz Special Collections

Above: The remains of the San Lorenzo River Bridge signals the final end of the Santa Cruz Railroad. — Courtesy: Harold Van Gorder Collection

Below: It is January 11th, 1884. Watsonville photographer Fell has just taken the last picture of the "Betsy Jane" before she is to be loaded on a flatcar and shipped out of the County forever. — Courtesy: Fred Stoes Collection

Railroad might just as well have closed up their operation and sold it for scrap.

While all still looked rosey to the general public, what many people didn't know was that the S.C.R.R. was sitting on a very precarious financial limb. Based on anticipated future earnings, the railroad had gone whole hog on constructing and equipping the line. In addition, a substantial amount of money had had to be spent in replacing the rail lost at sea and in repairing all of the damage which had been done by the Winter storm of 1875-1876. By the time the railroad had begun its operations in earnest, over $591,000 had been spent. This was over twice what F.A. Hihn had estimated it would cost to construct the railroad.

It began to be clear that once the South Pacific Coast reached Santa Cruz this money would never be recovered. With imminent catastrophy hanging over the head of the Santa Cruz Railroad, additional sources of financial aid suddenly began to dry up. In April of 1878, a $10 per share assessment was levied against all outstanding capital stockholders to meet ongoing operating expenses incurred during another severe winter. By June 15th, only F.A. Hihn had paid the assessment. Obviously, nobody was going to dump good money after bad. As soon as the county got wind of the situation, the last of the bonds were withheld pending a court investigation. Finally, by September enough unpaid assessed stock had been bought up by those stockholders still holding on that current operating expenses were able to be met. The railroad , however, was fast becoming destitute. According to the December 31, 1878, financial sheet, the following was the gloomy summary of conditions: net earnings amounted to $9,868.55. Still outstanding: bond principle payable October 18, 1880, $125,000; interest accrued, $16,525; bills payable, $60,231.17; other accounts, $74,564.

By the time the middle of 1879 rolled around, the financing of the Santa Cruz Railroad had become a one-man show. F.A. Hihn was paying most of the bills out of his own pocket just to keep the line alive. Oh, sure, the railroad was still in operation; in fact, had the S.C.R.R. not had all the financial burden hanging over it, some might have said that it was breaking even. This, however, could not save it from its inevitable demise.

By June of 1880, the South Pacific Coast would prove to be an immediate success, furnishing faster freight and passenger access into and out of Santa Cruz County than ever before. Also as expected, it would prove to be a devastating blow to the Santa Cruz Railroad. As with all drowning victims, the S.C.R.R. was able to keep its head above water for a time. Cost-cutting measures were begun. Engineer Garcelon had taken over duties as the lines superintendent in addition to running the train.

Service was cut to one train a day, and fortunately, the Winter of 1879-1880 had been a mild one. This stay of execution, however, would be short lived.

On January 21st, 1881, it began to rain in Santa Cruz County. By January 26th the Santa Cruz Railroad had experienced such extensive damage to its right-of-way that it ceased operations. On January 27th, the San Lorenzo River Bridge washed out to sea, and with it went the Santa Cruz Railroad.

With no revenue coming in, and precious little since the advent of the South Pacific Coast, there was just no money left to make the necessary repairs. On March 28, 1881, an assessment of $10 per share was again levied against all capital stock. By April 27, 1881, no monies had been received from the shareholders. Finally, in May of 1881, the railroad fell into the hands of the receivers and Santa Cruz County was to witness the end of its first railroad.

On May 4th, 1881, the following editorial appeared in the *Santa Cruz Weekly Courier* newspaper.

The Santa Cruz Railroad was an enterprise conceived, constructed, and carried on, in its earlier history, with much popular enthusiasm. The people of the upper portion of the county in particular fancied that the one thing lacking was a railroad. Outside capital was appealed to in vain, even when tempted by a subsidy, and but for the interest and public spirit of Mr. F.A. Hihn, supported by subscriptions from the greater portion of the men of means in the community at that time, it would have remained unbuilt to this day. The people of Santa Cruz, especially stockholders in the road, do not need to be informed that as a financial investment it proved from the beginning a disastrous failure. It was worse than a white elephant in the hands of its owners and managers. The problem of building and operating 20 miles of independent railroad, alongside of water competition for freight, and both steamship and stage competition for passengers, has never been successfully solved. Mr. Hihn was plucky and persistent, and when the South Pacific Coast Railroad seemed likely to absorb the lion's share of the limited business to be done, he still kept the road equipped and running, and advanced his own money to supply the deficiencies of delinquent assessments. The violence of the elements last winter was more than a match for his patient investments, and when the bridge across the San Lorenzo went out to sea, it was the death knell of the Santa Cruz Railroad.

The Santa Cruz Railroad. Reorganized

With the demise of the Santa Cruz Railroad, the obvious question on the minds of the local citizens was who, if anyone, would take it over? The South Pacific Coast had made no moves to do so, although many thought it would. The Southern Pacific was adamant about the matter. Likewise, the newly organized line that was once again trying to build the route of the Atlantic and Pacific, the San Francisco and Ocean Shore Railroad, wasn't saying anything. Finally, after two months of speculation by the local newspapers, the Pacific Improvement Company, a Southern Pacific land company and subsidiary, stepped forth and abruptly purchased most of the S.C.R.R. delinquent stock. In addition, it was announced that it would be advancing sufficient money to reopen the line and keep it running.

On the same day that the Pacific Improvement Company acquired the controlling interest, the Southern Pacific Company's General Superintendent, A.C. Bassett; Master Mechanic, J.F. Williams; Master Bridge Builder, Mr. Rice; and General Road Master, Mr. Murphy, all came down to Watsonville to inspect the storm-damaged S.C.R.R. and to lay out the necessary work to put it in running order. After a thorough examination had been completed, it was felt by all concerned that the damage could be repaired and that, within a few weeks, the narrow gauge line could again be in operation.

On June 4th, 1881, mixed trains, pulled by "The Jupiter," "The Pacific," and "The Neptune," once again began to make daily connecting runs between Santa Cruz and the S.P. depot at Pajaro. While the old S.C.R.R. had a new lease on life, the operation looked basically the same. The line was anything but a money maker. If the Southern Pacific was ever going to compete with the South Pacific Coast, it would have to do a lot more than just reinstate the train service. Of course, the S.P. realized this.

While A.C. Bassett was in Santa Cruz during the rebuilding of the railroad, he unloaded a bombshell on the local newspapers that put all of Santa Cruz County in an uproar. He informed the press that after service had been reinstated over the narrow gauge, the line would be prepared for broad gauging and the change would take place as soon as it could be conveniently performed. "Conveniently performed" meant at such time as the S.P. had gained full ownership of the line.

Once the line was broad gauged, the local folks knew that the Southern Pacific would be able to effectively compete with the South Pacific Coast. Also, they knew that the S.P. would be able to provide the businessmen of the county with almost nation-wide freight service which, unlike the South Pacific Coast, would require no change of cars. In addition, with a broad gauge line established to Santa Cruz, local speculation indicated that it wouldn't be long before the S.P. would build up the coast to San Francisco.

On November 10th, 1882, after more than a year of foreclosure proceedings and a strenuous effort to acquire all of the outstanding stock, title to the Santa Cruz Railroad passed into the hands of the Pacific Improvement Company. Shortly thereafter, the railroad was leased to the Southern Pacific for $31,800 per year. In this intermanagement lease agreement, the Southern Pacific was to pay all taxes, maintenance, and other operational costs. In return, the Pacific Improvement Company was to be responsible for the payment of any principle due.

Now that the Santa Cruz Railroad had been tucked neatly into the portfolio of the S.P., plans for its broad gauging could begin. Already, the Southern Pacific successor to the short-lived Monterey and Salinas Valley narrow gauge, the Monterey Railroad, had been broad gauged from Castroville to Monterey. Soon, the Santa Cruz Branch would also be broad gauged, and great things would lie in store for the communities along both branches. It was the Southern Pacific's intention to advertise the many tourist attractions around the Monterey Bay area and thereby compete with the South Pacific Coast for some of its lucrative passenger trade. By providing modern broad gauge trains, fast on-time service, a convenient time schedule, and many alternative tourist attractions, the S.P. felt that profit would soon be at hand. With this in mind, the Company announced that just as soon as the Summer tourist season of 1883 drew to a close, broad gauging of the Santa Cruz Branch would commence.

By the 1st of September, a small army of men were at work all along the right-of-way, replacing narrow gauge ties with broad gauge ties, laying 56-lb. iron rail, realigning small sections of track, strengthening old trestles and building new ones, constructing the necessary maintenance buildings, and building a new broad gauge turntable in Santa Cruz. Based on the effort being put forth, it wouldn't be long before the County would see its first broad gauge train arriving in Santa Cruz.

The 100 year old "Jupiter" reposes in Kennedy Park, Washington D.C. shortly before restoration.
— Ray Larsen

The original Santa Cruz Railroad narrow gauge locomotive, the "Jupiter," proudly displays itself in the Smithsonian Institute, Washington D.C., 1979. Out of the thousands of engines built in the U.S., the "Jupiter" still remains in 2002 the one to represent the era there. — Rick Hamman

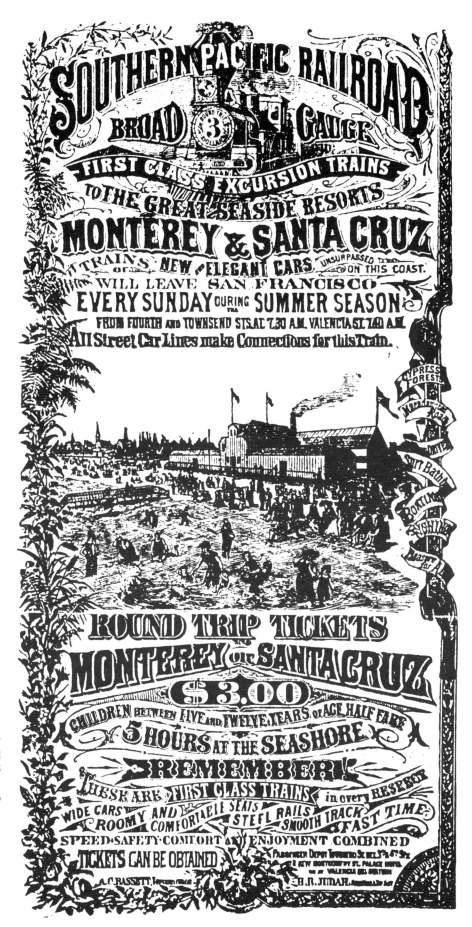

The "Daisy Trains" are now departing for Santa Cruz and Monterey; so states this 1885 S.P. advertisement.
— Courtesy: Palo Alto Historical Society Collection

Broad-Gauge Train Brought Through

The "Jupiter," by a long and loud whistle, as it crossed the trestle at the mouth of the river, Saturday evening, at 8:30 o'clock, bade farewell to the city to which it had been a daily visitor for the past six years. Behind this narrow-gauge Jumbo, with engineer Mynatt in charge, followed an express car, coach and smoker. Faithfully the men worked to get the track ready for the broad-gauge train Sunday, after clearing up the debris of the pioneer railroad to this city. At noon the depot platform and surrounding houses and steps were crowded by men, women and children. At half past twelve the last spike was driven by A.C. Stone and everything seemed ready for the train to make its appearance... The crowd continues to gather, and as the clock in the railroad office points to two, a strange whistle is heard in the distance... Then those on the top of the hill cry out - "HERE SHE COMES!" Smoke is seen curling up in the air and then engine No. 14, (The Red Eagle) with the cars of the S.P.R.R. is in sight. It crossed Locust street safely, and as the curve is reached it stops. Busy hands with hammers are soon at work, and the locomotive is surrounded by the curious in large numbers. The signal is given that all is ready, and the engine creeps cautiously forward to test the track; the freight cars are switched off; the turntable is tried and found to be in perfect order; the locomotive is coupled on, and at half past two Conductor Garcelon says "all aboard," and the broad gauge starts on her first trip from this city.

Santa Cruz Courier Item
Thursday, November 15th, 1883

And so, broad gauge railroading had become an established fact in Santa Cruz County. In no time at all, the Summer of 1884 would be upon the horizon and the Southern Pacific would know whether their $1,150,000 investment to broad gauge and equip the Santa Cruz and Monterey lines would show a return.

The Southern Pacific had gone first class all the way to insure that the Santa Cruz Branch and the Monterey Branch would be a success. In November of 1883, three new trains were put on order to be ready for the coming season. Each of these trains, later to be called the "Daisy Trains," consisted of a brand new high-speed locomotive, a baggage car, an express car, and six coaches. With the use of these new trains, it would be possible for the S.P. to run from San Francisco to Santa Cruz via Watsonville and take only ten minutes longer than it took the South Pacific Coast to come over the mountains. In addition with the broad gauging of the Santa Cruz Branch, travel time between Santa Cruz and Watsonville would be cut by over a half hour.

The Pajaro and Santa Cruz Railroad

During the period when the Santa Cruz Railroad was being broad gauged, another S.P.-created subsidiary, the Loma Prieta Railroad, began building a five-mile branch connection from Aptos, up Aptos Creek Canyon, to service the needs of the S.P.-controlled Loma Prieta Lumber Company. With the addition of this one more subsidiary, the financial and legal entanglements between this line and the Pacific Improvement Company managed Santa Cruz Railroad became so involved that some type of reorganization was deemed necessary. On June 3rd, 1884, the Santa Cruz Railroad and the Loma Prieta Railroad were reorganized under the corporate banner of the Pajaro and Santa Cruz Railroad. Its governing body looked something like the Who's Who of the Southern Pacific. Charles F. Crocker was the President; A.C. Bassett, its Vice-President; N.T. Smith, its Treasurer; and J.L. Willcutt, its Secretary.

With the evolution of the Pajaro and Santa Cruz Railroad, it became evident to all concerned that the Southern Pacific was solidly entrenched in Santa Cruz County. The "Daisy Trains," pulled by their new 6'4" high-drivered American type locomotives, had begun to make the heavily advertised mile-a-minute runs (in some places) from San Francisco to Santa Cruz and Monterey. In addition, two express and three local passenger trains had been put on each way between Pajaro and Santa Cruz. Also, daily mixed trains and weekend excursion trains were operating up Aptos Creek Canyon. Likewise, freight trains heavily laden with lumber products from F.A. Hihn's Valencia Creek Mill, sugar beets from the Soquel and San Andreas ranches, lime from the Cowell Kilns, and farm produce from the North Coast were daily operating on the Santa Cruz Branch. From all outward appearances, it looked like the S.P. had the Santa Cruz County coastal operations under firm control. If only they could do something about the pesky South Pacific Coast!

The Southern Pacific R.R. & Santa Cruz Co.

In late November of 1886, an unbelievable business opportunity was to present itself to the Southern Pacific. For years the South Pacific Coast narrow gauge had been an economic thorn in the side of the S.P. Now, because of unrelated external business pressures, James G. Fair would offer to sell the entire railroad, including the newly finished branch between Felton and Boulder Creek, to the company for $6,000,000. To make a long story short, by January 1st, 1887, the deal had been consummated,

Wagons line up to transport passengers, baggage, and express from the train which has just arrived in Capitola. — Courtesy: Harold Van Gorder Collection

and the Southern Pacific and its subsidiary, the Pacific Improvement Company, controlled the South Pacific Coast in total. Thus, in one small business transaction, the S.P. was able to eliminate all of its serious competition within Santa Cruz County.

From 1887 to 1892, process and progress would not change much in Santa Cruz County. The Southern Pacific had the county all wrapped up, and it was turning out to be a very lucrative business. First, there was the heavy weekday freight and passenger service going on over the Santa Cruz Mountains and around through Pajaro. Also, a significant amount of revenue was being generated from the Gharkey Railroad Wharf at Santa Cruz where the S.P. broad and narrow gauge tracks went right out to meet the moored ships. In addition to this revenue, probably just as much money was being derived from the weekend tourism.

There were the magnificent sights and tranquil sounds along the S.P. narrow gauge, the quaint little village of Aptos where Spreckel's famous Aptos Hotel had been reopened under new management, the beach at Santa Cruz where one found delightful accommodations at the fashionable hotels and the pleasures of the Neptune and Dolphin bathing baths if one were so inclined. Also, there was beautiful Camp Capitola where the babbling waters of Soquel Creek met the calm of the Pacific Ocean. Likewise, with the extension of the Loma Prieta branch two miles farther up Aptos Creek Canyon, the Loma Prieta-Monte Vista area was being billed as a camper's and picnicker's "Lost Horizon."

A Southern Pacific passenger train bound for Santa Cruz crosses the San Lorenzo River Bridge at the beach. — Courtesy: Louis Stein Jr. Collection

32

As the volume of business for the coastal broad gauge began to expand, many financial and material changes would take place. On May 14th, 1888, the Pajaro and Santa Cruz Railroad would be consolidated with the old Southern Pacific Company to become a division of the Southern Pacific Railroad. During the month of January, 1889, the entire line between Pajaro and Santa Cruz would be reworked. Many aging light-weight bridges would be replaced by stronger structures. Steel rail, 45-lb. straight sections and 52-lb. curved sections, would be spiked down in place of the original iron rail. In July of 1890, the S.P. would conduct an in-depth survey from Santa Cruz to San Francisco for possible future expansion up the coast. At about the same time, another survey would be carried out up Soquel Creek deep into the Hylands where F.A. Hihn and others had large timber holdings. Finally, in late 1892, a modern two-story passenger depot and a massive freight station would be constructed in Santa Cruz to replace the antiquated Cherry Street depot and the old S.P.C. & S.P. freight depots.

One should not get the impression, however, that this rosey period was not without its thorns. During the Winter of 1889-1890, Santa Cruz County would see over 124 inches of rain fall in the mountains. Because of this, monumental storm damage would be experienced by almost every local rail line. As a result, it would take much money for the railroads to dig themselves out of this accumulated mud and mire. Because profits were good during this time, however, none of the affected lines would close.

In 1893, the development and expansion bubble, which had been building since 1877, would burst. For years there had been a surplus of revenues over expenditures in the United States Treasury. Now, with the Dependent Pensions Act of 1890, the rapid construction of a new Navy, and the repayment of direct war taxes to the States, this surplus vanished. The country itself was in an agricultural depression because of poor crop management; thus, payments on farm mortgages were not being met. In addition, due to some very unsound financial practices, banks were failing all across the nation. Also, the railroad construction fever that had previously caught the expansionary dreams of the nation was now strangling it; there had been too many railroads built to too many places with no thought given to their profitability. As of the end of 1893, over 22,000 miles of railways were in the hands of the receivers and most new construction had been stopped.

The Panic of 1893 was in many ways a turningpoint in American history. It focused attention upon monetary questions, prostrated the silvermining states, embittered the already discontented farming regions of the west, produced an industrial chaos, out of which the stronger economic interests emerged with increased power by the absorption of embarrassed companies, and was accompanied by renewed labour troubles.[1]

For Santa Cruz County, the financial panic meant only one thing: "DEPRESSION!" The lumber industry almost came to a standstill. With the demand for lumber down, Santa Cruz lumber companies became very competitive with the larger mills in northern California and Washington State. When this happened, the price being paid for finished wood was almost as cheap as water. Men, when they could, worked for practically nothing. The only saving grace during this time was that some westward expansion was still going on. With that exception, this depressed condition would continue for almost two years before the pendulum would start to swing back towards more prosperity. This time, however, rules had been written and laws had been passed which would "HOPEFULLY" prevent another such panic from every happening again.

By 1897, all of the economic woes which had plagued the country had been resolved, and life in Santa Cruz County had just about returned to normal. All of the lumber mills were once again in full operation. The Santa Cruz Powder Works, up the San Lorenzo Canyon, had two hundred men at work turning out 700 kegs of blasting powder and 6,000 pounds of smokeless powder per day. Over in Watsonville, almost 2,500 carloads of apples from the Pajaro Valley would be shipped to various points around the country this year. In addition, the Pajaro Valley Consolidated Railroad would be incorporated from the Pajaro Valley Railroad and the Pajaro Extension Railroad. Soon thereafter, over 300 tons of sugarbeets per day would be shipped via the little narrow gauge from the Moro Cojo Ranch to the Spreckel's Sugar Refinery in Watsonville.

---

[1] Frederick Jackson Turner, Professor of History, Harvard University, Encyclopedia Britannica, 1911, *United States History.*

The Santa Cruz Beach & Boardwalk as viewed from the "Sea Beach" Hotel in the late 1890's. — Courtesy: California State Library Collection

With the coming of 1899, the end of the century was fast approaching. For years Santa Cruz County had been on the youthful verge of growth and development. Now, the tide of new events was beginning to ebb. The San Lorenzo Valley, the Aptos Creek Canyon, the coastline from Watsonville to Santa Cruz, and the "Hylands" in the Santa Cruz Mountains, had all become established regions with local town centers and accompanying industries. About the only piece of the expansionary dream which had not come to pass was a through rail line down the coast from San Francisco to Santa Cruz that would allow the North Coast region to be opened up. Even that was still a good possibility with

companies like the Southern Pacific in 1895, the West Shore Railway in 1897, and the Vanderbilts in 1899, firmly stating that each would soon be securing the necessary right-of-way to build such a line, and that construction was imminent.

Thus, with the beginning of a new century, Santa Cruz County would shuck its pioneer clothes of infancy and childhood which had been brought on by an expansionary dream; in turn, it would dawn the clothes of a contracting reality. Soon, it would be 1900, and the adult future of Santa Cruz County would depend on the steel wheel and a new contraption called the "AUTOMOBILE!"

Above: The new narrow and broad gauge Santa Cruz Depot is alive with activity as seen here around the turn of the century.
— Courtesy: Anne Locatelli Collection

Below: Several local folks relax in front of the first Southern Pacific, and possibly the Santa Cruz Railroad, Watsonville Depot.
— Courtesy: Harold Van Gorder Collection

An early S.P. mixed borad gauge train crosses Soquel Creek at Capitola. — Courtesy: Fred Stoes Collection

The second S.P. Watsonville Depot is seen as it appeared shortly after its 1895 construction. — Courtesy: Pajaro Valley Historical Association

It's the turn of the century. The Watsonville yard teems with action as the sugarbeet freight wagons line up for the Spreckel's sugar refinery, the reefers are being iced and packed with apples, and the afternoon train fron Santa Cruz and unloads its its passengers, baggage, mail, and express. — Courtesy: Charles Ford Company Collection

Aptos Creek Railroads

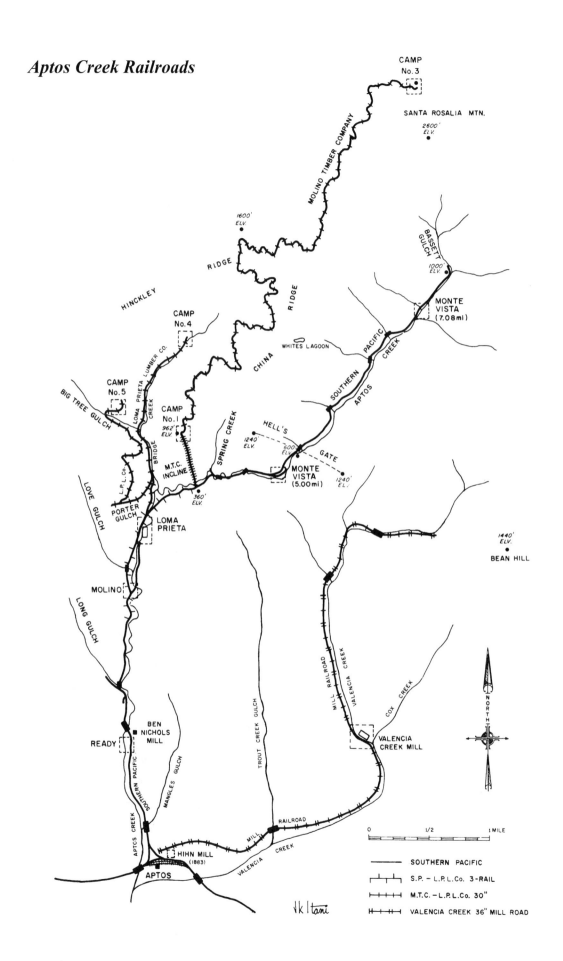

CAMP No. 3

SANTA ROSALIA MTN.
2600' ELV.

MOLINO TIMBER COMPANY

1600' ELV.

BASSETT GULCH

1000' ELV.

MONTE VISTA (7.08 mi)

HINCKLEY

CAMP No. 4

WHITES LAGOON

SOUTHERN PACIFIC

APTOS CREEK

RIDGE

RIDGE

CHINA

BIG TREE GULCH

CAMP No. 5

LOMA PRIETA LUMBER CO.

BRIDGE CREEK

CAMP No. 1
962' ELV.

SPRING CREEK

HELL'S
1240' ELV.
600' ELV.
GATE

MONTE VISTA (5.00 mi)
1240' ELV.

L.P.L. Co.

M.T.C. INCLINE

360' ELV.

LOVE GULCH

PORTER GULCH

LOMA PRIETA

1440' ELV.

BEAN HILL

MOLINO

LONG GULCH

VALENCIA CREEK

MILL RAILROAD

COX CREEK

NORTH

BEN NICHOLS MILL

READY

APTOS CREEK

SOUTHERN PACIFIC

MANGLES GULCH

TROUT CREEK GULCH

MILL

RAILROAD

VALENCIA CREEK MILL

VALENCIA CREEK

HIHN MILL (1883)

APTOS

VALENCIA CREEK

0   1/2   1 MILE

Jk Itani

——————— SOUTHERN PACIFIC

|—|—|—|—| S.P. – L.P.L.Co. 3-RAIL

|-|-|-|-| M.T.C. – L.P.L.Co. 30"

H—H—H—H VALENCIA CREEK 36" MILL ROAD

2

The Aptos Creek & The Loma Prieta Railroads

The Loma Prieta Railroad

Today, the grey squirrels are sporting in the treetops, and the speckled trout darting about in the pure waters of the Aptos. Tomorrow, the riven bodies of these forest trees will be lumber, and the brook a pool of liquid poison. This is progress ...

Santa Cruz Courier Item
September 20th, 1883

Ever since the time when millionaire sugar king Claus Spreckels had given up his plans for turning the local community into a second Santa Cruz, complete with racetrack and big hotel, and old Ben Nichol's mill, two miles up Aptos Creek Canyon, had burned to the ground, life in the little coastal village of Aptos had once again become a synonym for undisturbed tranquility. Except for those instances when one of the passenger trains bound for Santa Cruz or Watsonville would stop to discharge a group of fun-seeking picnickers or an occasional misguided traveler, this daily routine of timeless solitude was seldom interrupted. As the pendulum of time would continue its relentless swing through eternity, however, conditions would change. Aptos, according to the local gossip of the time, was about to become one of the largest timber shipping points in the county.

It was early in the summer of 1882. Rumors were flying thick and fast that several of the officers of the Southern Pacific and the Central Pacific railroads had just completed a big deal with the Watsonville Mill and Lumber Company and the Fallon family concerning their individual timber holdings up Aptos Creek Canyon.

Ever since the beginnings of lumbering in the Santa Cruz Mountains, the big trees in the Aptos Creek Canyon had been high on the timber magnate's list to feel the mighty blow of the lumberjack's heavy axe. Here on the steep mountain walls stood five hundred million board feet of prime uncut redwood and pine timber, along with hundreds of thousands of sixty- to eighty-foot-tall oak and madrone trees, just waiting to be cut into lumber and cordwood and sold for a handsome profit. Up to now, this had proven easier said than done because in order to get at the profitable timber, the brutal topography of the Aptos Creek Canyon would first have to be overcome.

Several attempts had been made in the past at logging these precipitous mountains, but all had failed for primarily the same reason. In order to get at this profitable timber, an expensive logging road or railroad of some type would have to be constructed into and through the canyon. Up to now, most of the lumber companies had been such small operations that they didn't have the ability to raise the necessary capital to do the job. That condition, however, was about to change.

On July 10th, 1882, Charles Crocker, A. C. Bassett, N. T. Smith, and J. L. Willcutt, of the Central Pacific and Southern Pacific, along with Alvin Sanborn, President of the Watsonville Mill and Lumber Company, filed articles of incorporation, in the County of Santa Cruz, under the name of the "Loma Prieta Railroad Company."

It was recorded that the railroad was to be constructed from Aptos along the meanderings of Aptos Creek to a point 3.7 miles up the canyon where the confluence of Bridge Creek and Aptos Creek took place. From here, the railroad was to be constructed 1.3 miles farther to an end point where a small meadow at the base of a large mountain would be encountered. In addition, the railroad was to be allowed to transport any and all freight and passenger business which might be generated by the lumbering activities about to be commenced in the area.

One of the biggest lumbering operations that would ever take place in Santa Cruz County was about to happen. Soon, the Doughertys of the Santa Clara Valley Mill and Lumber Company, the Sanborns of

Mount "Loma Prieta" (3,086 ft.) at the headwaters of Aptos Creek is the highest peak in the Santa Cruz Mountains. Its Spanish name means "Dark Ridge with a Broad Top." — Fred Stoes

All during the building of the Loma Prieta Railroad the pint sized Santa Cruz Railroad locomotive, the "Betsy Jane," did the honors on the construction train. — Courtesy: Bruce MacGregor Collection

the Watsonville Mill and Lumber Company, the Southern Pacific giants A.C. Bassett, N.T. Smith, and later, Timothy Hopkins (adopted son of Mark Hopkins), local businessmen Charles Ford and John T. Porter, and San Francisco attorney Thomas Bishop, would all come together and form the Loma Prieta Lumber Company. Coincidentally, many of the same individuals appeared on the directorate of the Loma Prieta Railroad Company.

Thus, the die had been cast. The primeval forest of Aptos Creek Canyon was about to be entered for the first time. Soon, the large forest monarchs of redwood and pine would be singled out to fall. Soon, their nude bodies would lie heavily upon the ground, waiting to be hauled off to a monstrous timber slayer, where they would be cut into various sizes of profit. Soon, the whistle of a portable steam donkey and the crack of the bullwhip would break the mistiful silence of the Aptos Creek Canyon. But, such was the case for progress. The noble forest would be sacrificed to the needs of the world.

> There were cities to be built
> And rail to be laid;
> There was timber to be had
> And a profit to be made.

By October of 1882, the Loma Prieta Railroad Company had acquired all of the necessary properties and capital such that the surveying, grading, and construction of the right-of-way could begin in earnest. In early 1883, the editor of the *Sacramento Bee,* J.M. Hawkins, filed the following report after visiting the survey and construction area while on vacation in Aptos.

Several months ago, Mr. Knox received orders to construct the road from Aptos to a certain place in the forest. Engineers were long engaged in selecting the route, because it is a precipitous one and has many curves and cuts, so many and so extensive as to make the work difficult, and to require an immense expenditure of money... A large force of engineers are now at work locating and determining the curves. The grading for the first four miles has been nearly completed. The track has been laid two miles and a half from Aptos and the construction train runs that far. Two hundred Chinese graders are employed. The choppers are Swedes. Carts were the only vehicles that could be used in the work. The first carts had to be hauled up by ropes, and even sure-footed mules could not find ways to get up until paths were dug for them. In many places the road-bed is from fifty to a hundred feet above the creek. There are various places where cuts

One of the many Loma Prieta Railroad bridges is going up across Aptos Creek. — Courtesy: Roy Graves Collection, U.C. Berkeley, Bancroft Library

sixty feet deep have been blasted in the rocky mountains and the sides have been dug out at other places in the sharpest curves ... The workers had to do a great deal of blasting in the rocks, and thousands of tons of powder were used to clear the route of stumps. At places the trees are so close together that a person may walk over several acres of ground and be unable to see the sun through the dense mass of branches and foliage above. The trees average six or eight feet in diameter, and some of them are even ten feet thick ...

With the coming of July of 1883, W.F. Knox of Sacramento and his two Chinese track gangs had construction operations well underway. Crew number one was clearing and grading the broad gauge right-of-way on to the mill spur at Molino while crew number two was feverishly laying ties and spiking down rails between Aptos and Bridge site number three at the first crossing of Aptos Creek.

Although it wasn't the longest or highest bridge on the right-of-way, bridge number three was a common landmark to the local folks because it crossed Aptos Creek at the site where the old Ben Nichol's mill used to stand. As a result, it served as a ready reference point. It, like the ten other bridges which would be built along the line, was being constructed by an expert crew of Chinese bridge builders under the watchful eye of master bridge builder Patridge.

At each bridge site, Patridge and his crew would first construct the wooden piers and approaches. Next the 80-foot wooden truss sections would be ordered to the site from the Southern Pacific bridge shops at Oakland where they had been prefabricated. Upon their arrival, they would be lowered into position and fastened down securely. As each of the eleven bridges was completed in this manner, W.F. Knox and one of his crews would then lay down track and extend it on to the next bridge site. Here, Patridge and his crew would begin the process all over again.

Every railroad has its own particular engineering problems which it has to face during its initial construction phase. In the case of the Loma Prieta Railroad, bridges were probably its single biggest undertaking. Not only did the right-of-way require a great number of bridges in a very short distance, but, also it required that they be constructed under the most precarious of conditions. It was for this reason that the five-mile Loma Prieta Railroad right-of-way would take the crews under Knox and Patridge over a year to complete.

On July I I th, the report went out that the exSanta Cruz Railroad narrow gauge locomotive, "The Betsy Jane" and her construction train had been seen up Aptos Creek as far as bridge number three. It should be pointed out here that originally management had decided the right-of-way was to be broad gauge so that freight could be shipped directly over the soon-to-be broad gauged Pajaro and Santa Cruz Railroad to the Southern Pacific mainline at Pajaro. Initially, however, until such was to happen, the railroad would be laid down as a narrow gauge operation on broad gauge ties. This would be done in order to allow for the speedy interchange of much needed construction materials and because the Loma Prieta Lumber Company did not want to wait until the right-of-way was broad gauged to begin their first season of lumber operations.

By the end of August, track work had progressed as far as Molino. Knox and his crew were in the process of clearing and grading the right-of-way on to end-of-track while Patridge and his crew were working on the 320-foot mill spur bridge across Aptos Creek. As soon as the bridge was completed and the spur extended to the proposed Loma Prieta Lumber Company mill site, construction would begin on the sawmill and the shinglemill. At the same time, a town, later to be named Loma Prieta, would be laid out about a half-mile above Molino at the confluence of Aptos and Bridge Creeks. Here, a railroad station would soon be erected to offer freight and passenger services to any and all interested parties.

By October, work had commenced on the final 1.3 miles of right-of-way. This last section would prove to be more difficult than the first to construct. It would have a ruling grade of 108 feet per mile, or 2%, and it would cross Aptos Creek no less than five times before it would finally reach the end-of-track at Monte Vista. Of these five crossings, two would be over 200 feet long and two would be accomplished by a single 280-foot curved trestle whose midpoint would be centered on a promontary on the opposite bank of the creek. Even by today's engineering standards, this last section of right-of-way, taking into account what was involved and what the crews of Knox and Patridge had to work with, would be considered quite a construction feat.

Now it was November. "The Betsy Jane" and her construction train had reached their final work assignment at end-of-track. Here, nestled in a small open meadow around which the Aptos Creek Canyon walls rose to a height of 850 feet in less than threeeighths of a mile, sat the second L.P.C.Co. mill site of Monte Vista. From here over 200,000,000 additional board feet of timber was expected to be cut and shipped to market.

Soon the last tie would be laid down, and the last rail would be spiked into place; soon the last bridge timber would be shored into position; soon the last carpenter's hammer would hit the datehead of the last nail into the last bent; soon it would be November l3th, 1883, and the Loma Prieta Railroad would be opened for any and all business which the Loma Prieta Lumber Company operations might provide.

The Loma Prieta Lumber Company

On November 14th, 1883, one day after the opening of the Loma Prieta Railroad, articles of incorporation were filed in the County of Santa Cruz under the corporate name of the "Loma Prieta Lumber Company." The capital stock of the company, all of which had previously been subscribed to by its officers and board of directors, was said to be $500,000. The company was to exist for 50 years, and it was to be allowed to enter into any and all business activities which involved the acquisition, manufacture, distribution, and sale of timber products.

In order to meet the anticipated open-ended demand for these timber products, the company initially acquired 7,000 acres of prime forest in the Aptos Creek Canyon. It was estimated at the time by a good authority that were all the trees felled, cut into cordwood, and piled upon the space occupied by the forest, every square foot of the ground would be covered to a height of eight feet. Thus it was easy to see why the L.P.L.Co. had been incorporated and what the future of these one-thousand-year-old forest monarchs was going to be.

Early in the Spring of 1884, after the winter rains had ceased to muck the trod ground, and the muddy waters of the Aptos had turned clear, the L.P.L.Co. brought in its first crew of white[2] laborers and construction was begun on their mammoth timber slayer at Loma Prieta.

Soon, the throbbing of the two massive steam boilers which powered the mill would pulse the ground like a pile driver; soon, the gnawing and cutting sounds

---

[2]There was much controversy being generated at this time by the white laborer who felt he was being cheated out of a job by the Chinese laborer who would work longer hours for less pay.

Locomotive #72, 2-4-2, was built by Stevens in the Southern Pacific Shops at Sacramento especially for this branch. It's shown here at Loma Prieta, circa 1885. — Courtesy: California Dept. of Parks & Recreation, Felton, Calif.

of the two niggerhead[3] circular saws, as they bit and ripped at the logs coming out of the millpond, would pierce the air in bursts of screaming numbness; soon, the canyon walls would reverberate with the thunderings and smashings of the logs as they rolled from the flatcars and disconnects into the millpond; soon, it would be June 2, 1884, and the mill would be well on its way to turning out 70,000 board feet of lumber a day during an 11-hour run.

From the summer of 1884 through the summer of 1887, not much change took place in the day-to-day lumber operations at Loma Prieta. Each season would see a mass of humanity swarm into the forests along the railroad right-of-way and around the mill to commence the work of turning the trees into furnished lumber products. First, the fallers and buckers would cut down and section the monstrous trees, whereupon the log chasers would line up the cut sections and attach the donkey cables. When this was done, the donkey boss would be called in to transport the trees, via drag line, to the railroad right-of-way such that they could be loaded onto waiting flatcars or disconnects and taken to the mill by one of the Pajaro and Santa Cruz saddle tank locomotives. Once at the mill, the logs would be off-loaded into the millpond and left to soak until such time as they had aged enough to be cut. When the logs were finally brought

from the millpond up the log slip to the saw, the log deckman would line them up and set the dogs for cutting. Once the sawyer had control of the incoming log, it wouldn't be long before the off-bearer would be sorting the various pieces of finished wood according to their individual sizes and shapes. Finally, the finished lumber products would be stored in the drying yard until such time as they were ready to be shipped out on the morning or evening mixed trains to Aptos.

In retrospect, most historians, when writing about events such as this, concern themselves primarily with those key figures who were financially responsible for its inception. While it is true that it took great sums of money to make the L.P.L.Co. a reality, it is also true that without the skills and abilities of the little people who had come west to put their own small scratch on the earth, the L.P.L.Co. would never have seen its first board foot of lumber.

It took men like millwright Alfred Buckley, whose mechanical understanding could keep a piece of machinery running better than any man alive. It took men like Frank Cook, with, a keen eye and experienced

---

[3]A "niggerhead" was a hook under the circular saw blade which rotated the logs as the saw cut them into various sizes and lengths.

Where once the peace and quiet of the forest reigned supreme, now stands the 1884 Loma Prieta Lumber Co. Shingle Mill at Molino. — Courtesy: California State Library

MOLINO.

"Molino" (Mill in Spanish) was the junction point at which a spur track was cut from the main into the Loma Prieta Lumber Company shingle, and later saw, mill area. — Courtesy: Stanford University Library, Timothy Hopkins Collection

The Loma Prieta Lumber Co. sawmill No. 1 lies in a narrow clearing at Monte Vista, 1886. — Courtesy: Stanford University Library, Timothy Hopkins Collection

judgment who could fell a tree so close to the mark that many times the log chasers would be left with nothing to do. It took men like Leslie Hoke, whose steady-handed sensitivity allowed him to operate a steam donkey with such finesse that you would think it was human. It took men like yardman Valla and finisher Hornberger and planing mill operator Cambiano, who made the finished lumber a quality product. Finally, and most important, it took men like mill foreman James Walker, whose word was undisputable, and who, because of it, had the respect of every man in the company.

Southern Pacific Aptos Branch 1887-1898

Just after the end of the 1886 timber season, management encountered a problem which they hadn't anticipated in their previous planning. Originally it had been decided that when most of the trees had been felled around the mill and along the right-of-way, the cutting operations would be moved up the canyon beyond Monte Vista. This was a good plan in theory; however, when construction of the skid road began, it became apparent that the topography of the Aptos Creek Canyon was not going to let this happen.

Just beyond Monte Vista lay an area, later to be known as "Hell's Gate," where the steep canyon walls rose to a height of 800 feet above the floor. Here one found deep fissures piercing the earth to indiscernible depths. Here one found tremendous evidence of massive landslides and great amounts of earth movement. Here one found the entrance to an indescribable tree-studded gorge, obviously carved out by the hand of God during the Creation. Here one

The Loma Prieta Lumber Co. sawmill No. 2 as it appeared below Loma Prieta in 1890. — Courtesy: U.C. Santa Cruz Special Collections

Saw logs fill the L.P.L. Co. No. 2 millpond as seen from the Loma Prieta Depot looking south in 1891. — Courtesy: Harold Van Gorder Collection

found that if these mammoth monarchs of aging redwood and pine were ever to lie in the millpond at Loma Prieta, it would not be via a skid road. To build and operate such a skid road would take more time, materials, manpower, and money than the standing timber was worth. Thus, the first stumbling block had been placed in the path of longevity for the Loma Prieta Lumber Company.

To the railroadmen of the L.P.L.Co. management, the solution to getting the timber out above Monte Vista was simple: extend the railroad farther up the canyon and write off the costs against the Southern Pacific. With this in mind, A.C. Bassett, in his annual report to the stockholders of December 1886, recommended that the Loma Prieta branch be extended a short two miles farther. He did not state that to build such a right-of-way would take a 4% grade with untold numbers of large cuts and massive trestles, and that completion of such a short addition would involve over a year of construction. As a result,

in spite of all this expensive engineering and construction, management ruled in favor of Bassett's proposal.

On March 5th, 1887, the following news story appeared in the *Santa Cruz Courier Item*:

Aptos Items
On Tuesday evening a party of surveyors of the Southern Pacific Company arrived from San Francisco to make a survey for the extension several miles further up into the timber section.

Thus, the scene was set. Engineer McCloud was called in by the company to carry out the survey and to commence the construction as soon as possible. While the task was easily arrived at in the minds of those who so ordered it, the actual work involved to accomplish the survey and the construction would prove to be both time consuming and costly. McCloud and his men were starting from scratch. There were no

Activity abounds in the Loma Prieta lumber yard as seen from the south looking north in 1891. — Courtesy: U.C. Santa Cruz Special Collections

roads or trails into the area. Each surveyor's stake would have to be put down into ground that was so steep one could barely stand on it much less take a bearing from it. From the start it became evident that in order for the line to climb 500 feet in two miles it was going to have to be constructed several hundred feet above the creek in many places. Also, there would have to be many large cuts dug and many massive trestles built because of the verticalness of the terrain and the numerous gulches which gouged the mountainside. In addition, the right-of-way would have to be constructed entirely without the use of fills because it always rained so heavily in the area during the winter season that any fill built would be washed away.

On March 14th, 1888, after over a year of construction, the line was finally opened between old Monte Vista and New Monte Vista.[4] Shortly thereafter, E.S. Harrison, while writing a brief history of Santa Cruz County for its then current Board of Supervisors, paused to make the following observation:

I have said that this is a wonderful pretty route,

and I will add that its completion is the consumation of a very difficult feat of engineering. One who had seen these forests in their virgin condition, unaquainted with the possibilities of railroading would never have dreamed that the whistle of the locomotive would some day break the deep stillness of these wild and rugged mountains.

Now that the S.P. was firmly entrenched in the local lumber business, the renewed success of the Loma Prieta Lumber Company was a certainty. Soon, telegraph and telephone poles, railroad ties, fence posts, and general lumber began stacking up in the storage yard to the tune of 70,000 board feet a day. It wasn't long before there were over 150 men working in the mill at Loma Prieta and another 80 men working

---

[4]The Southern Pacific, when they extended the line from the mill lite at Monte Vista (five miles above Aptos) to end of track at Monte Vista (seven miles above Aptos), never made a name distinction between the two locations. Therefore, for clarification purposes, "Monte Vista" as mentioned in the text here and following refers to the location seven miles above Aptos.

**Shown here is the Southern Pacific Loma Prieta Depot on the right and the C. Coates Saloon on the left as they were in 1887.
— Courtesy: Pajaro Valley Historical Association**

The crew and others pose with engine #80 and mixed train somewhere along the line between Aptos and Loma Prieta. — Courtesy: California Dept. of Parks & Recreation, Felton, Calif.

for the lumbering contractors of Baird and Dougherty in the forests near Monte Vista.' All in all, the Aptos Creek Canyon was fast becoming a beehive of activity.

Not all of this activity, however, was centered on the men who were working at the mill and in the forests. In order to provide the goods and services so necessary to meet the needs of the railroad, the mill, and their employees, towns had developed at Loma Prieta and Monte Vista. An example of this can be seen in the following letter from Bill Nye of Loma Prieta:

May 15th, 1891
Do not think because Loma Prieta is situated on the Santa Cruz Mountains that it is an isolated place; far from it, for here we have all the modern improvements to be found in a good sized village... Here is the hotel, store and main office,

where the genial secretary of the company, W.R. Porter, and the two bookkeepers, Messrs. Keeum and Rea, will be found at their respective desks. Adjoining is the store managed by J.B. Kent, who also has been busy replenishing stock for the season, even to the millinery line... There is a Wells Fargo express and a post office and a telephone communication with the offices of Baird and Dougherty, contractors, situated at Monte Vista, three miles distant from the mill, and William H. Hadner's situated opposite the mill. Thirty-six houses, all occupied, are situated adjacent to the mill, good houses, papered, painted and water inside and outside. Little garden spots of vegetation are everywhere noticeable... Adjacent to the hotel are the private cottages of J.L. Porter and Thomas Bishop, members of the company, while the commodious cottages of the directors adjoin.

A mixed train with crew and many Sunday passengers momentarily passes for the photographer somewhere along the downgrade between Monte Vista No. 1 and Monte Vista No. 2. — Courtesy: Pajaro Valley Historical Association

Work stops, people pose, the shutter clicks, and a view of Monte Vista (5 miles above Aptos) is captured for posterity. — Courtesy: California State Library Collection

A view of the second Monte Vista (7,083 miles above Aptos) is seen as it appeared in the late 1880's. If one looks carefully, three men can be seen in the middle of the photo and a locomotive to the right. — Courtesy: Pajaro Valley Historical Association

At Monte Vista, a small station along with various other buildings necessary to support the lumber contracting had been constructed. In addition, a dance hall and picnic grounds were built where on Saturday's and Sunday's tourists would come in by train and partake of the local activities offered - activities such as dancing to the music of the "Love's String Band" or indulging in a little alcoholic delight at the local tavern.

For the next seven years, 1891-1898, not much change was to take place in the day-to-day routine of life. Each day would see locomotive No. 1010 pulling a train of empty boxcars, flatcars and disconnects up the 4% grade to Monte Vista. Once the train reached Monte Vista, the logs, previously dragged in by oxteams from the surrounding cuttings, would be loaded on the flatcars and disconnects and the stacked cordwood of oak and madrone would be loaded into

the boxcars. As there was no turntable at Monte Vista, locomotive No. 1010 would always have to make the return trip to Loma Prieta backing down the canyon; when doing so, it operated on the head end of the train to prevent runaway cars. At Loma Prieta, locomotives No. 383 and No. 384 handled the necessary switching assignments at the mill and around Molino. Also, all the locomotives took care of the freight and passenger service into Aptos.

While the Loma Prieta branch was a short branch line as branch lines go, the amount of money it took to maintain it made it one of the highest priced per mile operations the Southern Pacific ever had. Each rainy season would see mountains of water come pouring down the various gulches and gullies, wiping out whole sections of right-of-way at a time. In addition, the San Andreas Fault at "Hell's Gate" was constantly on the move, causing many minor landslides and track realignments. The trains, according to one old timer, were always jumping the track at one point or another due to poor footing or a soggy right-of-way.

But such was life; the people who lived and worked in the Aptos Creek Canyon learned to sway with the punches and usually countered them with hard work and determination.

In early 1899, however, a punch was thrown that would prove to be devastating.

The Loma Prieta Railroad was so seriously damaged by the big storm of last month that it is said the portion above the mill will not be reopened for traffic, the amount of timber left being not sufficient to warrant the heavy expense of necessary repairs. The road is now being reopened from Aptos to the mill.

The Mountain Echo
April 8th, 1899

Nature, the referee, had counted to ten. The fight between man and the Aptos Creek Canyon was over. Man lay flat on the canyon floor never again to pass through "Hell's Gate." Never again would the crack of the bullwhip or the strain of the line break the silence in the little clearing at Monte Vista; never again would the sounds of the logs crashing down the mountainside into the holding pond at Monte Vista echo through the canyon; never again would the voices of small children and their larger parents, enjoying the picnic grounds, drift through the air in competition with the afternoon breeze; never again would the whistle of old No. 1010 or the bite of steel wheel on curved rail pierce the morning quietness as the train slowly climbed the tortuous grade to Monte Vista.

The battle was lost. With the closing down of the railroad to Monte Vista, all of the timber stands that

The shadows of late afternoon creep across the narrow canyon at Monte Vista No. 2. The train with its loaded disconnects is about to return to the pond at Loma Prieta to off load. — Courtesy: Harold Van Gorder Collection

The oxen have just arrived with a long skid train of saw logs which are about to be loaded on waiting disconnects. Monte Vista No. 2, circa 1895. — Courtesy: U.C. Santa Cruz Special Collections

the L.P.L.Co. owned had been cut. As a result, the L.P.L.Co. had no choice but to close down the mill at Loma Prieta and move on to new enterprises. In 1899 the mill was completely torn down and sold, piece by piece, to the highest bidder. The town, with the exception of the directors' cottages, was abandoned. The Southern Pacific ripped up the salvageable rail from old Monte Vista to new Monte Vista and shipped all of the locomotives out to see duty elsewhere.

For 15 years, the Aptos Creek Canyon had been pulsed with the sounds of human life as man, rightfully or otherwise, ripped and tore at the green and brown skin of this lush acreage to serve his own needs. Now, it was over. Once more the canyon would be allowed to return to its primeval state.

Two typical 1890's Aptos Creek Branch Southern Pacific shipping orders are seen: one from Loma Prieta Station and one from Monte Vista. — Courtesy: Paul Johnston Collection

S.P. #80 with open car arrives at Loma Prieta Depot (3.70 miles above Aptos) to pick up passengers bound for Monte Vista's one and two. — Courtesy: Roy Graves Collection, U.C. Berkeley, Bancroft Library

F.A. Hihn's Valencia Creek Mill

During the summer of 1883, most of the local excitement and attention around Aptos seemed to be focused on the ongoing construction of the Loma Prieta Lumber Company operations up Aptos Creek Canyon. It, however, was not to be the only major lumbering concern to operate in the Aptos area. Situated in a canyon one mountain range east of Aptos Creek, lay Valencia Creek. Here, Santa Cruz pioneer F.A. Hihn had acquired several thousand acres of prime timberland on which it was estimated there was over one hundred million board feet of timber just waiting to be cut. To that end, F.A. Hihn had recently established a 30,000 board foot capacity sawmill in Aptos.

By July of 1883, Hihn's mill had begun to run at capacity. Each day, with the use of steam donkeys, skid roads, oxen, mules, and large wagons, the cumbersome logs would come thundering down from the mountains to the mill. Once at the mill, it wasn't long before the logs were being shipped out the backdoor, via the Pajaro and Santa Cruz Railroad, as finished timber products.

While the operation was efficient, it did pose some problems. In order for the logs to reach the mill from the forest three miles away, they were having to be hauled by heavy, horse-and-mule drawn, freight wagons. This required a considerable amount of time, and it also kept the quantity of logs arriving at the mill to a minimum. To solve this problem, Hihn decided that, with the coming lumbering season of 1884, the mill would be relocated three miles up Valencia Creek into the current area of the canyon being cut. It would be a lot easier to ship the finished timber from the sawmill to Aptos rather than shipping the uncut log from the cutting area to the sawmill at Aptos.

With the beginning of summer, Hihn's mill was once again in full swing, cutting 30,000 board feet of lumber per day in a brand new location. Now, with the finished product rather than the uncut log being shipped to Aptos, one would think that increased profits would soon be at hand. This, however was not true. The over-all operation was still less than successful. In order to get the cut logs through the cramped confines of Valencia Creek to the mill, oxen and skid roads had to be used. In addition, once the logs had been cut into the finished product they still had to be hauled three miles into town before they could be shipped via the railroad. Together, these two problems had a tendency to reduce the output of the mill and thereby decrease its profits.

To alleviate the problems of timber access to the mill and at the same time speed up shipping to Aptos, Hihn decided a mule-drawn railroad was needed. With the coming of the spring of 1886, a 14,600-foot

narrow gauge line was laid out from the freight warehouse in Aptos to the mill on Valencia Creek. The first 9,300 feet of the line would be essentially level. From there, a 3% grade would be encountered for the next 3,400 feet. Normally this was a rather steep grade for mules, but it wouldn't pose any problems on this line because the loaded cars would always be going downhill. The last 1,900 feet of the right-of-way from the summit to the mill would also be level. From the mill the line would be extended into the woods at least another mile. The sharpest curve on the road would be twentyfive degrees.

By the middle of summer, the three-foot narrow gauge line had been completed and the mill was once again in operation. As a result of the mule-drawn railroad, the mill was now capable of turning out 40,000 board feet of lumber per day. While this wasn't much when compared to the massive operations going on in Aptos Creek Canyon, it was significant because it meant more jobs and more security for all of the local folks concerned.

On November 29th, 1886, the Valencia Creek mill was to come to an abrupt end. Before the day was over, the mill and most of the storage yard would burn to the ground. While any disaster caused by fire is unwanted, this one ironically had a good outcome. Because of the total loss of the operation, Hihn was forced to either give up logging Valencia Creek, or build a brand new mill. As times were good and the general lumber market was booming, he opted for the new mill.

After the winter rains had let up, the new mill began to be erected on the site of the previous one. This time, however, Hihn had decided that the new Valencia Creek mill would be similar in size and output capability to the Loma Prieta mill in Aptos Creek Canyon. To do this, the new mill would be set up to produce 70,000 board feet of finished lumber per day. In addition, a modern box factory and planing mill would be added to the facility. In order to meet the increased freight requirements brought on by a larger mill, a small saddle tank locomotive and some new flatcars were purchased.

By the time the summer of 1887 rolled around, the new operation was underway. In order to meet the ravenous appetite of the sawmill, Valencia Creek Canyon was being dismantled tree by tree. Once these giant monarchs had been cut, they would be sectioned and loaded aboard the four-wheeled totecars. From the forest they would be dragged by mule power to the pond where they would be off-loaded to await their fate. After each tree had been divided by the hungry saws and split into the appropriate sizes and lengths, the finished product would be stacked in the drying yard to await shipment. Once or twice a day, the little saddle tank locomotive No. 1 would be brought in, and

August 14, 1891. Mill workers and members of their families pose for the photographer at the F.A. Hihn Company millpond on Valencia Creek. — Courtesy: U.C. Santa Cruz Special Collections

the finished lumber products would be taken to Aptos over the three-mile narrow gauge. While the little locomotive was affectionately known as "The Betsy Jane" to the local folks, it was not the same locomotive which had previously worked on the Santa Cruz Railroad.

Probably the greatest years of operation for the Valencia Creek mill were from 1887 to 1892. One of the activities which made it so great was the constant competition going on between it and the Loma Prieta Mill. The men of both sawmills took great pride in pitting one mill's ability against the other. Day after day the men of each mill would push for total output

just to be able to say they were the best. Mid-August of 1888 was probably the finest example of this spirit: On August 17th, the Loma Prieta mill crew announced that they had cut 93,000 board feet of lumber after a ten-hour run. On August]8th, Hihn's Valencia Creek mill crew announced that they had cut 143,000 board feet of timber after the day's run. On August l9th, the Loma Prieta mill crew reported that they had cut 181,000 board feet of lumber in the unbelievable time of six and one-half hours. No doubt on August 20th in the local Aptos saloons, there were wagers paid and some fights fought over the entire event.

The second F.A. Hihn "Betsy Jane" pulls a train of loaded disconnects down the Valencia Creek Canyon to the millpond. — Courtesy: U.C. Santa Cruz Special Collections

The millyard of the Valencia Creek operations as seen looking upstream. — Courtesy: Pajaro Valley Historical Association

Chinese graders on the Valencia Creek right-of-way pose for a photograph. — Courtesy: Pajaro Valley Historical Association

With the closing of the Valencia Creek mill shortly after 1892, all of the equipment, including The Betsy Jane, went to Gold Gulch near Felton. Most of the men who had worked for the mill went to the Loma Prieta Lumber Company; as for the Valencia Creek Canyon, it began the ageless process of replenishing itself.

The Loma Prieta Lumber Company Transition Years

In 1901 the L.P.L.Co. leased a tract of land from Fred Hihn on Soquel creek and started a new operation at Hinckley Basin just over the ridge from Loma Prieta. The mill operated until the Winter of 1905, when a severe rainstorm caused substantial flood damage to the operation. It was in the process of being rebuilt when the earthquake of April 18th, 1906, hit. During the earthquake, the mountainside above the mill let go and buried it and seven employees under tons of earth. For a while they tried digging it out but finally gave up after recovering the bodies of those who had died in the slide.[5]

In 1907 the L.P.L.Co. started constructing a second mill in a flat above the site of the first mill at Hinckley Basin. They gave up on this idea, however, when it started getting too costly. What to do with all that uncut timber that had already been paid for???

In the spring of 1908, after considering all of the possibilities, management finally decided that the most economical way of getting the timber from Hinckley Basin was to build a second mill on the site of the first mill at Loma Prieta and drag the logs over the ridge to it. This would have some obvious advantages in that the millpond, dam, storage yard, and town were still in usable condition. In addition, unlike Soquel Creek where the finished products had to be hauled out by wagon to the railroad at Aptos before shipment, the Loma Prieta site offered the advantage of an S.P. branch line directly to the mill. Thus, by the summer

---

[5] To this day, the mill and all of its equipment still lies buried at Hinckley Basin.

F.A. Hihn work camp up Valencia Creek.— Courtesy: Pajaro Valley Historical Association Collection

Before the arrival of the F.A. Hihn Company's locomotive all of the work was done by mules such as those shown here. —
Courtesy: California Dept. of Parks & Recreation, Felton

of 1908, a second mill had been built and equipped on the site of the first at Loma Prieta, and the logs began to fill the millpond. After just a short time of operation, however, it was found that dragging the logs over the mountain from Hinckley Basin was proving to be much too costly in relation to the manpower and materials that it took to do the job. As a result, management again had no choice but to close down the second mill and go looking for new opportunities to present themselves. It wasn't long before such an opportunity happened.

By 1909, the Ocean Shore Railroad had built a spur line from their right-of-way on the coast, above Davenport, up to Swanton. It was here that the L.P.L.Co. purchased a tract of land on Mill Creek and began construction of a third mill. It was a smaller mill with only one boiler, but it was more than sufficient to meet the needs of the operation. By the Summer of 1910, the mill was in full production, rapidly shipping finished lumber products via the Ocean Shore Railroad to the Southern Pacific at Santa Cruz. It was just about this time when a second, and much larger, opportunity presented itself to the Loma Prieta Lumber Company back in the Aptos Creek Canyon.

The Molino Timber Company

All during the time when the Loma Prieta Lumber Company and the F.A. Hihn Company were logging the Soquel and the Aptos Creek Canyons, an 800-acre tract of timber on Hinckley and China Ridges, between the two canyons, had remained uncut. It wasn't that neither company wanted to go after the estimated 15,000,000 board feet of redwood lumber sitting on this tract - it was the fact that the rugged terrain surrounding the tract had made it financially unaccessible by all known forms of timber harvesting up to this time. Many schemes had been proposed over the years to scale the 600- to 800-foot canyon walls which led to the tract above, but all had been abandoned for one reason or another.

In the early days, broad and narrow gauge railroads had been proposed, but they were given up as too costly based on the engineering and construction necessary to complete such a grade. In addition to the railroads, highlines and cable runs were proposed, but again the terrain to the top prevented such possibilities. In 1908, when the second mill at Loma Prieta had been closed down after the failure of the Hinckley Basin operation, a scheme was proposed to turn the site into a shingle mill and bring the logs down in the form of split stuff on the backs of bull mules. This was tried for a while, but it was given up after a time when it proved to be too limiting in the amount of split stuff delivered to the mill.

In the spring of 1910, a group of long-time employees, familiar with Loma Prieta's failure to get at the lumber, approached the company with a new scheme to go after the timber on Hinckley and China Ridges. What made their scheme more plausible than the rest was the fact that it incorporated most of the good points of the previous schemes and none of their bad points.

The main points presented were that, first, the Loma Prieta Lumber Company would construct a 30-inch narrow-gauge right-of-way from Molino to a point approximately halfway between Loma Prieta and old Monte Vista, using the abandoned portion of the Southern Pacific Railroad wherever possible. Next, the group, in the form of a new contracting company, would build a 2,250-foot rail incline up the side of Aptos Creek Canyon from the point on the Loma Prieta proposed right-of-way to a point 657 feet up on Hinckley Ridge. Once on top, the narrow gauge rightof-way would be extended into the forests on Hinckley and China Ridges for approximately five miles. After the railroad was completed, the plan was to cut the redwood trees on the spot. The wood which was easily split would be cut into 2x2's, the wood not so easily split would go into posts. From here the wood would be loaded onto bull mules and carried to the railroad. Next, it would be loaded on flatcars and transported to the incline. Once at the incline, each flatcar would be lowered to the L.P.L.Co. right-of-way below. From there the split stuff would be taken to Molino for direct shipment via the Southern Pacific or to the mill for cutting into shingles.

Basically the plan as presented seemed feasible to the management of the L.P.L.Co., and so they agreed with the group to purchase the wood by the carload once it had been delivered to Molino.

Therefore, on May 28th, 1910, O.E. Chase of the Chase Lumber Company; Alfred Williams, secretary of the L.P.L.Co. and director of the Big Creek Timber Company; F.G. Severance, director of the L.P.L.Co.; Alberto Stoodley, bookkeeper and clerk for the L.P.L.Co.; and Fred Daubenbiss, manager of the L.P.L.Co.'s general store at Opal Cliffs all came together and incorporated under the name of the Molino Timber Company. The stated purpose of the company was lumber contracting, the prime contract being with the Loma Prieta Lumber Company.

Basically the plan for getting the wood off Hinckley and China Ridges was financially sound, but there was to be one major drawback which would make the entire operation highly speculative. The operating capital to complete the whole project and get the company rolling was listed at $20,000. This meant that all of the timberland, construction, equipment, rolling-stock, materials, and manpower would have to be purchased at minimum costs. Because of this cost factor, many things, not normally done when constructing a railroad, would have to be done to save money.

First, it was decided that all flatcars, railroad ties, bridges, timbers, cribbing, and line poles would be made by the employees of the company. In addition, as the gauge was only 30 inches and the equipment relatively light, it was decided there would be no need for ballast. Also, it was decided that by making the flatcars only 16 feet long the wheel bases could be kept short, thus allowing for the construction of shallow cuts and sharp curves.

When surveying, engineering, and construction was finally begun, cost savings was still the name of the game. Right off the top $8,000 had been spent to lease the land and to buy the timber rights from the F.A. Hihn Company. This left only $12,000 with which to try to complete the project. "An impossibility," many had said, but those connected with the company and familiar with the lumber business knew otherwise.

To cut costs on the surveying, M.T.C. hired Arnold Baldwin, then a surveyor for the County of Santa Cruz, to come in during his spare time on the weekends to layout the right-of-way. While it took

This is the 1915 joint shipping and receiving plant for the Molino Timber Compnay-Southern Pacific at Molino .— Courtesy:
Woods Mattingley from the A. Stoodley Collection

This is the 1915 joint shipping and receiving plant for the Molino Timber Compnay-Southern Pacific at Molino. — Courtesy: Woods Mattingley from the A. Stoodley Collection

The hoisting engine used on the M.T.C. incline. — Courtesy: Woods Mattingley from the A. Stoodley Collection

longer for the survey to be completed, the cost savings was substantial.

To cut costs on the engineering, Homer Kinsman from New York was hired to be the chief engineer and foreman of M.T.C.'s entire operation and to take charge of the initial engineering and construction line. In order to keep M.T.C.'s right-of-way costs to a minimum, Homer Kinsman started out by purchasing used 16-lb. rail in 15-foot lengths from a firm in San Francisco. While the rail caused many connection and switching problems, its initial cost per ton more than offset any difficulties. Next, in those places where the narrow gauge and the S.P. broad gauge shared a common rail, he designed and built all of M.T.C.'s three-rail switches rather than pay a premium price for

same. In addition, he specified that, since the flatcars were only four feet wide, the right-of-way need not have a clearance of any greater than five feet. As a result, he was responsible for many of the narrow cuts and flatcar-width fills situated along the right-of-way.

By the end of the summer of 1911, Homer Kinsman had the Molino Timber Company's incline and ridge-top railroad well on its way to completion. About the only item of business left on the agenda, which still involved a significant cash outlay, was the purchase of a steam locomotive to operate above the incline. Whatever locomotive was to be chosen, it had to be one that could climb M.T.C.'s 4% ruling grade, negotiate its extremely tight curves, be very light, and be cheap.

Stacks of grapestakes and split-stuff line the upper landing and storage yard of the M.T.C. incine. — Courtesy: Woods Mattingley from the A. Stoodley Collection

After thoroughly examining all of the many attributes of the different steam locomotives available from the various manufacturers, M.T.C. finally decided on a little two-truck, 11-ton, wood-burning Shay for $2,750.00. It was a gutsy little engine that arrived at Loma Prieta from the Lima Locomotive Works in mid-November of 1912. It had two 5x8 inch cylinders that delivered 90, tractive effort, horsepower through a 3:1 gear reduction to the 20-inch wheels below. Lima of Ohio claimed that it was capable of climbing up to a 15% grade under its own power and still have enough steam left to blow its whistle. In addition, the mechanic who came with the little sidewinder said it had the flexibility to run around any tree stump on the Molino Timber Company property. While these were exaggerated claims, the ability of this little engine was more than enough to match any assignment M.T.C. would ever order its way.

By the following Spring of 1913, the little engine had been moved to the top of the incline and the Molino Timber Company lumbering operations were well underway. Each day would see 20 to 30 men hard at work in the forest — cutting, splitting, and stacking the various sizes of redwood, oak, and madrone split stuff along the right-of-way to await shipment. When the timber was cut some distance away from the railroad, the logs would first have to be dragged to the right-of-way by bull donkey and spool donkey before they could be split and stacked. In those places where steam donkeys couldn't be used, the logs would be split on the spot and then the mule teams, operated by the five King brothers, would be brought in to carry the finished split stuff to the right-of-way.

Once enough split stuff had been stacked along the right-of-way, the little shay, with engineer Brown at the throttle, would come up the 4% grade, pushing

The Loma Prieta Lumber Co. motorcar #3 pushes a load of supplies up from Molino to the base of the incline. — Courtesy: Woods Mattingley

The men and equipment of the M.T.C. pause for the camera click at one of the camps on top. — Courtesy: Harold Van Gorder Collection

four empty flatcars to be loaded. The cars were always pushed ahead of the locomotive to prevent runaways. This sometimes caused problems, however, in that engineer Brown couldn't see possible dangers such as slides, trees, or rocks on the right-of-way. To help alleviate this problem, orders were given that train lengths were to be kept at a minimum of four cars each.

Along the five-mile right-of-way, in addition to those places where the various amounts of split stuff had been stacked to await the arrival of the little sidewinder and its four empty flatcars, there were three M.T.C. support camps. Camp No. I sat at the -top of the incline where there were a blacksmith shop, a storage shed for hay for the mules, a railroad repair facility, a small rail yard, and housing for the Rossi family who operated the steam donkey on the incline. Camp No. 2 was situated about halfway between Camp No. 1 and Camp No. 3. Here, there was a cookhouse, many year-round dwellings, and a short railroad siding. At Camp No. 3, located at the end-of-track in an open meadow on top of China Ridge, were more year-round dwellings and support facilities. Camp No. 3 was known to the men as "Sheep Camp" because M.T.C. had leased the surrounding meadow to a local sheepman for his sheep. In addition to these three camps there was a floating camp of Japanese who moved from area to area depending on where there was work.

Two or three times a day, the Shay and its train could be seen making its way between the camps taking down loaded cars and returning with empties. Once the train reached Camp No. 1, the cars would be uncoupled and then lowered, one by one, to the Loma Prieta right-of-way below. Joe Rossi did the honors on the steam donkey while his son served as brakeman on the cars going down.

Joe Rossi, when operating the steam donkey, could not see to the bottom of the incline. As a result, a crude two-wire bell system had been installed to allow the men below to notify Joe when loaded cars

had reached the bottom or when empty cars were ready to be drawn up to the top. When the crew at the bottom wanted the steam donkey to be started, the two wires would be touched together once. This would ring the bell at the top, signaling Joe to go; when they wanted Joe to stop the steam donkey, the wires would be touched together twice. While this was a crude communications system, it did the job, and that was all that was necessary.

Once the flatcars had reached the bottom of the incline, they were stacked in a small railroad yard until such time as the gasoline-powered Hall-Scott switcher, operated by Bernard Klink, came along and pulled them to Molino and the mill. When the cars reached their final destination, they were unloaded and then returned via the Hall-Scott switcher to the incline.

Basically, the Molino Timber Company operation was to continue more or less unchanged in this fashion until its closing after the summer season of 1917. While the scope of the operation had never been anything to write home to mother about, its place in the history of Santa Cruz County was obvious. Here, a small group of men had gathered together to conquer what many before had been unable to do. Here, with limited means but lots of intestinal fortitude, a battle was won. Here, with the sweat of the brow and the flexing of muscle, men were able to turn untapped resources into human needs. Here, for a short five years, the Molino Timber Company operated one of the crookedest, short-line, narrow-gauge railways ever to exist in the colorful history of California.

Thus, by the spring of 1918, the rails had been ripped up and the locomotive and all of the rollingstock had been lowered to the bottom of the incline. Shortly afterward, the rails, rolling-stock, and locomotive were sold to the Loma Prieta Lumber Company to be used on their recently opened right-of-way up Bridge Creek.

M.T.C.'s Shay stops for a brief moment on "Lone Tree" trestle. — Courtesy: Woods Mattingley from the A. Stoodley Collection

A trainload of shingle bolts makes its way along China Ridge in the summer of 1913. — Courtesy: Woods Mattingley from the A. Stoodley Collection

Above: Some of the side clearances along the M.T.C. right-of-way, such as this cut between the Bridge Creek and Hinckley Creek areas, were narrow to say the least. — Courtesy: Woods Mattingley

At right: It's the close of the M.T.C. operations. The Shay sits at the bottom of the incline for the very last time. Soon it will work for and belong to the Loma Prieta Lumber Co. — Courtesy: Woods Mattingley from the A. Stoodley Collection

Owners of the company view the cabins of the split-stuff makers along the M.T.C. right-of-way. — Courtesy: Woods Mattingley Collection

The Bridge Creek And
Big Tree Gulch Operations

During the period of time from 1883 to 1898, the Loma Prieta Lumber Company logged off all of the Aptos Creek Canyon and its tributaries except for a 700-acre tract of land up Bridge Creek Canyon that belonged to the F. A. Hihn Company.

About the time the Molino Timber Company operations were coming to a close on Hinckley and China Ridges, and the F. A. Hihn Co., realizing that if the 15,000,000 board feet of timber sitting on the Bridge Creek tract wasn't cut now, it never would be, offered to sell the Loma Prieta Lumber Company the property for ten dollars per acre. This meant that if the company did buy the property, their mill at Loma Prieta, which had been previously converted into a shingle mill in 1912, would now have to be converted back into a sawmill capable of handling large-diameter logs. In addition, the topography of Bridge Creek Canyon, being similar to Aptos Creek Canyon, was such that some sort of method to bring the cut logs down off the steep mountainsides and then to the millpond would have to be devised.

After thoroughly reviewing the entire proposal Homer Kinsman, then with M.T.C., convinced the L.P.L.Co. management that here too steam donkeys and a narrow gauge railroad, such as M.T.C.'s, could be used to get the large redwood trees out. After taking Kinsman's recommendation under advisement and reviewing the current lumber market, the L.P.L.Co. decided it was time to get back into the lumber business.

In early 1917, the company purchased the 700-acre tract of land, and soon Homer Kinsman began laying out the new right-of-way from the junction of Bridge and Aptos Creeks to a point up the narrow box canyon known as "Chalk Point" or Camp No. 4. The entire 30-inch narrow gauge right-of-way would be less than a mile long when it was completed, and with the exception of a 3% ruling grade and two medium-sized trestles, one across Porter Gulch and one across Big Tree Gulch, its construction posed no real engineering problems.

With the right-of-way started, the L.P.L.Co. next turned its efforts to finding a locomotive to operate on the new line. Since M.T.C. was still in operation at the time, and therefore using its little shay that had been

Now working for the Loma Prieta Lumber Co., old M.T.C. No. I pulls a load of split-stuff down to the mill. — Courtesy: Harold Van Gorder Collection

In this rare photograph, Mrs. Harvey West and her father pose in front of the Loma Prieta Lumber Company's Shay No. 2. —
Courtesy: Woods Mattingley Collection

Hoffman's Camp or Camp #5, 1920, Loma Prieta Lumber Co. — Courtesy: Woods Mattingley Collection

promised to the company when M.T.C. closed, the L.P.L.Co. went looking for a second locomotive to work on the Bridge Creek tract. It wasn't long before they found that the Empire City Railway at Strawberry, California, was selling a used 14-ton, oilburning Shay for $4,000 that would just fill the bill. Shortly after the little six-by-ten-inch twin-cylinder Shay arrived, the right-of-way was completed to Camp No. 4, and the railroad commenced operations.

By early summer, the redwood-ladened flatcars and longer disconnects, pulled behind the little rail hanger with George Short at the throttle, began rolling down the line to the millpond at Loma Prieta. There wasn't much to this, less than a mile long, railway operation, but without it, the giant redwoods, some of them eight to nine feet in diameter, would never have reached the mill to be cut into the needs of man.

By the end of the 1917 summer season, the operation in Bridge Creek had just about filled the

millpond. The Southern Pacific was now bringing in freight cars and gondolas twice a week to be loaded with finished lumber, railroad ties, grapestakes, posts, pickets, shingles, and wood. Bob Stewart, station agent at Aptos, took care of all of the company's shipping, while Guss Shroder usually served as engineer between Aptos and the mill.

Unlike the 1890's operation, there was no formal Southern Pacific passenger service to the mill from Aptos. Instead, Elmar Soaper operated a companyowned, six-passenger, Fairbanks-Morse rail speeder that once a day made the round-trip into Aptos to pick up mail and supplies. In addition, on Saturday nights after the mill had closed down, it was also used to take the men into town who were interested in a little "rest and relaxation." On Sunday nights, it returned to Aptos to pick them up. If you missed it, according to Karmany West, it was a long, cold, and often sobering walk back to the mill in the dark.

76

Right: Mr. & Mrs. Hoffman at Big Three Gulch cookhouse. Mr. Hoffman was Woods Superintendent while Mrs. Hoffman was the camp cook. — Courtesy: Woods Mattingley from the Paul Johnston Collection

Left: The S.P. Loma Prieta train crew poses along the branch in the 1920's. The man with his elbow on the side rod is engineer, Gus Schroder. — Courtesy: Woods Mattingley from the Paul Johnston Collection

In addition to the lumber mill operations going on at Loma Prieta, there were also a couple of smaller operations taking place in the Aptos Creek Canyon. About a mile below Loma Prieta sat the settlement of Schillings Camp. Schillings Camp was run by the Schilling family who had a pack train outfit that hauled out shingle bolts, pickets, posts, ties, and cordwood from the surrounding area. The camp consisted of the Schilling family house, a large cookhouse, bunkhouses for the employees, a small landing with rail siding, and a large barn and corral for mules and bay. Just below the steel bridge and about a mile south of Schillings Camp, there was a rail siding known as the "Hihn Spur" or "Ready." Here the L.P.L.Co. had built another mill on a tract of land they purchased from Mrs. Ruth Ready, a Hihn family relative. The mill, compared to the Loma Prieta operation, was much smaller in scope in that it only turned out split stuff, ties, and sorted lumber. The combination of the three -Schillings Camp, the mill at Ready, and the larger operation at Loma Prieta - made the Aptos Creek Canyon a pretty active place during this period in time.

In 1918, the Molino Timber Company closed down its five-mile ridge-top and incline railroad operation and sold off all of the company's equipment to the Loma Prieta Lumber Company. This included the little 11-ton Shay loco, the flatcars, and all of the rail. In anticipation of this closing, Homer Kinsman had already been making plans on what to do with the equipment once the company had acquired it. As a result, the little shay, its cars, and the rail they ran on, didn't sit around collecting dust and rust for very long.

In harvesting the Bridge Creek tract, the company had run into a problem. Off of Bridge Creek was a tributary known as Big Tree Gulch. Big Tree Gulch was a very long, very narrow, and very steep canyon that just happened to have some very large redwood trees in it; four in particular, were over 16 to 18 feet in diameter. The problem this posed was that getting these large redwood trees down to the Bridge Creek right-of-way below presented a logistics situation that would tax the mind of the greatest general. How do you get large logs around tree stumps just as large? How do you use a steam donkey to drop logs 80 feet straight down? How do you load flatcars off a 30-foot cliff? Generally, you don't.

As a result, Homer Kinsman decided that the only way to get the trees out was to go in after them. This involved building a two-mile-long switchback railroad operation up the side of the mountain that would eventually put the railroad in Big Tree Gulch 250 feet in elevation above the Bridge Creek right-of-way. Not much is known about the construction of the right-of-way, 60 years later, except that it took two switchbacks, eight trestles, and one

heck of a lot of cribbing to reach end-of-track, or Camp No. 5 as it was known in those days. In two places, they used over 6% grades, and in one place, I wouldn't even want to hazard a guess as to what the grade was. All in all, it was quite an undertaking.

By July of 1918, the Big Tree Gulch operation was in full swing. Early in the morning, the men would be brought up by train from Loma Prieta or down from Camp No. 5 to the day's work site. Here 25 to 30 men, under superintendent Hoffman, would make feeble attempts to turn the giant trees into movable sections that could be carried back down to the mill. Some trees were so large that they had to be split in half before they could be hauled away. You talk about work! "Whew!" Once the trees had been cut into shipable sizes and lengths, the steam donkey, with an inch-and-a-half cable, would be brought in to pull the trees to the right-of-way. After the trees had been loaded on waiting flatcars, engineer Brown and fireman Karmany West, aboard one of the little shays, would carefully transport the logs down the steep and twisting right-of-way to the millpond at Loma Prieta. From here the logs would soon be finished lumber, sitting aboard an Aptos-bound Southern Pacific freight train.

Shortly after the Big Tree Gulch operation began, the cutting in Bridge Creek was completed. Camp No. 4 was then abandoned and the line was closed to the point where the Big Tree Gulch branch began. For the next three years, all of the timber operations would take place along the Big Tree Gulch right-of-way, and above Camp No. 5.

Unlike Camp No. 4, which had been comprised of just a few shanties, Camp No. 5 or Hoffman's Camp, sometimes called "Camp Comfort" by Mrs. Hoffman, was quite a substantial village. Here there were several bunkhouses with adjoining showers and washrooms, a cabin for the cook and his helper, a large warehouse on the low line spur, a mule barn with large fenced corral, several stump animal shelters and smaller corrals next to the mule barn, two other stable buildings, a blacksmith shop, half a dozen bathrooms, twelve cabins, and a community meetinghouse. In addition, there was a small two-track yard where one spur was for empties and the other spur was for loading.

At the end of the 1920 timber season, the Big Tree Gulch and the surrounding area above Camp No. 5 had just about been logged off. The mill had been shut down for the winter with just a little over half a season's logs still lying in the pond. The shays had been stored in their shed for protection, and the town of Loma Prieta, with the exception of the three L.P.L.Co. directors' cottages, was mostly in moth balls. Although no one knew it at the time, the mill had seen its last board foot of lumber to ever be processed.

With the coming of the 1921 season, the L.P.L.Co. management decided there wasn't enough timber left to warrant reopening the mill. The final curtain had fallen. Now, it would just be a matter of time before all of the equipment would be sold off, and once again the Aptos Creek Canyon would return to its perpetual silence.

The first thing to go was the uncut logs in the millpond. They were loaded aboard flatcars and hauled to their new owner, the San Vicente Lumber Company, on the other side of Santa Cruz. Next, most of the mill equipment left for the various companies that had purchased it. The buildings were left behind, as they were of no value. Finally, the two Shay locomotives were put up for sale for $700.00 each.

While the price was right, no one at that particular time wanted a used 30-inch, narrow gauge Shay locomotive. After an extended period of time, the little rail bangers went back into storage at the mill site. For the next four years, the little locomotives sat unused. During that time, the bell of one locomotive was stolen; the bell of the other locomotive went to the San Jose-Milpitas Ranch owned by Harvey Bassett. In 1925, Clarence Srock, then a caretaker for the company at Loma Prieta, sold the little shays to a lumber company at Oakhurst, California that was just about to build a 30-inch narrow gauge railroad out onto the "Soquel" at Sugar Pine flats near Bass Lake. With the shipment of the shays, railroading in the Aptos Creek Canyon was about to come to an end.

In 1928, Columbia Motion Pictures filmed a movie entitled "One Way Trail" at the millpond and along the Southern Pacific right-of-way. In it was a great train wreck, the only real wreck of any consequence to ever occur in the Aptos Creek Canyon. Finally, after more than 45 years of Southern Pacific operation in the Aptos Creek Canyon, the line to the mill was ripped up. Never again would the sound of a railroad, or anything else for that matter, interfere with the natural order of things in the Aptos Creek Canyon.

On October 28th, 1963, most of the land that had originally belonged to the Loma Prieta Lumber Company was deeded to the State of California, for a park, by the Marks family of Salinas. The park was appropriately named "The Forest of Nisene Marks." The only stipulation in the gift was that the park would remain in its natural condition except for a small section of land, known as the "Timothy Hopkins Area," which could be minimally developed as the State so chose.

Today the grey squirrels are once again sporting in the tree tops, and the speckled trout are darting about in the pure waters of the Aptos. The small imprint that man has made on the land has just about receded into eternity. The forest is as it was in the beginning.

In contemplation of the scene the mind pauses - the consciousness of a sublime silence is borne in upon the soul by every sense. The stillness brings a reverential hush to the spirit; the mighty forest monarchs are lifting their heads hundreds of feet toward the heavens, each a spire from this leafy temple; the atmosphere rises with the sweetness of incense toward the blue vault above; every instinct of nature impels to worship, every impulse of the soul inclines to adoration.

The Santa Cruz Courier Item
September 20th, 1883

The remains of a narrow gauge trestle in Bridge Creek Canyon are seen 55 years after the last train crossed it. — Rick Hamman

*S*lowly, but surely, the forest is reclaiming the Aptos Creek Canyon. Except for this author's hand, this unknown piece of metal has not seen life for over 80 years. Someday the forest will have hidden it entirely. — Courtesy: Bruce MacGregor Collection

Today, most of the Aptos Creek Canyon is part of the California State Park "Forest of Nisene Marks." Where once the lumberjack and the oxen ruled supreme, now the hikers and backpackers roam. Shown here are four hikers: Bill McClung, Bob Armbruster, Ed Stephenson and Jim Ewing who accompanied this author on a 13-hour grueling journey up the canyon in search of Monte Vista No. 2. — Rick Hamman

Santa Cruz to Los Gatos & the San Lorenzo River Basin Railroads

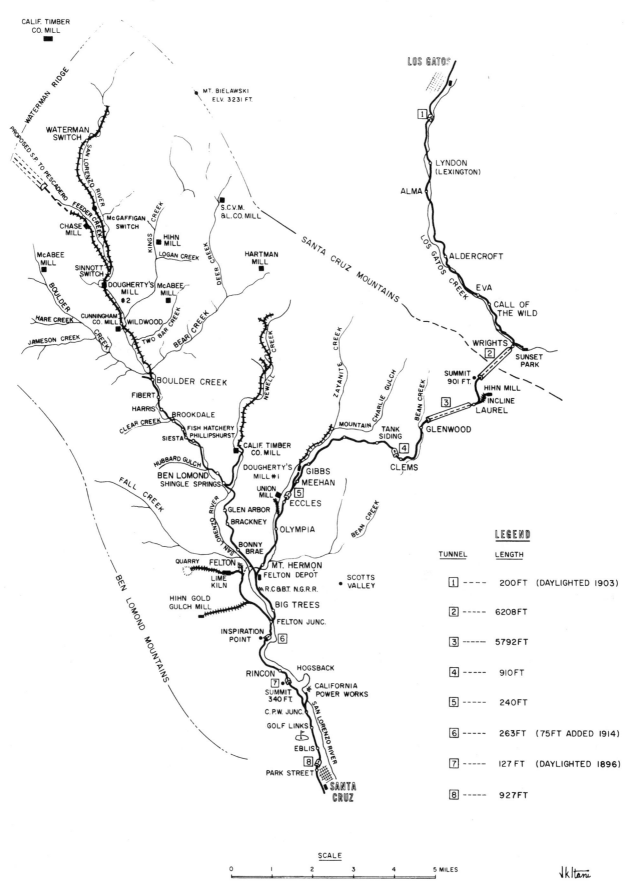

LOS GATOS

CALIF. TIMBER
CO. MILL

WATERMAN RIDGE

WATERMAN
SWITCH

PROPOSED S.P. TO PESCADERO

MT. BIELAWSKI
ELV. 3231 FT.

FEEDER CREEK

SAN LORENZO RIVER

LYNDON
(LEXINGTON)

ALMA

McGAFFIGAN
SWITCH

KINGS CREEK

CHASE
MILL

HIHN
MILL

S.C.V.M.
BL.CO. MILL

ALDERCROFT

McABEE
MILL

LOGAN CREEK

EVA

SANTA CRUZ MOUNTAINS

SINNOTT
SWITCH

DOUGHERTY'S
MILL
#2

DEER CREEK

HARTMAN
MILL

CALL OF
THE WILD

McABEE
MILL

LOS GATOS CREEK

WRIGHTS

BOULDER CREEK

HARE CREEK

CUNNINGHAM
CO. MILL

WILDWOOD

TWO BAR CREEK

BEAR CREEK

NEWELL CREEK

ZAYANITE CREEK

CHARLIE GULCH

SUNSET
PARK

JAMESON CREEK

SUMMIT
901 FT.

BEAN CREEK

HIHN MILL

INCLINE

BOULDER CREEK

LAUREL

FIBERT

HARRIS

BROOKDALE

GLENWOOD

CLEAR CREEK

FISH HATCHERY

SIESTA

PHILLIPSHURST

MOUNTAIN

TANK
SIDING

BEAN CREEK

CALIF. TIMBER
CO. MILL

CLEMS

HUBBARD GULCH

DOUGHERTY'S
MILL #1

GIBBS
MEEHAN

FALL CREEK

BEN LOMOND
SHINGLE SPRINGS

UNION
MILL

ECCLES

SAN LORENZO RIVER

GLEN ARBOR

BRACKNEY

OLYMPIA

BEAN CREEK

BONNY
BRAE

QUARRY

FELTON

MT. HERMON

BEN LOMOND MOUNTAINS

LIME
KILN

FELTON DEPOT

R.C&B.T. N.G.R.R.

SCOTTS
VALLEY

HIHN GOLD
GULCH MILL

BIG TREES

FELTON JUNC.

INSPIRATION
POINT

RINCON

HOGSBACK

CALIFORNIA
POWER WORKS

SUMMIT
340 FT.

C.P.W. JUNC.

GOLF LINKS

SAN LORENZO RIVER

EBLIS

PARK STREET

SANTA
CRUZ

LEGEND

TUNNEL	LENGTH
1 -----	200 FT (DAYLIGHTED 1903)
2 -----	6208 FT
3 -----	5792 FT
4 -----	910 FT
5 -----	240 FT
6 -----	263 FT (75 FT ADDED 1914)
7 -----	127 FT (DAYLIGHTED 1896)
8 -----	927 FT

SCALE

0   1   2   3   4   5 MILES

JK Itani

82

3

The San Lorenzo River Basin Railroads

From its small beginnings nestled deep in the Santa Cruz Mountains, the San Lorenzo River, bounded on the west by the Ben Lomond Mountain Range and on the east by the Santa Cruz Range, descends 1,200 feet in 21 miles before it finally reaches its mouth on the Monterey Bay at Santa Cruz. The river and its six major tributaries, Two Bar Creek, Kings Creek, Bear Creek, Boulder Creek, Newell Creek, and Zayante Creek, comprise what is known as the San Lorenzo Valley Basin. It is that basin and the history of railroading that took place within it which follows:

Little by little, the footprints of man had crept into the unexplored and awe-inspiring lands along the San Lorenzo River and its tributaries. First, it had been the Indians hunting and trapping and living within the ecological limits imposed upon them by the area's conditions. Next, exploration parties such as those led by Fremont and others were to chart the area and record its qualities. Finally, early pioneers and settlers would come to eke out a living and establish a homestead with an eye toward the future.

It was early in 1853 when one such settler, John Hines by name, happened to be doing some digging in a gulch approximately six miles above Santa Cruz. All of a sudden he gazed up at the side of the bank where his shovel had just struck. Here, before his very eyes were some bright metallic flakes, the likes of which he had never seen before. It wasn't long after that before John Hines was in town filing a mineral claim at the local land office. When asked by the clerk what the mineral was, he said with a grin, "Gold!!!"

And so it was that the early history of the San Lorenzo Valley began to be written. As soon as the magic word "gold" began to roll off the tongues of the local people, the area, later to be known as Gold Gulch, was crisscrossed with mineral claims. Before

it was all over, several companies, including the most successful one, the San Lorenzo Gold & Silver Mining Co., would be mining gold at up to $500 per ton. As for John Hines, he was able to successfully work his claim, taking out over $28,000 in gold from a cut about the size of a small log cabin.

Just above Gold Gulch on the San Lorenzo River, there was a quiet little meadow surrounded on three sides by mountains. It was here that several people, attracted by the gold and the area in general, had established a "no name" settlement over the years. It was also here that a owner of extensive lands had staged a costly court battle over some disputed property. In 1858, the case was decided in his favor and in tribute to his hard-working San Francisco attorney, John B. Felton, the land owner named the no name settlement after him. Thus, Felton, the first community of any size, was established in the San Lorenzo Valley.

As time went on, the search for gold subsided. While much gold had been found, the yield was not sufficient to keep large companies in profitable operation. As a result, many of the Felton residents, rather than pull up stakes and move on with the industry, went looking for other enterprises. While previously combing the surrounding hillsides looking for gold, other materials had been found that in many ways were just as good. Large limestone deposits had been located in several of the nearby areas along with significant amounts of sand and clay. In addition, there was another untapped resource in the San Lorenzo Valley that was also worth just as much as gold. This resource was uncut redwood, pine, oak and madrone trees. The entire valley was one vast forest where millions of dollars of forest products stood waiting for the knock of opportunity.

Unfortunately, this financial opportunity, both from lumber and from lime, was not as easily arrived at as one might think. It was seven long miles down a tortuous and winding San Lorenzo Gorge from Felton

An assessment notice for the San Lorenzo Rail Road Co. has been presented to Mr. Bartlett. Probably the first of many. — Courtesy: The Tumbleweed

to Santa Cruz. At that time, the only good toll road into and out of Felton was a 10% grade that went across Captain Isaac Graham's property southeast of town and then followed the east rim of the gorge into Santa Cruz. While the road was passable, and in fact well traveled, because of the grade it posed monumental problems when it came to moving heavy freight loads.

Realizing the situation, but at the same time being spurred on by the lure of the almighty dollar, several prominent Santa Cruz area businessmen came together in 1861 to see if they couldn't come up with a solution to the problem.

The San Lorenzo Valley Railroad

On May 20th, 1861, a group of Santa Cruz's finest entrepreneurs led by F.A. Hihn incorporated under the name of the "San Lorenzo Valley Railroad." It was their stated purpose to build a railroad from Santa Cruz, 16 miles up the San Lorenzo River, to a point known as the "Turkey Foot" where Boulder Creek, Bear Creek, and the San Lorenzo River all came together. Of the capital stock listed at $200,000, an initial amount of $47,500 had been subscribed to. It was hopefully predicted that soon the balance would also be subscribed to and the affairs of the road could get underway.

While the railroad looked good on paper, and

most agreed it would be a fine financial investment for all concerned, coming up with $150,000 more was no easy task. Several obstacles stood in the way of such a project. First, there was still much dispute going on over the validity of certain properties within the county which had once been part of the massive Spanish land grant system. Second, while California had become a state, there were still many legal questions left unanswered as to County-State relationships. Third, with the country in a heated conflict over slavery, no one was anxious to tie his assets up during such uncertain times. In retrospect, it wouldn't be until early 1866 that the concept of the San Lorenzo Valley Railroad, or any railroad for that matter, would finally receive much local public attention.

On January 6th, 1866, F.A. Hihn wrote an editorial suggesting that Santa Cruz County needed a railroad connection with the outside world. On January 19th, 1866, Mr. Seyante of the Felton area recommended in a *Sentinel* editorial that the San Lorenzo Valley Railroad should not only be built, but that it should also be extended from the headwaters of the San Lorenzo River through the Santa Cruz Mountains to Saratoga and Mountain View. Shortly thereafter, on February 3, the first official Santa Cruz County Railroad meeting took place. As a result of that meeting, it was decided that one, a rail connection was needed with the outside world, and two, that continued investigation into all possibilities, including routes both via Watsonville and through the Santa Cruz Mountains, should be undertaken. On June 19th, Mr. William J. Watson, Chief Engineer for the Stockton and Copperopolis Railroad, at the request of the Railroad Committee, delivered a preliminary survey of Mr. Seyante's mountain proposal. In it he stated that the road could be built with a ruling grade of 90 feet per mile at a cost of $28,000 per mile. He further stated that a half-mile tunnel would be needed to penetrate the Santa Cruz Mountains but that timbering would not be expensive as it was easily arrived at along the right-of-way. While the proposal proved interesting, without any capital investment, it was just so much research. As history would later reveal, public sentiment was more convinced that a right-of-way via Watsonville would be the easier to construct.

While the recommendations from Mr. Watson's survey were never carried out, they did, however, rekindle substantial interest in the original San Lorenzo Valley Railroad project. By early 1868, enough new stock had been subscribed to such that construction of the railroad could begin.

It was the plan of the S.L.V. management that initially the railroad would be built from Santa Cruz to Felton with the line being extended to the Turkey Foot at a later date. Thus, with the coming of Spring of 1868, work was begun on the grading, culverting, and bridge building of the San Lorenzo Valley Railroad. The grade was set at 40 feet per mile. There was to be one tunnel, approximately 900 feet long, near the site of the California Powder Works through what was known as the Hog's Back. This was a granite finger of land that jutted out from the side of the canyon such that the river went all the way around it and then doubled back to its original position. As the grade was to be kept as close as possible to the San Lorenzo River, trestling would be kept to a minimum.

By mid-summer all was going according to schedule. Much of the grading had been completed satisfactorily, and now bridge and culvert work had begun. Acquiring the necessary timber for the work was no problem because the railroad right-of-way was loaded with loggable trees. As a result, it simply became a matter of cutting what you needed.

It was this one point of tree cutting by the railroad, however, that didn't sit too well with a couple of parties. Mr. Isaac E. Davis and Mr. Henry Cowell, both of whom owned large areas of land along the right-of-way, had had condemnation proceedings carried out against particular pieces of their property by the railroad. While this was deemed necessary, and agreed to by all parties concerned, the two gentlemen thought they also should be paid for the standing timber on the property; the railroad, of course, felt otherwise. On July 27th, 1868, Mr. Davis

and Mr. Cowell asked for and received a preliminary court injunction halting construction of the line until the matter could be straightened out.

On August 11th, 1868, the defendants, the San Lorenzo Valley Railroad Co., presented an affidavit declaring that a petition had been filed in the County Court to condemn the said land for a railroad track, and had procured an order under the 34th section of the Rail Road Act of 1861, amended in 1863, permitting it to occupy and use the land sought to be condemned during the pending of the proceedings for condemnation, and that the work it was doing on the land was only the excavation of its railroad track. The judge ruled in favor of the San Lorenzo Valley Railroad Co. by dissolving the injunction.

With that problem taken care of, so the company thought, construction resumed. A short time later, the company was served with a second injunction, this time from the Appellate Court. Once again construction was halted. it would be almost 18 months before the case would be heard. When it finally was heard, the court ruled in favor of Davis and Cowell and against the S.L.V.R.R. This was an obvious setback to the company. Long drawn-out court cases and the time wasted in waiting have a tendency to spend much more money and lose financial backing. Such was the case for the S.L.V.R.R.

It was now March 6th, 1871. The San Lorenzo Valley Railroad, in an effort to keep its corporate shell intact and its franchise, recertified its existence with the County Clerk. It had a new board of directors and slightly different officers, but the company was the same. In a further effort to win public support and opinion, the railroad announced that it would be extending its line, once completed, to San Jose. Also, in an effort to solve its legal problems, the long-standing battle with Mr. Cowell and Mr. Davis would be taken to the California Supreme Court.

With obvious victory on the minds of the S.L.V. management and its supporters, it was a sad day for all, two and a half years later, when the final word was received from the California Supreme Court. In a landmark case (No. 1828) that affected all of the future railroads which would ever be built in the State of California, the Supreme Court gave the following ruling:

Section 34 of the Railroad Act of 1863 makes no provision for the compensation of such temporary undertaking (taking of private property for public use without just compensation) and therefore the Act is declared unconstitutional.

Henceforth and forever more railroads would have to pay for all usable assets contained on or in land taken under condemnation proceedings.

This decision prostituted the S.L.V.R.R. Co. It

Update for the 2002 edition: San Lorenzo Valley Rail Road

The original text for the San Lorenzo Valley Rail Road was largely based on a few newspaper articles, court records, and other official documentation generated over 130 years ago. Like so many early railroad companies it seemed more a reality on paper than in physical plant.

After the book originally came out, I had the opportunity to work as a crew member for many years on the Santa Cruz, Big Trees, & Pacific Railway going up and down the canyon of the San Lorenzo River. After repeatedly seeing many old cuts and fills that did not fit any of the previous railroad history, several of us started exploring the canyon more closely.

We discovered that the San Lorenzo Valley Rail Road had, in fact, made the cuts and fills plus some grade for three miles from Felton down to where the railroad would have crossed the river for the first time. Plus, we found additional sections that had been started further down the canyon. Thus, it was determined that the San Lorenzo Valley Rail Road was much more than just a paper railroad.

Today, most of that 130-year-old grade lies within Henry Cowell State Park. You can check it out. The full story remains to be completed.

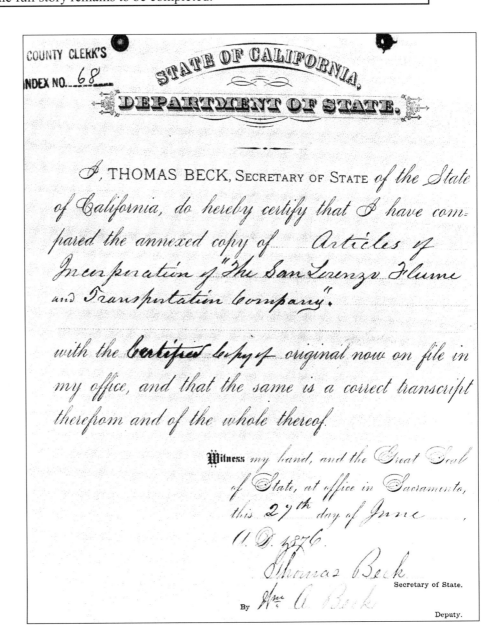

The San Lorenzo Flume & Transportation Company Incorporation. — Courtesy: Santa Cruz County Clerk's Office

was now January of 1874, and the railroad was broke and unbuildable. With nothing left but its dreams of the past and the pressing future, it threw in the towel, released its franchise, and ceased to exist.

The San Lorenzo Flume & Transportation Company
The Santa Cruz & Felton Railroad Company

Life has a way of continuing on with or without planned progress. So it was with the San Lorenzo Valley Basin during that 13-year period, from 1861 to 1874. New roads had been completed, including a heavy wagon road down the tortuous San Lorenzo Canyon. Several small shingle mills, sawmills, and splitstuff operations had been set up by local lumber companies. Two limestone operations were begun near Felton. The California Powder Works had started shipping various types of black powder from their site at the Hogsback to a newly completed wharf in Santa Cruz. The Homestead Act had opened up most of the upper valley to 160-acre tracts of land, and a second settlement known as Lorenzo had been established about a mile below the Turkey Foot.

With this development and expansion had come many new businessmen who, like their S.L.V.R.R. predecessors, were acutely aware of the potential wealth this area had to offer. Likewise, these same businessmen realized that wagons drawn by horses, mules, and oxen were just not adequate enough to handle the volume of lumber, lime, and other products that could be generated in the San Lorenzo and surrounding canyons. Thus, with the demise of the San Lorenzo Valley Railroad, it came as no surprise when in just six short months another group of entrepreneurs had stepped to the forefront and incorporated to do it all over again.

In late October, the Santa Cruz newspapers announced that a new organization informally known as "the San Lorenzo Company" was about to incorporate to build a narrow gauge railroad from Santa Cruz to Felton and an eight-mile lumber flume from Felton to the vicinity of Alcorn's old place near the Turkey Foot. Once at the Turkey Foot it was planned to extend smaller branch flumes up Bear Creek, Boulder Creek, and the San Lorenzo River to a point where sufficient water could still be found to fill each flume. It was estimated that the project would take two years to complete and that it would be in operation by the time the Santa Cruz Railroad was ready to open. While no specifics were given, the newspapers hinted that this would be the biggest business concern yet to take place in the county and that, judging from the investors involved, the project was bound to succeed.

It wasn't very long after the October announcement before the San Lorenzo Company had formally incorporated under two separate entities to carry out its plan as previously presented. The first incorporation was that of the Santa Cruz and Felton Railroad Company. The railroad was to run from a wharf, soon to be built on Monterey Bay, up River Street and Pacific Avenue in Santa Cruz to Bay Street near the cliffs of Mission Hill at the town's northernly limits. From there it would follow a route somewhere between the wagon road and the San Lorenzo River until it reached its terminus in Felton. The second incorporation was that of the San Lorenzo Flume and Transportation Company. It was this company's responsibility to build the V-framework flume from a point about two miles above the Turkey Foot, where they were building a $12,000 lumber mill, to Felton. It was estimated that the railroad would cost about $500,000 to build and that the flume would cost about $2,500 per mile for its construction.

While the Santa Cruz & Felton had big plans for it's financial future, they suffered from a rather skimpy beginning. Originally, the railroad was to follow a portion of the easy San Lorenzo Valley Rail Road grade of 40 feet to the mile. This would have taken them through the powder works and into a 900-foot tunnel which traversed the Hogsback. That was a good idea except when the narrow gauge's management started realizing what it would cost them to tunnel through solid granite they opted for an alternate plan. Instead, they laid out a twisting, winding, 3.5% grade out of Santa Cruz that bypassed the powder works and crossed the Hogsback at a point where only a 127-foot tunnel through soft soil would be required. From this point, known as "Summit" and later "Rincon," the line was four miles of level to slightly downhill grade into Felton. In a second cost-cutting measure, the S.C.&F. decided to use rail as light as 20-lb. iron in some places rather than 35-lb. iron as originally called for.

By the time early Spring of 1875 dawned upon the county, both the railroad and the flume were well into construction. Already, the right-of-way for the railroad had been surveyed and partially graded, and now ties were being laid into position to await the coming of the rail. While the railroad was progressing at a beehive pace, the flume was an even greater scene of activity. Two miles of flume had been completed from the company's mill above the Turkey Foot down to the town of Lorenzo, and over 200 men were hard at work on the rest.

The erection of the flume was under the direction of Mr. Levi Hammell, a noted expert in California flume building. It was considered by most to be more of an engineering feat than was the railroad. The entire structure was elevated anywhere from 30 to 50 feet above the ground and at the six places where the flume

Light freight engine for 25 or 30 lb. rail.

Cylinders, 9½ inches diameter 14 inch stroke.

Wheelbase,	7ft. 3 inche
Diameter of drivers,	30 or 33 "
Weight in working order,	20,000 lbs.
Water capacity of tender tank,	500 gals.

Above: The advertisement for the H.K. Porter Co. was designed around a locomotive #218 which was to go to the Chester & Lenoir R.R. That same locomotive, however, because of a mix-up, became the S.C. & F.s "Santa Cruz"engine. — Courtesy: Stanford University Library

Right: The "Santa Cruz"locomotive as it appeared in Felton during opening ceremonies, October 13, 1875. — Courtesy: Roy Graves Collection, U.C. Berkeley, Bancroft Library

A view of Pacific Ave. in downtown Santa Cruz as it appeared in the early 1880's. Originally, the Santa Cruz & Felton RR used this track to leave and enter town. — Courtesy: Fred Stoes Collection

crossed the San Lorenzo River, arches of from 125 feet to 210 feet were necessary. Adding to the degree of difficulty was the design requirement which called for a constant decrease in elevation of five inches in every 80 feet. The V-framework of the flume itself required approximately 125,000 board feet of 2"x6' scantling to the mile. All construction lumber was floated down the completed portion of the flume from the company's 30,000 board foot capacity mill to the current section being worked. In this manner, material costs could be kept at a minimum because all lumber was supplied by the company to the company.

The railroad and the flume were not the only areas the San Lorenzo Co. had ongoing construction taking place. By the middle of April, the company's $25,000 wharf had begun to be erected at the beach. It was predicted by its builders, the Pacific Bridge Company, that the 1,278-foot single-ended structure would be completed and in use by June 15th.

By the time the scheduled opening of the wharf took place, the affairs of the San Lorenzo Co. were well on their way toward completion. The flume was progressing rapidly toward its terminus with the

S.C.&F. at Felton. Rails had now been laid for almost four miles out of Santa Cruz, and the tunnel and bridge work was about completed. In addition, several 24-foot by 7-foot Carter flatcars had arrived from Sausalito and had now been put into horse-drawn service doing construction work. . .

The day, July 5th, 1875. Evidently most people had recovered from the various activities of the Fourth and were now looking forward to next year's Centennial celebration. But, even more than next year's celebration, many local folks were looking forward to today. For the last few years, railroads and railroad construction had been the topic of discussion around Santa Cruz. Now, the Santa Cruz Railroad and the Santa Cruz & Felton Railroad were nearing completion. Soon, the birth of progress and productivity would be a reality for the county. As with all expectant mothers, the first sign of movement within the womb holds special meaning. And so it was that today would be that day for Santa Cruz County.

All day long, a heavily laden freight caravan had been making its way from Watsonville along the county road. By early evening, it had reached its destination, the Santa Cruz Railroad's end-of-track at Aptos. With strain and pain and tackle block and anchor, the caravan's cumbersome cargo was placed on the track for shipment to Santa Cruz.

There it sat, 15 tons of cold, silent steel waiting for the breath of life to stir within its boiler. Engineer Pope climbed aboard and lit the firebox. He watched the brass and glass pressure gauge slowly climb, 10 lbs., 15 lbs., 20 lbs., 30 lbs. . . . more cordwood was added to the fire. In no time at all, the sounds of hissing began to come from within. It wasn't long thereafter until Pope once again eyed the pressure gauge. Steadily it had climbed to 90 lbs. Steam was now coming out of the POP valves. People were standing around in the warm early evening atmosphere listening to the panting of the boiler and feeling and smelling the soft cloud of steam that permeated the air around them. All were waiting for that moment when Pope would ease back on the reins of this iron horse and give it its head. And then it happened. The first burst of steam filled its cylindrical lungs and the mighty steed gave out with a belch of fiery smoke as it lurched under its own power. All onlookers gave out with a cheer of enthusiasm as the Santa Cruz and Felton's first motive power gave forth to life.

After thoroughly inspecting his mount, Pope deemed it ready for the run into Santa Cruz. While all the men had been paying attention to the masculinity of this H.K. Porter 0-6-0 steam locomotive, a freespirited young lady had been decorating this beautiful little "Santa Cruz" engine with flowers. Pope, seeing what she was doing and being caught up in the euphoria of the event itself, asked her if she would like to accompany him in the cab on the way to Santa Cruz. Without hesitation, she accepted. And so it was on that gentle summer evening that a full-sized narrow gauge steam locomotive, with a man at the throttle and a woman on the whistle cord, announced to the world that the wheels of progress and productivity had just seen movement for the very first time in Santa Cruz County. . .

On October 9th, 1875, the community's management placed an ad in each of the local Santa Cruz newspapers announcing that a "gala" event was to take place on Wednesday next, and that all were invited to partake of the festivities which were to start on River Street at 9:30 a.m. The following is a firsthand account of that event as told by a local reporter:

The general invitation extended by the Board of Directors to the public, through the columns of last week's journal, met with a most hearty acceptance, and when on Wednesday morning the whistle of the "Santa Cruz" sounded on River street, a general rush was made in the direction of the cars. Speedily they were filled, or rather let us use a more expressive word, and say crammed, with their precious freight of happy humanity ... Seven cars were thus filled, and Tucker, the fireman of the locomotive thinking of the heavy grades before him, wiped the perspiration from his manly brow with the back of his hand, and groaned a ghastly groan . . . The first train has left Santa Cruz, and seven hundred of her people are whirling away towards the mountains ... Pope lets her work briskly, for there are heavy grades ahead, and with the load we are hauling it will not do to crawl towards them. Now we are in the old Mission Orchard, one more curve and we are on the long tangent, which will bring us past Gharkey's vineyard. Steadily, Pope, my friend; and you, Tucker, pile on your wood, for in a moment more we commence to climb 126 feet to the mile. Now we are upon it; the engine seems to know what is required of her; she struggles bravely. You can hear her exhaust for a quarter of a mile. Slowly we climb - slowly but surely. Pope views his engine affectionately: "There is a terrible load behind you, little one, pull manfully;" and she does. There is a sharp curve in front of us. The wheels turn slower and slower; she pants heavily. We look ahead anxiously; the merry laugh is silenced, and each one holds his breath. Will we make it? No! one more laborious revolution and we stop. Do not chide her, gentlemen, she has done her duty. "Give her a drink," yells a voice in the crowd, and a drink she gets, although it is rather oily. Suddenly the whistle sounds 'off brakes,' and she makes a struggle, pants once or twice, and stops again. "More steam, Tucker, my man, you are our only salvation now! Steadily the needle drops over the face of the indicator, 100, 110, 120, 130. "Now, Pope, once more!" Off go the brakes again, and with a cheer that made the old woods ring we bounded forward briskly. She will not falter again, "not if we know ourselves," say those two fellows in the cab. Once more the merry hum of voices rises, and the "Santa Cruz" whistles cheerily as she works ahead. The Powder works are below us now, nestling cosily in their pretty valley, the flags flying to welcome our approach. We pass through the tunnel, 127 feet long, and the top of the grade is reached. Every one draws a long breath. Pope gives her a little more oil, and we go ahead again. Soon we strike the river bank once more. Below us bubbles the noisy waters over their bed of granite boulders. Above us towers the almost perpendicular hill side, clad in all the verdure of a California forest. We cross the "slide" now; the most difficult piece of work on the road was done here. These walls of rock are as hard as adamant; that Howe truss over the central chasm has a span of seventy-five feet... The vertical distance from this truss to the river is 150 feet... Men say to each other the road is splendid. A magnificent engineering achievement... A few more heavy curves and long trestles and we reach the toll house point, and leave the river... It is only a short distance from here to Big Trees... Mr. Silent has had the underbrush cut away, a stand erected for the band, and long rows of tables for the benefit of the public, beneath whose lunches the planks soon groan heavily. The place is alive with people, and every one appears to be enjoying himself... The afternoon passed as pleasantly as the morning, and when at half past four the train left, it carried as happy a crowd as ever a locomotive pulled. Six o'clock found us in front of the St. Charles Hotel once more. Three rousting cheers were given, and the jolliest day we have ever seen, came auspiciously to an end. And here, before we close, let us pay this one compliment to the care exercised by the company: There were over 2500 people at the picnic, and not one returned home with so much as a scratch...

It had taken the S.C.&F. only eight months to complete the rail line from Santa Cruz to Felton. Likewise, its sister organization, the San Lorenzo Flume and Transportation Company, had also been constructed in about the same amount of time. Together, they now formed a 16-mile transportation system that stretched from the "Gharkey" railroad wharf and the future Santa Cruz Railroad yards into the heart of the San Lorenzo timberlands.

What had been a dream for F.A. Hihn and others in May of 1861 had become a reality for the group known as the San Lorenzo Company on November 4th, 1875. The first through freight, 30,000 board feet of lumber for Hugh Sheer of Oakland, had just been shipped from the head of the flume to the sea. It had

traveled the flume from the company's mill to Felton at the rate of 5,000 board feet per hour. From Felton it was loaded onto waiting flatcars and brought to town by the "Santa Cruz." At the city limits, the engine was cut off and the cars were drawn by horses through Santa Cruz to the wharf. Thus, the combined operations of the San Lorenzo Company were begun.

It should be noted that all was not peaches and cream when it came to the final leg of the operation. The City of Santa Cruz had placed some severe restrictions on the S.C.&F. when it came to operating trains through town. The original ordinance had stated that if and when a horsecar company is incorporated within the City of Santa Cruz, the Santa Cruz and Felton must allow that company the use of its right-of-way down Pacific Avenue for up to 600 feet. It also stated that, from that time on, all freight and passenger cars could be drawn only by horse over that section of track. In addition, the railroad had to agree to install and maintain a seven-foot-wide strip of wooden planking wherever its tracks shared city streets. Not so ironically, a horsecar company incorporated on the very same day as did the Santa Cruz & Felton. As a result, life was not so pleasant for the railroad when it came to downtown operations.

In order to alleviate this bottleneck and at the same time improve operations, the S.C.&F. management decided to build a 900-foot tunnel through the chalk walls of Mission Hill and bring their right-of-way in behind the City of Santa Cruz. This

The scene is the end of the flume and the beginning of the railroad at Felton around 1876. — Courtesy: California State Library

Above: The flume stands stalwart at one of the many crossings of the San Lorenzo River above Felton. — Courtesy: Bruce MacGregor Collection

Below: Mr. & Mrs. Harmon relax at home near the line of the flume above the town of Lorenzo. — Courtesy: Sue Meschi Collection

"Lorenzo," later part of Boulder Creek, as it looked in 1875 when the flume first arrived. — Courtesy: U.C. Santa Cruz Special Collections, photographer: S.P. Sanborn

Once upon a time there was to be a Felton and San Lorenzo Railroad Co. — Courtesy: Santa Cruz County Clerk's Office

was done in short order, and before the beginning of 1876, the Santa Cruz & Felton had seen the last of Pacific Avenue.

It was just about this time that Superintendent A. Williams had left the employee of the Santa Cruz & Felton and had gone to work for the Santa Clara Valley Railroad at Dumbarton Point. With the rumor circulating that the S.C.&F. was going to continue its line into the Santa Clara Valley through the Santa Cruz Mountains in the near future, many no doubt saw Mr. Williams' leaving as a further step in that direction.

By early Summer of 1876, the S.C.&F. had received its second locomotive from H.K. Porter which had appropriately been named the "Felton." In no time at all, it and its sister locomotive, the "Santa Cruz" were hard at work moving the company's 34 flatcars, six boxcars, and two passenger coaches up and down the San Lorenzo Canyon.

The Felton & San Lorenzo Company

By the end of the first season of operations, the San Lorenzo Company had come to a rather unhappy conclusion about their flume. It only had a certain capacity for the shipment of lumber, beyond which it couldn't go. Unfortunately, the prospects for future business dictated that there would be much more lumber to ship than the flume could handle. As a result, until something was done to change this situation, the lumber business up the San Lorenzo would not be able to develop.

On November 8th, 1876, men from the Board of Directors of both San Lorenzo Company subsidiaries came together and incorporated under a new banner to be known as the "Felton and San Lorenzo Company." Its capital stock was listed at $500,000 of which only $40,000 had been subscribed to. It was the intention of its management that the narrow gauge S.C.&F. be extended from Felton to the town of Lorenzo. Once the line reached Lorenzo it was to break into three branches. The first branch would turn west and follow Boulder Creek for approximately ten miles. The second branch would turn east and follow Bear Creek for seven miles. Finally, the third branch would continue up the San Lorenzo River for about eight miles to its headwaters.

While the "Felton and San Lorenzo Railroad" was a feasible concept, and no doubt a money-maker, the possibilities of raising another $460,000 from the local community were looked upon by most as slim for the present. Already, over $1,500,000 had been paid out by local investors in Santa Clara and Santa Cruz Counties to build the flume, the S.C.&F. Railroad, and the Santa Cruz Railroad. To approach them for more was a waste of time. If the railroad was going to be built at all, about the only way it could happen would be to attract some large San Francisco investors.

The South Pacific Coast Railroad

About the time brokers were out beating the bushes for investors for the Felton and San Lorenzo Railroad, plans were beginning to take shape for a far larger operation over in the San Francisco Bay area. By May of 1876, formal articles of incorporation for the South Pacific Coast Railroad to build and operate a rail line from Alameda to Santa Cruz via San Jose had been filed with the County Clerk's Office. The stated brass were A.E. Davis, President; Joseph Clark, Vice President; George H. Waggoner, Secretary and Treasurer; R. Romain, Auditor; Thomas Carter, Superintendent; and Carry Peoples, ex-Santa Clara Valley Railroad Director and current S.P.C. honorary director. The capital stock, all of which had been subscribed to by Davis and Fair except for six shares which belonged to the other Davis APPOINTED directors, was listed at $1,000,000.

Because all of the stock had already been subscribed to and because much of the land had previously been purchased by the acquired Santa Clara Valley Railroad, the South Pacific Coast was able to begin surveying and construction of the Dumbarton Point-Newark to San Jose portion almost immediately. By January of 1877, this section had been completed to the outskirts of San Jose, and people in Santa Cruz County were beginning to believe that this upstart South Pacific Coast Railroad was a for-real concern.

Building the South Pacific Coast[6] from Dumbarton Point to San Jose of course, had been one thing; building it from San Jose to Santa Cruz, however, was going to be quite another. On the one hand, much of the grading and culverting had already

---

[6]The text for the S.P.C. as written here will be abbreviated. As there are already two very fine publications, *South Pacific Coast* and *South Pacific Coast: A Centennial* by Bruce A. MacGregor, the intent of this section will be only to add continuity to the chapter and to release new information.

The Gharkey Railroad Wharf basks in the Monterey Bay moonlight one warm 1890's evening. This picture, made from the original glass plate, is very rare because night photography as of this time was almost technically impossible. — Courtesy: U.C. Santa Cruz Special Collections

been accomplished when the Santa Clara Valley Railroad had been taken over. All that had been required to finish the line to San Jose was to clean up the 1875-1876 storm damage and continue on. As for obstacles, there weren't any. The right-of-way was essentially straight and level, and no heavy bridging or tunneling had been necessary. On the other hand, in order to continue the line from San Jose to Santa Cruz, a 2,000- to 3,000-foot mountain range was going to have to be crossed. No matter how the S.P.C. was to go about it, extensive tunneling, bridging, grading, and culverting would be required before a South Pacific Coast steam locomotive would ever sound its arrival in Santa Cruz.

Thus, the first question, of course, was how would it cross the mountains? Originally, many had thought the best way was to go through the range from Saratoga and drop into the headwaters of the San Lorenzo and then down into Santa Cruz. This plan was shortly deemed infeasible, however, after realizing the tremendous amount of deep trestling across narrow gorges, tight radius curves around sharp contours, and numerous long tunnels through granite that would be required. The second plan, encouraged by anxious farmers and ranchers in the San Tomas area and some of the large property owners along Los Gatos Creek, was to be the one finally adopted by S.P.C. management. It called for the right-of-way, once it left San Jose, to enter the Santa Cruz Mountains near the town of Los Gatos. At that point, it would first traverse through two short tunnels in the Los Gatos Canyon and then stop at Lexington where the Santa Clara Valley Mill and Lumber Company had its sawmill in full swing. From Lexington, the right-of-way would follow Los Gatos Creek on to a point at the base of the Santa Cruz Mountains, later to be known as "Wright's." Next, it would pass through a 6,200-foot tunnel into the headwaters of Soquel Creek and stop at a spot to be named "Laurel." It was at this location that Santa Cruz millionaire Fred A. Hihn had much of his timber holdings. Upon leaving Laurel, the right-of-way would drop through a 5,800-foot tunnel into Glenwood Basin. Here, the Glenwood Lumber Company already had a large concern in operation; in nearby Scott's Valley, the El Dorado Lumber Company also had a substantial mill going. In addition, many wine grapes were being grown in the area. After leaving Glenwood, the right-of-way would continue on through another 900-foot tunnel into the Zayante Creek Canyon and next stop at a place to be known as "Dougherty's." At this spot, the Santa Clara Valley Mill and Lumber Company would build a mill to service the harvesting needs on its 5,000 acres of timberland. Finally, the line would descend into Felton where it would make connections with the Santa Cruz and Felton Railroad at "Big Trees."

While it was easy to think about and to talk about building the South Pacific Coast from San Jose to Santa Cruz, the actual job of doing it brought all concerned to cold sobering reality. Initially Chief Engineer, Thomas Davis (nephew to Hog Davis) had estimated construction costs through the mountains at $20,000 per mile. After finally getting out and doing the engineering survey and then commencing construction, he found that it was going to cost more like $100,000 per mile. Fortunately, backer James Fair didn't seem to get too excited about the "slight" cost over runs, and the money for the project, as many outsiders noted, kept coming from some inexhaustible well.

It should be noted here that Fair and Davis had much greater ambitions for the South Pacific Coast than just a short line from Alameda to Santa Cruz. Eventually it was planned that the S.P.C. would build east and join the narrow gauge Denver & Rio Grande which was presently moving west. To that end, both men had spent a considerable amount of time with the brass from the Denver & Rio Grande in formal discussions concerning such a transcontinental link.

By June of 1878, through service from Alameda to Los Gatos had started, and construction in the Santa Cruz Mountains was well underway. Probably of all the problems encountered in building this narrow gauge mountain right-of-way, the biggest headache would be tunnel No. 3, or Summit tunnel, at Wright's. This 6,200-foot tunnel would take almost two years to construct and would claim the lives of over 30 men in the process. While long tunnels had been dealt with before, never one that crossed an earthquake fault such as this one crossed, the San Andreas. Because of it, tunneling crews encountered coal deposits, shifting sandstone, granite slabs, natural gas which sometimes violently exploded by accident, and excessive amounts of water.

On September 6th, 1879, the first train crossed the San Lorenzo River bridge into Big Trees on that portion of the S.P.C. right-of-way that had been completed from the Santa Cruz and Felton Junction to new Felton. As the train pulled up in front of Big Trees, Johnny Hooper, who kept the trees, came out with a bottle of champagne and treated all hands to a little afternoon delight. From this day forward, track laying and ballasting would continue on up to the Summit tunnel from the Santa Cruz side at a much faster pace. In just a short nine months, it would be May of 1880, and the narrow gauge South Pacific Coast "Santa Cruz Division" would commence operations. Within a few more months, the railroad would have most of the freight and passenger business and Fred Hihn's beleaguered little Santa Cruz Railroad between Pajaro and Santa Cruz would turn belly up and die.

South Pacific Coast locomotive #5 poses with train and crew on three rail track in Santa Cruz. Crew left to right: Conductor, "Daisy" Hollenback; Engineer, Fred Reynolds; Baggageman, "Brick" Roy, and unknown fireman. — Courtesy: Fred Stoes Collection

The S.P.C., because it was narrow gauge and because it was financed primarily by only one man, was initially looked upon by many as a spur of the moment, less than first-class operation. This, however, couldn't have been further from the truth. The line, as most would later come to realize, was a very well planned and very well thought out railroad. Right from the start the maximum ruling grade had been set at 90 feet to the mile, a comparatively easy grade even in those days. The right-of-way itself was comprised of 50-lb. rail spiked to redwood ties grounded in a firm foundation of high quality ballast. The equipment consisted of all brand new rolling stock built by Carter Brothers of Newark and ten brand new Baldwin, 4-4-0, 22-ton steam locomotives. Adequate maintenance facilities and station sites had been provided along with three first cabin ferries to transport passengers and freight from San Francisco to Alameda. As a final measure, much of the original Santa Cruz and Felton right-of-way had been

realigned and beefed up with the addition of a new tunnel at the slide area and several small bridges. As a whole, the S.P.C. was a first-quality concern the likes of which were only to be duplicated in Colorado.

With the coming of the summer season of 1882, once again came the realization that the flume was just not adequate enough to handle all of the freight that could be generated both now and in the future north of Felton. The Santa Clara Valley Mill and Lumber Company, in addition to their Zayante Creek property at Dougherty's, had large parcels of timberland in the Newell Creek Basin and in the San Lorenzo and Bear Creek Canyons above the Turkey Foot. Plans were now being readied as to how to harvest these holdings once the Zayante Creek operation was complete. Without some better form of transportation, other than the flume, production capabilities could never be met. Besides the S.C.V.M.&L.Co., other interests were developing along the flume that further added to its burden. Cunningham and Company had recently built

97

A 6-car S.P.C. passenger train descends the San Lorenzo Gorge grade, circa 1905. — Courtesy: Francis J. Carney Collection

Train approaching Rincon on the narrow gauge. — Courtesy: Harold Von Gorder Collection

a 40,000 board-foot capacity sawmill about two miles above the Turkey Foot on the San Lorenzo River where they were working 2,000 acres. Also, they had two shinglemills in operation, one on Kings Creek, and one on Boulder Creek. In addition to the Cunningham mills, there were many other smaller operations going on in the area such as the Comstock Mill, the Union Mill, Joseph Perry's Mill at Lorenzo, and the Chase and Company Mill. At Pacific Mills, later to be called Ben Lomond, J.P. Pierces' concern was busily turning out extensive quantities of finished lumber products.

It should be added that there were increased transportation demands, other than for freight, being created by the area. Because of the Homestead Act, many new families had moved into the hinterlands of the San Lorenzo Valley to claim their 160-acre tracts of government land. Also, many hunters, fishermen, and campers were continually coming to examine and

explore the wilds of the area. In addition, all those single and married lumbermen who were gainfully employed locally provided an increased population base. In support of this expanding population, new and larger communities were being established. First, there was Boulder Creek, an informal little town that was developing around the Turkey Foot. About a mile below Boulder Creek sat the already well-established and ever-expanding community of Lorenzo. A short distance from Lorenzo, there was another new milling community known as Clear Creek. From here it was just two miles to Pacific Mills where more development was taking place. With all of this increase in population being brought on by the homesteading and cultivation of the outlying areas, the continuing tourism, and the expansion and establishment of new communities, better passenger, mail, and express transportation was also becoming a dire necessity.

Inevitably, from what was happening, the next event was almost a virtual certainty.

The Felton and Pescadero Railroad Company (S.P.C.)

On Thursday, June 21, 1883, the Santa Cruz Courier Item newspaper reported that several of the well-known gentry had come together under the incorporated banner of the Felton and Pescadero Railroad Company. Their stated purpose was to build a narrow gauge line between the communities of the same two names. Among those prominently listed were A.E. Davis and G.H. Waggoner of the South Pacific Coast and Superintendent R.M. Garrett of the S.P.C. subsidiary, the Santa Cruz and Felton. The capital stock of the company, all of which had been subscribed to by its stated directors and silent backer(s), was listed at $500,000. Hopefully, the article went on to say, Santa Cruz would have a connection to Pescadero via Felton within two years.

While Pescadero was to be the eventual goal of this new railroad, at present its management's only concern was the building of the line as far as the Turkey Foot. Almost immediately property in the towns of Boulder Creek and Lorenzo began to skyrocket in price. Everybody wanted to be on the mainline, and everybody wanted to be near the terminus. The only question left unanswered, of course, was where was the terminus to be? Many thought Lorenzo was the logical place because it was a larger community and because Joseph Perry, a man of much influence, had a sawmill and a shingle mill in operation there. At the same time, however, others felt that Boulder Creek offered the best location. Here, there was much more level open space such that a good-sized railroad yard could be laid out. Also, Boulder Creek sitting right on the Turkey Foot provided a better outlet should expansion ever take place into any one of the three canyons. The decision wasn't very long in coming. After a careful examination of the two locations, the management of the Felton and Pescadero Railroad announced that henceforth and forever more the company's terminus would be Boulder Creek.

Thus, the end points of the line had been chosen, and now all that was left to do was select the best route and buy the property. It had been the intention of management to begin the extension of the line from the old Felton yards, go across the San Lorenzo river, and proceed up its right bank to Pacific Mills. From Pacific Mills, the line would have to cross the river two more times before it reached Clear Creek and then four more times before it terminated in Boulder Creek. While there was an increase in elevation of only 200 feet between Felton and Boulder Creek, the line, due to the topography of the San Lorenzo Canyon,

would have to be engineered like a rollercoaster. In some places, a ruling grade of 2.5% would be necessary to jump from flat spot to flat spot, while in others a succession of curves, cuts, and fills would be the standard rule of thumb. No tunnels would be required.

About the time the Felton and Pescadero started buying up property out of Felton they ran into an unexpected situation. The local townsfolk who owned the property in question were asking exorbitant prices for same. After many unsuccessful negotiation attempts, the railroad said to heck with the townsfolk and decided to begin the Boulder Creek branch from the new Felton station on the S.P.C. line over the hill.

By the end of the 1883-1884 rainy season, the route had been selected and secured, and surveying and construction under W.P. Drumm of the S.P.C. had begun. With the exception of a bad sandstone area about a mile out of Felton where several Chinese workers would lose their lives in a landslide, no major obstacles or encumbrances would slow completion. In just a little over a year the Boulder Creek branch would be complete, and operations would commence to Pacific Mills (Ben Lomond in 1887), Clear Creek (Brookdale in 1902), and Boulder Creek.

On Sunday, April 26th, 1885, a double celebration commemorating the 66th anniversary of the I.O.O.F. and the opening of the Felton and Pescadero Railroad was held. It included a special excursion aboard the first passenger train to Boulder Creek and then a gala picnic. On hand was Engineer Pete Simon who did the honors in the cab along with Conductor Henry "Daisy" Hollenback, who looked after the train's management.

On April 28, 1885, scheduled freight and passenger service commenced over the S.P.C. subsidiary, the Felton and Pescadero Railroad. In a few short months, Boulder Creek would come to be known as the timber-shipping rail center for western central California, and the once progressive town of Lorenzo would fade into history.

The South Pacific Coast Railway/ Southern Pacific

The mountains were awakening to the sounds of humanity as it gouged and cut and hacked and chopped its way toward progress and profit. While black powder from the Santa Cruz Powder Works in the San Lorenzo Canyon, lime from the H.T. Holmes Company and the I.X.L. Company at Felton, and fruit and produce from the Glenwood, Laurel and Wright's areas would be sold and shipped in great quantities, lumber would prove to be the biggest money-maker for the South Pacific Coast. By 1886, the company's mainline and its branches were operating at peak conditions. Each month, hundreds of carloads of timber products were now coming out of the yards at

Originally, the Santa Cruz & Felton RR right-of-way passed around Inspiration Point through a sharp cut pictured on the right. When the S.P.C. took over they dug tunnel #6 to straighten out the fine. In later years, during the widening of the tunnel for broad gauging, the track was once again temporarily laid through the cut and trains run there on. — Courtesy: U.C. Santa Cruz Special Collections

Felton and Boulder Creek. At the same time, passenger trains, especially on weekends and holidays, were bulging at the seams as they carried their happy throng of excursionists to the many tourist points along the right-of-way. Taken as a whole, the S.P.C. was, and would continue to be, an obvious financial success for its management and an obvious thorn in the side of the Southern Pacific's broad gauge line into Santa Cruz via Pajaro.

Shortly before the end of 1886, as previously mentioned, in a move that caught everyone by surprise, James G. Fair would sell his active interests in the South Pacific Coast to the Southern Pacific for $6,000,000. In order to make it easy on the S.P., he would turn right around and buy back $5,500,000 worth of 50-year 4% redeemable gold bonds issued

as a first mortgage against the S.P.C. line. In effect, he simply turned the management of the South Pacific Coast over to the Southern Pacific and bought himself a guaranteed return on his money of $220,000 a year. If the S.P. fell into hard times, for whatever reason, the line would revert to him, as he held the first mortgage. Evidently after a short period of time had passed, however, Fair, for reasons known only to himself, decided he didn't want anything more to do with the railroad business. In the normal course of business procedures over the next few months, he sold his bonds to the Farmers Loan and Trust Co. for their face value plus a "little" profit. This move would sever Fair from the South Pacific Coast forever.

Because of Fair's back and forth business transactions and because of the disarray of the many

On Monday, May 11, 1903, President Theodore Roosevelt visited "Big Trees." In his honor, one of the giant monarchs was dedicated and bears his name to this day. A collector's ribbon. — Courtesy: George Hildebrand Collection.

S.P.C. subsidiaries, such as the Felton and Pescadero and the Santa Cruz and Felton, the Southern Pacific decided to put it all under one corporate umbrella. On July 1st, 1887, the South Pacific Coast Railway was incorporated to consolidate the various interests of the South Pacific Coast Railroad. Needless to say, with the consumation of this incorporation, all vested interests of the South Pacific Coast and its subsidiaries were now under the firm control of the Southern Pacific, and those individuals who were involved in its conception and projection had been bought out.

For the next 18 years, the Southern Pacific's South Pacific Coast Railway would remain the successful operation it had been ever since its inception. Although sporting a somewhat different name, the narrow gauge trains would ramble the rails of the Santa Cruz Mountains without seeing much change in their day-to-day routine. Lumber companies would come and go, tourist spots would change, but the resourcefulness and the popularity of the line would project itself far beyond its founding fathers' wildest dreams. Before the line would finally begin to be broad gauged in 1905, the South Pacific Coast would encompass an operation comprising 25 steam locomotives, over 600 freight cars, and 75 passenger cars.

The People and the Places

While corporate history and financial success are interesting, the real story behind the narrow gauge, and later the broad gauge, was that of the folks who earned their livelihood because of it and the people and the places that were served by it. William H. Anderson

With the opening of the railroad between Santa Cruz and Los Gatos, and the beginning of service on the San Lorenzo River branch, three Santa Cruz mountain towns would emerge as major commercial shipping centers. The first of these would be Wright's, the second would be Felton, and the third would be Boulder Creek.

Wright's

In 1870, James Richard Wright, a retired minister; his wife, the former Sarah Vincent; and their ten children moved into the upper Los Gatos Creek mountain region to settle on a 48-acre tract of land they had been given as repayment for an old debt. Seven years later, the South Pacific Coast came along and purchased a portion of Wright's land on which to build their railroad.

It was early in 1877 when O.B. Castle and his Chinese tunnel gangs first arrived at the Wright's property at the site where work would soon begin on a 6,200-foot bore through the Summit Range of the Santa Cruz Mountains. In almost no time at all,

Above: President Roosevelt descending the station platform steps into the grove. — Courtesy: California State Dept. of Parks & Recreation, Henry Cowell "Big Trees" Park: **below, the S.P.C. narrow gauge crew, Engineer, Robert Elliott; Fireman, Jack Crole; Conductor, Tom O'Neil and Brakeman, George Osgood posing in front of the President's train.** — Courtesy: Harold Van Gorder Collection

The Glenwood railroad yard and depot area seem idle on this particular day. — Courtesy: Octagon Museum, Santa Cruz County

construction buildings, workmen's shanties, and a cookhouse had gone up around the tunnel site. Shortly thereafter, track layers working up the completed grade from Los Gatos had reached the tunnel portal with rail. Within a few weeks, construction trains were running back and forth between Los Gatos and the tunnel camp. As was common practice of the day, endof-track quickly picked up the name of its original property owner and current neighbor, "Wright's."

Once the railroad had become well established at Wright's, the farmers and fruit growers in the surrounding areas began to become anxious about shipping their goods via rail. As a result, it wasn't long before the S.P.C. started scheduled freight and passenger trains to Wright's to meet this demand and, at the same time, to bring in additional revenues. Ironically, it would be the tunnel that determined Wright's as the major shipping center for the Summit area of the Santa Cruz Mountains. Because the tunnel would take almost two years to construct, end-of-track would be at Wright's for some time. During this period, hotels and stores would be built, freight warehouses would be erected, and a post office would be established. By the time the tunnel was completed .and the rail line opened farther, there was no need to establish another shipping center — Wright's was it.

Wright's was to see its greatest years as a commercial center from 1880 to 1915. Each season there would be as many as fifty wagons a day lining up at the boxcars in Wright's to off-load their fruit. In addition, the two local packing houses, the Earl Fruit Company and the Pioneer Fruit Company, shipped as many as 200 extra cars a year to the canneries at San Jose. The fruit consisted of table grapes, Bartlett pears, apples, cherries, and plums. Besides the regular freight, the farmers used to ship their fancy fruits via the Wells Fargo express cars on the 5:00 p.m. evening passenger train to San Francisco.

Not only was the fruit shipped locally, but in later years after the line had been broad gauged, it was also shipped nationally. Jeanette (King) Andrus, daughter of James King - once known as the Champion Plowman of the World - recounts the following story: "In the old days, the railroad would notify my father when refrigerator cars would be on the siding at Wright's. He and the other local ranchers would then take their fruit and produce down and load the cars. Usually the cars would be picked up by the night freight from Felton. Sometimes the fruit would go all the way to New York. I knew this because when I was a little girl I used to help fill fruit crates. On the bottom of some of the crates I would leave a letter telling who

104

I was and from where the fruit was coming. I received many replies to my letters, some from as far away as New York. I once even received a silver bracelet from a man who assumed I must have been a rich California farm girl. When father found out, he put a stop to my letter writing."

Wright's besides being a commercial center, was also well known as a tourist center. Across Los Gatos Creek next to town, a picnic area known as "Sunset Park" had been established in the early days. For over twenty years, it served as the place to go whenever a picnic was the order of the day. Here, there were a dance floor, picnic tables, and a barbeque area. On hot summer days, train after train would leave their happy groups of people to follow the wild pursuits of life at Sunset Park. As long-time resident Johnny Woods recalled: "There used to be gang fights at Sunset Park once people got to drinking pretty good. Ladies would remove their stockings and fill them with rocks to help their boyfriends out. Usually the Sunday train back to San Jose was a pretty wild ride with lots of fist fights and broken windows." It should be noted here that all was not as violent as it seemed. By 1908, the local property owners had had it up to their hair lines with all this tomfoolery, however, and under pressure the Southern Pacific was forced to close Sunset Park.

Fortunately, Sunset Park was not the only attraction at Wright's. There were also many resorts in the Summit area which used to send wagons to meet the daily trains. In those days, people came to stay for a long period of time rather than just a couple of days. The Wright and the Miller families, among others, had resorts. Also, Dr. Goldman of San Jose had a convalescing home in the area. In addition to the resorts, one of the finest rifleman's clubs in California was to be found at Wright's. Finally, the town had a bar and a dance hall if those were your pursuits, and a general store and post office where Charlie Squire gave out mail and sold Sunday papers if you were so inclined.

Empty S.P.C. narrow gauge cars await the arrival of mountain fruit from the Summit and Hylands area while a relaxed mood, perhaps a Sunday, seems to prevail over the community of "Wright's." — Courtesy: Harold Van Gorder Collection

Felton

The South Pacific Coast, and later the Southern Pacific, considered Felton to be two separate locations. The first location, identified as "Old Felton," was near downtown where the early Santa Cruz and Felton terminated its line at the flume. Originally the site contained a four- to five-track yard, a turntable, and a depot, among other structures. After the flume had been taken down and the branch to Boulder Creek opened, the yard became a loading area for the local lime companies, tanbark operations, grape growers, and sawmills. The second location, across the San Lorenzo River from Old Felton, on the Santa CruzLos Gatos mainline, was known as Felton. Here, there was a four-track holding yard, a large freight depot , a turntable, and a passenger station. It would be from this place that most narrow gauge trains going over the hill or down to Santa Cruz would be made up.

Each night, barring bad weather conditions, the evening freight with its heavy load of forest products would work its way down from Boulder Creek to Felton. Also, during the day, a mixed freight would make a round-trip over to Old Felton via the junction below Big Trees and pick up the cars in the yard and at Hihn's lumber mill in Gold Gulch. In addition, a daily freight from Santa Cruz would bring cars up bound for Los Gatos and Boulder Creek and return with others destined for the wharf. Finally, after all of the cars from these previous trains had been sorted in the Felton yard, the night freight from Boulder Creek would continue on to San Jose, taking loaded cars over and returning with empties in the morning. This was more or less the freight operation that went on out of Felton all during the narrow gauge days.

As for passenger service, Felton was the tourist gateway to Boulder Creek, Henry Cowell's Big Tree Park, the sights and sounds found along the San Lorenzo River Gorge, and later Mount Hermon. It was from here that one made connections out of the San Lorenzo Valley for San Francisco, San Jose, Oakland, and Santa Cruz, among other points. It was also from here that Nick Sinnott offered chartered stage service to many of the local resorts found in the surrounding hillsides and mountains.

Boulder Creek

With the establishment of the railroad in the upper San Lorenzo Valley, the town of Boulder Creek grew and prospered. Soon becoming the lumber center for the area, it took on the building of a main street where several stores, saloons, hotels, and other various places of trade lined the avenue. What had originally been Stephen Crediford's hotel, stable, general store, and post office in 1875 had become by 1890 a fullfledged town of 650 people, complete with railroad depot, school, church, and jail. As with most early California lumber-railroad towns, it had its typical social split. On the one hand, there were the numerous saloons and whorehouses that supported the recreation of the hard-working lumberjacks; while on the other hand, there were the God-fearing families who were trying to raise decent children in a healthy environment. Curiously, all were able to work together under most conditions except when the church would occasionally burn to the ground for some unexplained reason or when a drunken fist fight would break out downtown.

Depending on whose statistics you believe, at one time Boulder Creek was somewhere between the second and the fourth largest lumber-shipping point in California. Each season, thousands of cords of firewood, millions of board feet of finished lumber, shingles, shakes, split stuff, fence posts, telegraph poles, railroad ties, and bridge timbers would line the crowded yard. According to the memoirs of Joseph Aram, Station Agent at Boulder Creek from 1885 until 1924, there were enough timber products on hand such that every single night, year-round, a narrow gauge freight train of at least 40 cars could and did depart from the Boulder Creek yards.

On the evening of Saturday, July 29th, 1899, the all-time champion narrow gauge train load left Boulder Creek for Felton. The following newspaper account by W.S. Rogers, editor of the *Mountain Echo,* tells the story:

> The record was broken last Saturday evening in the matter of daily freight shipments from Boulder Creek and the largest train ever yet known went over the line on that evening. It consisted of 7 3 loaded freight cars, I -caboose and engine No. 13 and tender. Its total length was 2,413 feet or only 227 feet less than a half mile and was taken from this place to Felton by only one locomotive under the guidance of engineer Mat Crole and Fireman Fred Reynolds, with conductor Frank Brundage in charge and brakemen George Ely, Bill Clouette and Jim Partenscky to assist in regulating the speed. Thanks to Agent Aram we are enabled to give the following data concerning this phenomenal train load: It consisted of ten cars redwood cordwood - 99 cords; 6 carloads pine wood - 50 cords; 15 cars sawed lumber — 94,476 feet; 1 carload box bolts - 8 cords; 4 carloads of slab wood - 37 cords; 37 carloads railroad ties — 7,160 individual ties or 229,120 feet lumber measurement; making the total tonnage of the train-load 2,017,620 pounds.

By today's standards, there is nothing out of the ordinary about operating a 73-car freight train. This, however, was no easy task in those days. Automatic couplers and airbrakes were unknown items on freight equipment. Trains were hooked together with link and pin couplers. When it came to braking, the train crew had to jump from car to car, while the train was

For over half a century the lime kilns at Felton, shown here in the early 1900's, was a heavy producer of carload freight for the railroad. — Courtesy: Mrs. George Ley Collection

moving, setting and releasing the brakes per the whistle instructions from the engineer up front. One missed link and pin coupling and you could be hopelessly caught between two freight cars like a vise. One unheard braking command and you and the rest of your train crew, along with the train, could be in the throes of dire disaster momentarily.

A classic example of the foregoing would be what took place after the record train reached Felton. Before going over the hill to San Jose, it was decided to run 53 carloads of railroad ties down to Santa Cruz. About a mile out of Felton on the down grade, the Santa Cruz train came uncoupled 13 cars back from the engine. With link and pin couplers, it was impossible to hook the train together while it was moving. The 40-car second section began to pick up speed. It was important at this time that the engineer kept his 13-car train with engine well ahead of the second section, because ill the second section caught him, there was the possibility of a derailment. This, of course, didn't make life too easy for the engineer because the curves were tight, and if he took them too fast he and the fireman would shortly have to join the birds. To make matters worse, if the second section was not stopped in

the next two and a half miles, both sections would be on the 3 -1/2 % down grade into Santa Cruz. All that would be necessary if that happened would be to record the results of the disaster. Fortunately, the expert crew were well experienced at this game, having played it many times before, and were able to stop the second section shortly before the down grade at Rincon.

Another interesting aspect of Boulder Creek was the fact that many of the town's citizens worked for the railroad. Being the end of the line up the San Lorenzo Valley, all freight and passenger trains began and ended here. Because of this and because Boulder Creek was a small community, most of the townsfolk knew the local railroad employees on a first-name basis. While there are many stories to tell about men like engineers Jim Quill, Bill Dow, Charlie Glass, Bill Clouette; brakeman George Hickey; and Baggageman Brick Roy, among others, no doubt the one that best shows community attitude is the one concerning conductor Daisy Hollenback.

Late one night in 1891, a fire started in the backroom of a local Boulder Creek saloon. Before people realized what had happened, it was out of control. The fire started consuming buildings one by

ENGINE... S.P.C. RY. ...TRAIN NO. 422 EAST BOUND
...BOULDER CREEK DIVISION
IN THE DITCH AT BEN LOMOND CAL.
MAR. 3, 06

Our local train had a narrow escape from a bad wreck on its downward trip last Saturday, just before noon, in the town of Ben Lomond.

It was just after the tremendous downpour of rain of that forenoon which washed a large amount of sand on the track at the crossing of the old Love Creek county road just back of the Episcopal church in our sister town. M.H. Hopkins, of Ben Lomond, happened to notice the obstruction on the track just as the train was approaching and signaled the engineer with a bandana hankerchief. Engineer Hughes was at the throttle and he at once shut off the steam, but hardly had he done so before the engine struck the sand and at once leaped from the track, with the tender and front combination car following. The engine plowed its way for a distance of 54 feet through the sand and finally careened over against an oak tree just as it was ready to come to a standstill. Both the engineer and fireman stayed with the engine but fortunately neither were injured. Conductor Hollenback, Baggageman Roy, Brakeman Kent and Mail Weigher Davis were all standing in the baggage room of the rear combination car and all were thrown to the floor by the jerk of the sudden stopping of the speed of the train. Several passengers were also quite severely jolted in their seats, but fortunately no one on the train was injured beyond slight bruises. Had the train not been signaled by Mr. Hopkins just in time the accident might have been a much more serious one. As it was, traffic was stopped on our branch road for the day and the silence of the grave prevailed in the railroad yards here Saturday afternoon.

A wrecking crew was sent from San Jose and they succeeded in getting the locomotive — No. 14 — back on the track Sunday but little the worse for its side trip. — Courtesy: Mrs. Carl Tyree (Aram) Collection, Boulder Creek Historical Society

108

Above: The gentlemen line the Ben Lomand platform waiting for the afternoon train. — Courtesy: Pat Liebenthal Collection

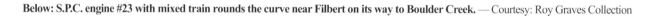

Below: S.P.C. engine #23 with mixed train rounds the curve near Filbert on its way to Boulder Creek. — Courtesy: Roy Graves Collection

one on the railroad side of town. After several hours of firefighting, it was decided that all of the east side of Main Street, including Daisy Hollenback's house and the Dougherty-Middleton store which contained almost $40,000 worth of merchandise at 1891 prices, was going to be a total loss. Realizing that the Dougherty-Middleton store was the mainstay of the community, Daisy came up with an idea to stop the fire short of their emporium. He quickly went to the engine house, got steam up in one of the passenger engines and brought it out onto the closest railroad track to his house. At the same time, several of the lumbermen brought in heavy logging cables and strung them around Daisy's house. When Daisy arrived with the engine the cables were attached and the house was literally dragged off its foundation, contents and all. This single action on Daisy's part proved to be enough to create a firebreak and the Dougherty-Middleton store was saved. Needless to say, all of the lumber for Daisy's new house came from the Dougherty mill, "no charge."

The San Lorenzo River Basin Lumbering Industry

While the redwood logging industry of the San Lorenzo River Basin was in no way as large as that found in the northern California Counties of Humbolt, Mendocino, Del Norte, and others, it still was one of the prime suppliers of quality lumber products all during the growth years of the late 1880's and early 1900's. Unlike its northern California counterparts where much of the land and the logging operations were controlled by large corporations such as the Lagoon Lumber Co., the Pacific Lumber Co., or the A.B. Hammond companies, most of the San Lorenzo lumbering industries were a product of local initiative.

With the exception of the Santa Clara Valley Mill & Lumber Co., the F.A. Hihn Co., and the I.T. Bloom concerns, most of the local operations were small businesses long on backbone and intestinal fortitude and short on capital. These included the McAbee Brothers, Homer Rider, the Harmon's, Duffey & Longley, the Hubbard & Carmichael Brothers, the Hoffmans, the Hartmans, and the Joseph Perry mills. At any one time in the San Lorenzo Basin there would be at least four to five of these small operators turning out 20,000 to 40,000 board feet of timber products per day during the season. One of the factors which led to their success was that they were portable. In a matter of weeks any of these small concerns was capable of tearing down their operation at one location and setting it up on another. Thus, they didn't have to own a lot of property, or the timber rights to it. Instead, they could buy or lease one tract of land at a time, cut it, and then move on to the next. In this manner much of the timberlands, especially along the tributaries of the San Lorenzo River, Boulder Creek, and Bear Creek, were cut.

The redwood logging season for most of the big and small companies normally began about the middle of February. A crew of around 12 men, including a cook, several choppers, a few sawyers, and peelers, would go out into the area to be logged and establish a working camp. From here, they would work the forest until they had cut enough logs to keep the mill in operation for another year.

First, the head chopper, usually a man of good judgment and lots of experience, as well as being an excellent axeman, would select the trees to be cut. Next he would have to mark out a bed for each tree to fall in where it would cause the least amount of injury to itself and the other standing trees. After this had been accomplished, the actual work of cutting the tree could begin. In some cases where the redwoods were very large, they would have uneven swells at their bases. As a result, a staging platform for the choppers to work from would have to be erected six to ten feet above the swells.

Choppers usually worked in pairs. They started by making an undercut on the side of the tree toward which it would fall. This was accomplished using double-bitted, three- to four-pound, 42-inch axes. In making this cut, great care had to be used to make certain that the sides of the cut were equidistant from the center point of the fall. With the undercut completed, the choppers would move to the back of the tree and start sawing, using a two-man, 12-foot crosscut saw, at a point slightly higher than the undercut. As they sawed the tree, steel wedges were driven into the kerf to remove pressure on the saw and also to steer the tree in the right direction. As the saw ate into the tree more and more, additional wedges would be driven in until enough pressure had been created to force the tree to fall. Once the tree was on the ground, the sawyer would size up the fallen monarch as to how it should be cut to provide the best millable saw-logs. At this point, the peeler would remove the bark at those places chosen by the sawyer and the tree would be cut. After cutting, the peelers would remove the rest of the bark from each saw-log and then they would be hauled to the mill to be turned into finished products.

One of the largest saw-logs ever to be cut and processed in this manner was done so at I.T. Bloom's Park Mill in Big Basin during the 1904 milling season. Before the milling was completed, a 25-foot section had been turned into 86 telegraph poles of the same length and 36,000 board feet of finished lumber.

Finished lumber, of course, was not the only end product to come from the San Lorenzo forests. Also, there were numerous shingle mills, split-stuff

South Pacific Coast locomotive #13 Poses with the elite of the local Boulder Creek Railroadmen in 1892. Left to Right: Boulder Creek Station Agent, Joe Aram; Mr. Wiley; Fireman, Charlie Glass; Car Repairman, Mr. Larsen; Fireman, Johnny Stocker; In gangway, Fireman, Fred Reynolds; In cab, Engineer, Bill Dow; On running board, Charlie Chase and Brakeman, Sam McKean; On ground, Conductor, Henry Amaya. — Information courtesy: Doug Sarmento, Photo Courtesy: Fred Stoes Collection

operations, and box factories operating in the area. In addition, the leather-tanning industries were consuming a lot of tanbark oak trees. Likewise, the laurel tree, the madrone tree, the oak tree, the pine tree, and especially the redwood tree all fell prey to the cordwood harvesters.

In retrospect, most people find it hard by current standards to relate to this early-day woodsman of the forest and of the mill. Here was a person who got up at 4:00 a.m. each morning, worked in the scorching sun for I I to 12 hours a day, six days a week, lived hard, fought hard, struggled to survive, and was able to find happiness without all the required necessities of today. While our minds tend to make "Paul Bunyans"

out of such men, in truth they were not. Basically, they were men of endurance and of average stature who put in a hard day's work for a day's meager pay.

A classic example of this endurance was demonstrated on March 6th, 1899 at Duffey and Longley's mill. It was on this particular Monday that two men, T. O'Connor and M. Quinby, using nothing but hand tools, cut and split and stacked seven cords (a cord of wood is four feet high by four feet wide by eight feet long) of fir wood in one day. For their efforts, they each received 75 cents per cord and a 35-cent bonus for a good day's work. Ironically, even with the advent of the chainsaw and other modern equipment, their record has yet to be broken.

Above: The town of Boulder Creek as seen from the S.P.C. railroad yard in the early 1890's. — Courtesy: Doug Sarmento Collection

Below: The town of Boulder Creek is seen from a nearby hillside as it appeared shortly before the earthquake. — Courtesy: Vince Locatelli Collection

Boulder Creek Depot, circa 1895
Published by Boulder Creek Historical Society, 1976

A different time, a different place, a different day, Boulder Creek remembered through the artistic abilities of Rachael Bachrach.
— Courtesy: Boulder Creek Historical Society

The Dougherty's
The Santa Clara Valley Mill &
Lumber Company

It was 1858 when a young Missouri man named William Patrick Dougherty first settled in the Santa Clara Valley. With a few dollars in his pocket, this 26-year-old, strong-willed but fair-minded Irishman had come to eke out a new life in the West. With him he brought the abilities of a good farmer and a fine lumberman. Not quite ready to settle down yet, he began his career by working a very small lumber mill in the Santa Cruz Mountains. After only one year, he was able to save enough money to buy and equip a farm and settle down. This he did, and for the next five years he worked the old Naglee place in San Jose. During this time a pretty young Irish Miss named Jane O'Connor caught his eye, and it wasn't long before they were married. Shortly after his marriage, William Dougherty started to become despondent about his farm. While he had all the things the average man could hope for, a wife, a child on the way, and a good piece of land, the rural occupation of a farmer just didn't seem to sit well with him. At the same time, friends he used to have in the lumber business who were now successful, the growth and development that was taking place in the Santa Cruz Mountains, and the inward drive to succeed, all began to gnaw at him. Finally, after much pro and con, he decided he was going back into the lumber business, and that's all there was to it.

In the Fall of 1864, he sold his farm and started a small retail lumber outlet in San Jose and a mill near Lexington in the foothills of the Santa Cruz Mountains. Shortly thereafter, his younger brother, James Dougherty, who had just been discharged from the Union Army at the end of the Civil War, joined him in the lumber business. To the operation James Dougherty added a keen insight into manpower and materials and a very good engineering ability. For the next five years, the undeclared firm of Dougherty & Dougherty grew and prospered. William Dougherty looked after the retail yard in San Jose and the business affairs of the company while James Dougherty ran the lumber operations in the Santa Cruz Mountains.

From 1869 to 1873, the success of the Dougherty Brothers was beyond belief. First, an interest in the business was sold to C.K. Hobbs and Samuel McFarlane wherein the name of the concern became "Hobbs, Dougherty & Company." Next, Hobbs was bought out by William Hall and the firm became "W.P. Dougherty & Company." In 1870, the sash factory and planing mills of Metcalf & McLellan and of W. Pratt along with the lumber business of McMurtry & McMillin were acquired. In 1871, the

William P. Dougherty and his pregnant wife, Jane, pose before the camera shortly after they were married. — Courtesy: Mrs. Robert P. Mudd

cares of the company had expanded such that an entire city block was taken over between Third and Fourth streets in downtown San Jose. By 1873 the firm had grown so monetarily that formal articles of incorporation were filed with the State of California.

The name of the new corporation, which now comprised several mills and retail operations, was to be known as the "Santa Clara Valley Mill & Lumber Company." The Officers of the Company were as follows: President, William P. Dougherty; Manager, James Dougherty; and Secretary, James M. Thorp. In addition to the officers, the directors included B.P. Rankin, Jacob Lenzen, W.W. Pratt, and W.H. Hall.

While many companies would experience severe hardships during the four-year period following the financial panic of 1873, such would not be the fate of the Santa Clara Valley Mill & Lumber Company.

Because the West was in a state of development and growth, and because the demand for lumber was always on the increase, the S.C.V.M.& L. Co. continued to expand in spite of itself. By 1877, they had become the largest lumber concern in the Santa Clara Valley and in the foothills of the Santa Cruz Mountains behind Los Gatos.

Dougherty's Mill: Zayante Creek, 1880-1886

During this time of expansion, the company had acquired ownership to over 8,000 acres of timberland in the Zayante Creek and Newell Creek basins. In order to log it, a steep wagon road (later to be known as Bear Creek Road) had been cut from Lexington to the top of the Santa Cruz Mountain Range where their property began. On a small scale, they had tried to work certain sections of this land without much success. Unfortunately, the rugged terrain of the area offered a great deal of resistance when it came to moving large quantities of both raw and finished wood products. Thus, it was with great enthusiasm that the Doughertys greeted the news of the plan to build the South Pacific Coast Railroad to Santa Cruz through the mountains. Although there is no written evidence to prove it, the **S.C.V.M.&L.** Co. probably had a great deal of influence on the final S.P.C. right-of-way alignment through their timber holdings.

In conjunction with the completion of the S.P.C. Railroad, the company began to make plans for harvesting their holdings on a very large scale. The first item of business, of course, was to pick a mill site somewhere along the projected S.P.C. right-of-way. After examining all of the many possible locations, the point finally chosen lay about three miles above Felton on Zayante Creek. As the mill at this point was almost a hundred feet below the S.P.C. Railroad, a gradual one-mile spur had to be constructed to overcome the difference in elevation. At the junction where the spur and the mainline came together, a depot was established, appropriately named "Dougherty's Mill." (Today, almost one hundred years later, the original long forgotten station site at Dougherty's Mill Junction remains as an official U.S. Geological Survey Bench Marker.)

By 1880, all things as planned had come to pass. The S.P.C. had been completed and the Dougherty Mill was in full production. Already there were 20 men at work in the mill turning out 30,000 board feet of lumber per day, and 35 more men in the woods feeding the hungry millsaw's appetite. In addition, there were another 50 men cutting split stuff along with 10 more men who were gulching and loading. As if this weren't enough, a box factory employing I I men had also been established that was turning out over 2,000 boxes a

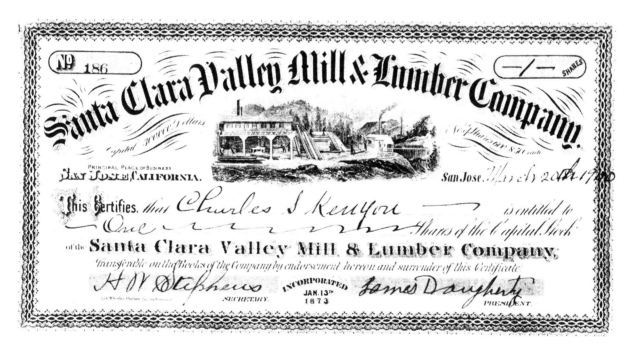

One share of the Santa Clara Valley Mill & Lumber Co. stock valued at $500.00 was a considerable amount of money as of 1900 when this was issued.-Courtesy: San Jose Historical Museum

The Dougherty Folks pose with the Felton, or more locally known as the "Dinkey," near end of track in 1892. Left to right: John Nelson, Fireman; "Little" Brown, Brakeman; Nick Sinnott, Conductor; in the cab, Engineer Alex Skelton; in the gangway, 6-year-old Walter Skelton. — Courtesy: Roy Graves Collection

day. Altogether, the combined operations were shipping out at least 100 carloads of wood products a week. Besides these shipments, an additional 10 to 12 carloads of cordwood a week were being shipped to the company's brick kilns at Lovelady's Station between San Jose and Los Gatos.

Because of the size of the Dougherty operation, a two-mile narrow gauge railroad running into the company's timberlands was also in operation. It was the prime mover of most the logs, split stuff, and cordwood from the woods to the mill and from the mill to the siding on the South Pacific Coast. (Not much information is available about this railroad 95 years later. There are no known photographs. The only accountable facts, supported by newspaper copy, are that it required a lot of trestle work and that at least one locomotive was buried in a landslide in 1884 and is still there, somewhere, today. For the most part, only a few traces of the original right-of-way exist, the rest being reclaimed by the forest.

By the end of the 1886 season, much of the original acreage had been cut over. There was some question as to whether there was sufficient timber for the mill to reopen in 1887. This, however, was a question which would never have to be answered. Late one Fall night, a fire started in a pile of rubbish, and before anyone realized what was happening, the entire mill was in flames. To make a long story short, the mill, with the exception of the boilers and most of the yard, was lost to the fire. The Dougherty's, now with no mill and not much loggable timberland, decided to move on to new horizons.

Dougherty's Mill #2
(above Boulder Creek 1887-1902)

It was early in the Spring of 1887 when the Dougherty Brothers first arrived in Boulder Creek ready to take on their next big lumber venture. Recently, the S.C.V.M.&L. Co. had acquired 7,000 acres of lush timberland along the upper portion of the

116

San Lorenzo River and over the ridge into the headwaters of Pescadero Creek. Now, with the newest and most modern lumber equipment available and lots of good green capital, the brothers were busily laying out plans on how to harvest this prime timber.

Four miles above town at a spot soon to be known as "Dougherty's," a 50,000-board-foot capacity sawmill complete with millpond and supporting lumber camp was being laid out. At the same time, a cookhouse and several bunkhouses along with 30 fourroom cottages and a combination schoolhouse and meeting hall were being erected to provide the necessary comforts and conveniences for the company's single and married men and their families. Likewise, a schoolmarm, Miss Gilday by name, had been retained to teach the twenty some odd school children enrolled in the Dougherty School District.

Because of the large daily output of the mill, the tremendous amount of acreage involved, and the fourmile distance from Boulder Creek to Dougherty's, it was decided that the only feasible form of transportation would be a narrow gauge railroad. First of all, it would allow for the direct interchange of loaded flatcars from the mill at Dougherty's, through Boulder Creek and Felton, to the company's yard in San Jose. Second, a railroad from the logging camp to the mill would provide the necessary means with which to keep the pond well filled with logs; and third, it was the only economical way to deal with the volume of freight traffic the S.C.V.M.&L. Co. had in mind.

James Dougherty was the Chief Engineer for the railroad. He had it laid out and constructed in a matter of months. During the construction there were few

This is believed to be the only known view of the Dougherty Mill at Zayante. Photographed by Fell. — Courtesy: Pajaro Valley Historical Association

117

obstacles encountered. The four-mile grade from Boulder Creek to the mill was a gentle 1%. The one-and-a-half-mile stretch from the mill to the logging camp only increased in grade by a half a percent. For the most part, the railroad followed the San Lorenzo river from town to the mill, crossing it only three times and then three more times from the mill to the logging camp. The only stringent requirement placed upon the railroad during construction was that it conform to South Pacific Coast standards such that equipment could move freely from railroad to railroad. This meant the curves were of as wide a radius as possible, the roadbed was well laid down, the ties were of redwood, and the rail was 50 lb.

By mid-August of 1887, the railroad had been completed and the mill was ready to commence operations. In order to handle all of the freight cars on the company railway, soon to be officially known as "The Dougherty Extension Railroad," a secondhand steam locomotive was purchased from the S.P.C. As it so happened, it turned out to be the old Felton engine from the Santa Cruz and Felton Railroad. To run her, an engineer by the name of Alex Skelton was hired. Before long, the two had become accustomed to each other, and what would turn out to be a long term of events together, began.

From 1887 to 1896, the logging camp above the mill served as the main base of operations. It was from here that the trees around the mill, along the right-of-way, and at the camp itself were logged off. It should be noted that Patrick J. McGaffigan was the company's Superintendent in charge of the operations in the woods and at the camp. During this period, he built a beautiful home on the side of the canyon overlooking the camp that was the envy of everyone for miles around. Because of this house's influence on the area, the logging camp below it soon came to be known as "McGaffigan's Switch." (Now, some 85 years later, McGaffigan Mill Road still wanders back into the old camp area, a product of its forgotten history.)

One of the problems which had plagued the S.C.V.M.&L. Co. for years was the continual threat of fire. Sawmills by their very nature were highly combustible. As a consequence, insurance rates were very high, and few sawmills, including the Dougherty's, were ever insured. After the company had lost their Zayante mill in 1886, they had taken every precaution possible to prevent the same thing from happening again. Among other things, the new mill at Dougherty's had an iron roof to protect it from failing sparks. In addition, it had a steam-pumped sprinkler system fed by a 10,000-gallon water tank and a 30,000-gallon backup supply housed in a nearby ravine. Even with protection such as this, however, it was still not enough. Late one Saturday evening

during the summer of 1888, the new mill caught fire and was reduced to charcoal and ash in less than a half hour. Undaunted, the Dougherty Brothers rebuilt it, this time making it even bigger and better. On October 24, 1891, the mill burned to the ground for a second time. Again it was rebuilt. It was estimated that the 1888 fire had caused $40,000 in damages and that the 1891 fire had caused $50,000 in damages. While heartbreaking and exasperating, these accidents were looked upon as part of the cost of turning out lumber, and so they were primarily ignored.

In 1894 William P. Dougherty (known to the men as W.P.) died of heart failure. Over his local span of 30 years, he had grown from a small farmer to President of the Santa Clara Valley Mill & Lumber Company, now a multi-million dollar institution; a member of the board of directors of the Loma Prieta Lumber Company; President and owner of the San Jose Brick Company; part owner in the Hotel Vendome in San Jose; and a partner with Henry L. Middleton in several mercantile ventures in Santa Cruz County and timberland speculations in Mendocino County. With his death, he left his brother James in control of all of his enterprises.

In early 1897, the Dougherty Extension Railroad was pushed two miles farther into the San Lorenzo Canyon to allow for the logging of its headwaters. At the same time, the logging camp was relocated from McGaffigan's Switch to end-of-track. For the next four seasons, most of the logs for the millpond came from this upper San Lorenzo area. With the headwaters cleared by the end of the 1900 season, the company moved their cutting operation to two large parcels of timberland just outside of Boulder Creek which they had recently acquired from the Harmon family. This property was harvested during the 1901 season.

All during this time from 1887 to 1901, the Dougherty Extension railroad did its job. With Engineer Alex Skelton at the throttle of the "Felton," more commonly known to the local folks as the "Dinkey," Fireman William Gregory chucking wood, and Conductor John Gaffney leaning heavily upon the brake wheel, the little train made its round-trip run from the mill to Boulder Creek twice a day. It should be noted that the Dougherty Extension Railroad provided freight service to and from Boulder Creek for more than just the S.C.V.M.&L. Co.; about a half a mile above Dougherty's Mill, at a place known as "Sinnott Switch," a spur had been constructed up Feeder Creek to the Chase lumber mill. Chase had a small 25,000-board-foot capacity operation that was harvesting most of the two-mile-long Feeder Creek Canyon. From here an additional three to five carloads a day of wood products were shipped. About halfway between Boulder Creek and Dougherty's, the railroad ran right through the middle of the J.W. Cunningham

Above: The S.C.V.M.&L. Co. Dougherty Mill in 1895, four miles above Boulder Creek on the San Lorenzo River. — Courtesy: G.G. Gaffney Collection

Right: February 15, 1904. Three gentlemen of the times pose in the lower end of the Boulder Creek yards where transfers from the Dougherty Extension Railroad to the South Pacific Coast took place. — Courtesy: Mrs. Carl Tyree (Aram) Collection, Boulder Creek Historical Society

It is the 4th of July, 1897. Usually the Dougherty & Middleton mercantile in downtown Boulder Creek is a place of much activity. On this day, however, the camera has captured the opposite.—Courtesy: Rick Hamman from the Skelton Collection

One of the many concerns which used the services of the S.C.V.M.&L. Co. RR was the Chase lumber mill on Feeder Creek, shown here circa 1895. — Courtesy: Santa Cruz Octagon County Museum

The Dinkey running light poses along the right-of-way for Oakland Photographer Cheney. — Courtesy: Vernon J. Sappers Collection

& Company milling operations. From here, too, daily shipments of from three to five carloads of finished lumber were sent. At Two Bar Creek just below Cunningham's, the McAbee Brothers also had a spur where lumber and split stuff was loaded. In addition, there were various shingle mills, split stuff, and cordwood operations along the line at one time or another that also took advantage of the railroad. Sometimes when the freight traffic really became heavy, the S.P.C. narrow gauge would make a special round-trip up to Dougherty's and back just to ease the load. Many's the time that locomotives No. 13 or No. 20 with Engineers Dow, Reynolds, or Glass at

the throttle were seen up the extension.

A continual headache for Engineer Skelton was the problem of poor footing or fallen debris caused by the 60 to 70 inches of rainfall the forest received per year. During the operation of the railroad, there were several incidents where the "Dinkey" jumped the tracks and ended up in the river or where a fallen tree or large branch would lay across the right-of-way, thereby doing damage to the train. As a consequence, the "Felton" spent much of her time in the S.P.C. narrow gauge shops in Newark being repaired or refitted while leased S.P.C. engines No. 2 or No. 3 would be brought in to take her place. A typical

The Felton stands lifeless near Bear Creek Road in Boulder Creek after 40 years of faithful local service. Ironically, this last glimpse shows her with B.C.&P. RR lettering waiting on broad gauge ties ready to go over a dream railroad which never happened. — Courtesy: Louis Stein Jr.

example of such incidents was the following accident which occurred on September 28th, 1897:

The Mountain Echo
Thrilling Accident - Narrow Escape

Tuesday morning last, as the Dougherty extension freight train was coming down from the mill it was stopped in a most thrilling and unexpected way. Suddenly from behind a bunch of brush on the curve, there burst the startling sight of a prostrate tree across the track but a short distance ahead of the locomotive. Taking in the situation, quick as a flash, engineer Skelton whistled "down brakes" and reversed the engine, behind the locomotive and tender were four heavily loaded flat cars... It was but a few seconds and while the train men were still applying the brakes that the groaning engine struck the tree about midway from top to butt... This caused the first contact to be against the headlight. Then the smokestack was struck and torn off at the boiler. Also the sand box was demolished and the whistle annihilated... The sudden smash against the top gear of the engine must have tossed the tree upward, as it passed clear over the cab in which were the engineer, fireman and a young lady - Miss Della Wente of Santa Cruz. This alone saved these three people from either being killed or terribly injured... As soon as possible after everything had been done to stop the train, Mr. Skelton seized Miss Wente and jumped, quickly followed by fireman William Gregory, who had applied the tender brake. Although the wheels of the engine in front and the four cars of freight behind remained on the track, the tender and drivers of the locomotive were derailed in a peculiar manner. This was done by the broken off smokestack falling on a sloping bank and rolling down against the tender. Here it caught, one end against the tender the other against the bank, and before it was crushed raised one side of the tender and one set of drivers up and forced the whole mass, including the rear end of the engine over about a foot, the flanges of the wheels clearing the rails and the wheels themselves dropping onto the ties, on which they bumped until the train stopped. . . Conductor J.E. Gaffney was on the rear car and as quick as the brakes were applied and the train stopped, he ran forward and seeing the wreckage scattered by the way, expected to find death and suffering about the engine. He was greatly surprised and relieved to find his friend Miss Wente and his train associates unhurt. Engineer Skelton says, that as the tender and cab were raised bodily upward on one side by the broken smokestack, he thought the engine was going to upset. This clinched his resolve to jump with his passenger burden for their lives.

As a postscript, it should be added that within two weeks the doughty little pioneer engine was at work again as frisky as ever.

On July 28, 1900, James Dougherty, after a prolonged illness, was to die from lip cancer. This left the company in the hands of his wife, Katherine. While a capable women in her own right, she definitely needed help with the cares of the business. By August 11th, much of the company's stock had been sold by herself and the former Mrs. W.P. Dougherty to outside interests in order to preserve the company. It was at this time that a special meeting was held to elect new officers and to reorganize the directorate. The results of the meeting were as follows: Timothy Hopkins, President; Henry Middleton, Manager; H.W. Stephens, Secretary; and M.A. Keefe and Charles S. Kenyon rounding out the group. The Dougherty wives, while remaining stockholders were silent partners.

With the end of the timber harvesting season of 1901, most of the Santa Clara Valley Mill and Lumber Company's property in the upper San Lorenzo River Basin had been logged off. What little there was left was not sufficient to warrant another year of operation. Thus, the company would now have to go after their last remaining piece of property in the upper Pescadero Creek Canyon. This would prove to be a major undertaking, because between the railroad and the property lay the 1,267-foot Waterman Gap Ridge.

While the ridge was only 520 feet higher than the railroad or the property, transporting saw logs across it in some form or fashion that was economically feasible would be no easy task. Unfortunately, there was only one year's worth of standing timber on the property. Therefore, anything calling for a large cash expenditure was immediately ruled out. Obviously, a railroad was not the answer, and ox-teams wouldn't work because the ridge was too steep. Finally, Company Superintendent J.W. Cunningham hit upon the solution. First, a mile-long skid road was built from the Dougherty Extension Railroad, at a place known as Waterman Switch, over the ridge at its low spot to the property. Along it a two-inch water line was laid the entire distance with taps about every 150 feet to continuously lubricate the skids. Next, one of the largest stationary steam donkeys in Santa Cruz County was leased from the Union Mill at Big Basin and placed in position at Waterman Switch. Finally, a system of pulleys, winches, and steel cable was laid along the route and the Dougherty Wire Cable Logging Road was ready for business.

The operation involved hooking up to 15 saw logs at a time together and dragging them over the top with 7,000 feet of one-inch cable. To return the cable from Waterman Switch to the property, a smaller steam donkey with 14,000 feet of five-eighths-inch line would pull it back. As luck would have it, the system worked beyond everyone's expectation, and the operation was successful.

With the end of the 1902 season, all of the original property had been logged off, and the mill at Dougherty's would shut down for good. Although lumbering for the S.C.V.M.&L. Co. in the San Lorenzo and Pescadero Canyons was over for the most part, they weren't through yet. In 1903, much of the mill and equipment was moved far up Bear Creek to a large track of land on Deer Creek. Here, they would operate from 1904 to 1907, removing some of the last big trees around. While the operation, because of its location, was not on a scale equal to that of the mill at Dougherty's, it too proved to be financially successful.

Shadows of the late afternoon sun gently veil the Dougherty right-of-way and the ladies and children strolling thereon at Wildwood, perhaps to signal the close of an era. — Courtesy: U.C. Berkeley, Bancroft Library Collection

Today, some 60 years later, there are still signs of the old Dougherty Railroad such as this piece of rail and right-of-way near Waterman Switch and this remains of a San Lorenzo River trestle just above the mill site .— Rick Hamman

From an 1875 advertisement.

Friday, October 9, 1914: Longtime S.P. Station Agent Joseh Aram, representing the Boulder Creek Board of Trade, presents a key of "Friendship" to railroad trust busting California Governor Hiram Johnson at Brookdale. — Andrew P. Hill.
Courtesy: Mrs. Carl Tyree (Aram) Collection, Boulder Creek Historical Society

At left: This station agent's badge belonged to Joseph Aram, who for over 40 years was a credit to first the South Pacific Coast and later the Southern Pacific at Boulder Creek — Courtesy: Mrs. Thomas (Alberta) Aram

Below: Typical of the many turn of the century Boulder Creek Saloons fraternized by the local gentry was this one belonging to M.C. Sarmento. Left to right: Charlie Wing and his dog; Bar Keep & Owner M.C. Sarmento; Joe Mello; Bull Puncher, Mr. Cousins. — Courtesy: Doug Sarmento Collection

The mill and woods crews relax for a moment at the Hartman Mill on Deer Creek in 1902 and allow the camera to capture a glimpse of history. — Courtesy: Jimmy Hartman

Under the direction of the Bull Puncher, oxen drag a heavy saw log over a well greased (with water) wooden skid road in the Bear Creek area above Boulder Creek for Isaiah Hartman & Co. — Courtesy: John Holm Collection

Typical of the many inclines which worked the Santa Cruz Mountains was this one at the Hartman Tie Camp, Section 22, up Boulder Creek. — Courtesy: Anne Locatelli Collection

The California Timber Company

Shortly after the Loma Prieta Lumber Company was organized in 1882, Timothy Hopkins and A.C. Bassett together purchased an eight-mile-long tract of lush timberland in the Pescadero Creek Canyon for $12.50 an acre. For over 18 years, they sat on the land, not allowing any of it to be harvested. Finally, in the early part of 1900, they founded the Pescadero Lumber Company with the idea of beginning its cutting. A few weeks after its incorporation, Henry L. Middleton, then manager of the Union Lumber Company, combined forces with Hopkins and Bassett and reorganized the two companies under the name of the "Big Basin Lumber Company." With the two concerns now combined, most of the Big Basin and the Pescadero Creek Canyon was owned by one syndicate. It was the intention of the Big Basin Lumber Company management to first log off Big Basin and then go after Pescadero Creek. Unbeknown to the company, the now famous artist and photographer, Andrew P. Hill, and his "semperviron" associates had other ideas for some of the virgin timberland in the Big Basin. After two years of negotiations with the Hopkins, Bassett, and Middleton Company; the state of California; and lots of interested people, 3,800 acres of the Big Basin became the "California Redwood Park." It was the first state park to ever be established in California. With a large portion of its land now in public trust, the Big Basin Lumber Company reorganized its objectives.

It was during this time that the Santa Clara Valley Mill and Lumber Company ceased its operations at Dougherty's. With the two companies, the Big Basin Lumber Company and the S.C.V.M.&L. Co., sharing a common management, and the two Dougherty wives holding much timberland previously willed to them in the Newell Creek Basin above Ben Lomond and in Pescadero Creek canyon, everyone involved saw a common denominator.

On April 4th, 1903, formal articles of incorporation were filed with the County Clerk's Office concerning the California Timber Company. While the company's home office was in San Francisco, as were its directors and officers, everyone knew that Mr. Hopkins, Mr. Bassett, Mr. Middleton, and the Dougherty wives were all liberal stock holders in the listed capital assets of $1,000,000. As this company was well funded and well organized, with immediate goals in mind, it didn't take long for planned developments to start happening. The first endeavor would be the Waterman Creek mill in Pescadero Creek Canyon, and the second endeavor would be the Newell Creek Mill near Ben Lomond.

By June of 1903, the mill on Waterman Creek in the Pescadero Basin had begun operations. As predicted, it was one of the most modern facilities to cut lumber in the Santa Cruz Mountains. It had a daily output of from 50,000 to 75,000 board feet, and it had a two-mile-long logging tramway that brought saw logs

Deer Creek Mill, the last of the S.C.V.M. & L. Co. operations in Santa Cruz County. — Andrew P. Hill. — Courtesy: The Redwood Keg from the Louis Gho Collection

C.T. Co. locomotive the "Kitty" poses on three-rail track at the Newell Creek mill. — Courtesy: Harold Van Gorder Collection

from the woods to the mill to maintain that capacity. For the time being, anyway, a wagonroad had been cut from the mill over the ridge to Waterman Switch where flatcars were loaded with finished lumber and then taken to Boulder Creek on the Dougherty Extension Railroad. While this transportation system worked adequately, the management of the California Timber Company knew that the only way Pescadero Canyon would ever be logged was if there was a railroad from Boulder Creek to Pescadero.

Shortly after the 1904 lumber season began at the Waterman Creek Mill, the California Timber Company started its second planned development on Newell Creek. Using the equipment from the old Enterprise Mill, a mill site was established up Newell Creek at the entrance to the forest about a mile and a half from the South Pacific Coast right-of-way. It was estimated that the Basin contained from 50,000,000 to 60,000,000 board feet of standing timber and that it would take at least ten years to cut it all. Originally, back in the late 1870's, the Dougherty's had attempted to work the Newell Creek Basin from the top without much success. Now, the offshoot of their beginning concern was back to go after it all. Like the Waterman Creek Mill, the Newell Creek Mill when completed would have a daily output of from 50,000 to 75,000 board feet, it would employ over 80 men, and it would use the most modern and labor-saving equipment available.

With Timothy Hopkins and A.C. Bassett having close ties to the Southern Pacific management, it was no problem at all for the California Timber Company to have a spur track laid from the S.P.C. at Shingle springs up to the Newell Creek Mill site. In addition, once the line reached the mill, it would be initially extended two miles farther into the woods to allow for the transportation of saw logs to the millpond.

On May 1st, 1905, the Newell Creek Mill, under the general supervision of Ed Longley, began its

operations. To aid in its initial timber harvesting, the "Dinkey" with Alex Skelton at the throttle was brought in from Dougherty's to haul saw logs from the forest to the mill. Once the pond was full with enough logs to keep the mill in business for the season, the "Dinkey" would return to the Dougherty Extension Railroad to transport the finished timber from Waterman Switch to Boulder Creek.

By mid-August, both the Waterman Creek Mill and the Newell Creek Mill were running at capacity. A camaraderie was developing between the two mill crews which was especially beneficial to the California Timber Company. Both operations had started competing with each other for daily output. It wasn't long before the crews from each mill were putting out 65,000, 70,000, and 75,000 board feet per day. On August 10th, 1905, the Newell Creek Mill, with a lot of preplanning and presetup the day before, turned out 85,115 board feet of competitive product.

Of course, the challenge went out to beat it. Finally, on August 31st, after several unsuccessful attempts, the Waterman Creek Mill put the contest to rest by turning out 109,441 board feet in a ten-hour run. It shouldn't be left unsaid that this kind of output was generating one heck of a lot of business for the South Pacific Coast Railway.

While competitive spirit was lining the lucrative pockets of the California Timber Company, it, like its Dougherty Brothers predecessor, would fall prey to a fiery disaster. On October 26th, 1905, the Newell Creek Mill and most of its yard would burn to the ground. Fortunately, none of the 3,000,000 board feet of uncut saw logs in the pond were affected. Within six months, the mill had been reconstructed, and the 1906 season was looked forward to as being even bigger and better. This year the company was planning to purchase a second steam locomotive to help things be even better.

Above: The California Timber Company Newell Creek Mill circa 1910. — Courtesy: U.C. Berkeley, Bancroft Library **Below: Woodsmen pause and pose while loaded narrow gauge flatcars along the Newell Creek line await the arrival of the Kitty to haul them to the pond.** — Courtesy: Rick Hamman Collection

The California Timber Company Waterman Creek Mill circa 1910. — Courtesy: Octagon Museum, Santa Cruz County

The Race, The Earthquake, and the Coming of the Broad Gauge

During the construction of the Waterman Creek Mill in March of 1903, the Dougherty Extension Railroad Engine No. 1, the "Dinkey," was replaced for reboilering purposes by S.P.C. 4-4-0 No. 3. Upon its return from the Newark shops in June, a possible prophecy of the future was revealed. Lettered on the side of the "Felton's" tender were the characters "B.C.&P. R.R." When properly translated, it read the Boulder Creek and Pescadero Railroad. Almost immediately, the question that formed on the minds of the local populace was "of what is this an omen?"

For years the Southern Pacific had nonchalantly talked about broad gauging the South Pacific Coast. They bad begun to plan for this eventuality as early as August 3 1st, 1897, when they ordered that henceforth all new bridges constructed and all ties replaced will be done so as to accommodate broad gauge trains. While this was a step in the right direction, it was a long way from following through. Now, events were shaping up that caused the S.P. management to take a real look at this proposition. First and foremost, with the opening of the California Redwood Park (later Big Basin), the upgrading of Big Trees, the establishment of several new resorts in the Santa Cruz Mountains, and the building up of the beach area in Santa Cruz and Capitola, passenger service was increasing beyond the capacity of the narrow gauge equipment. Second, several companies had recently incorporated to build a competing broad gauge line into Santa Cruz down the coast, and it looked like one of them might eventually succeed. Third, there was a need to standardize facilities and upgrade equipment over the entire branch. In these days of knuckle couplers and airbrakes, the narrow gauge was fast becoming a bit of an oddity. Finally and most important, by 1902 most of the San Lorenzo Valley, with the exception of Newell Creek, had been logged off. If the Southern Pacific wanted to continue its lucrative freight business out of the area, they were going to have to extend their line out of Boulder Creek and into the virgin Pescadero Creek Canyon.

While in 1899 the first section of three rail track was laid from San Jose to Los Gatos due to the heavy traffic between the same points, the actual plan to broad gauge the entire South Pacific Coast narrow gauge didn't come to the forefront until late November of 1902. Just after Thanksgiving, the S.P. announced that the initial work of laying the third rail would begin on December 15th, with the line between Wright's and Los Gatos. As soon as that was completed, the Alameda to San Jose portion and the Santa Cruz to Boulder Creek portion would be next. The last section between Felton and Wright's would take somewhat longer due to the necessary widening of two and a half miles of tunnels between the points.

The broad gauging of the S.P.C. was not the only plan the Southern Pacific had in mind at this time. Shortly after the 1903 New Year had begun, the S.P. sent Company Surveyor C.S. Freeland and a crew of twelve men into Pescadero Creek Canyon to study the possibilities of building a railroad from Boulder Creek through the Waterman Switch Gap to the coast at Pescadero. Their prime purpose as stated by Mr. Freeland was to "get grades, altitudes, distances, resources, etc. of the proposed route so that the railroad company can formulate estimates on the feasibility, cost, and profits of a railroad through that region." Obviously, they were going after all the redwoods in the Pescadero and Butano Basins and the rich farming areas around Pescadero and up the coast.

The following is a synopsis of broad gauge events that took place from the beginning of 1903 to the beginning of 1906.

April 4th, 1903: The 200-foot tunnel No. I above Los Gatos was daylighted, and broad gauge trains now run around it to the end of three rail track.

April 26th, 1903: The first double-headed broad gauge excursion trains ran straight through from San Francisco to Wright's this day. There were a total of four trains comprised of 50 cars carrying approximately 4,000 people.

July 25th, 1903: The survey from Boulder Creek to Pescadero is completed. The cost is estimated at $500,000, for which bonds will be issued; the S.P. will take half the bonds and the California Timber Company the other half.

September 26th, 1903: The first steel bridge is now under construction across Clear Creek at Brookdale; orders have also been given to begin construction of a second steel bridge at the first crossing of the San Lorenzo River below Boulder Creek.

November 7th, 1903: Surveyor C.S. Freeland is back in Pescadero Canyon conducting a second and more precise survey.

Another of the railroad's many customers, both narrow and broad gauge, was the California Powder Works. Shown here, the spur into Magazine #5 sits empty. The large wooden structure to the right is filled with sand to absorb shock should the magazine explode. — Courtesy: Santa Cruz City Museum

With the conversion of gauges it was necessary to reroute the line into Old Felton along a route next to the covered bridge. Shortly after the new RR bridge was completed and broad gauge trains run across, it began to sag due to too much weight. It wasn't long before a new pier was added to the bridge middle. — Courtesy: Ted Toft Collection

South Pacific Coast engine #2033 poses on the first broad gauge train into Boulder Creek. This and engine No. 2007 were the only broad gauge locomotives known to be on the S.P.C. roster. — Courtesy: Bob Willey from the Mickey Shannon Collection

December 5th, 1903: 35 broad gauge fruit carshave left Wright's this season.

October 22nd, 1904: 250 narrow gauge freight cars have been sent to Nevada. From now on, there will be no more narrow gauge freight over the hill due to the shortage of cars. Instead, all freight will be taken to Santa Cruz and transferred to broad gauge cars.

November 5th, 1904: All sidings in the Santa Clara yards have been equipped with three-rail track.

November 12th, 1904: The Southern Pacific has begun broad gauging from Santa Clara to Alameda.

December 30th, 1904: Surveyor C.S. Freeland has found a better alignment via Feeder Creek to Pescadero. The third survey is now under-way.

January 21st, 1905: Construction began on a 200-foot steel bridge across the San Lorenzo River at Big Trees.

February 5th, 1905: Broad gauging has started from Santa Cruz to Wright's.

March 11th, 1905: A 105-foot-high concrete retaining arch has begun construction near tunnel No. 6. Its purpose is to throw the track out away from the slide and lessen the curve.

March 18th, 1905: The Mission Hill tunnel is being broadened four feet by four feet. The dirt is being used to fill in around the low portion of the Cowell Trestle at Big Trees.

April 21st, 1905: The S.P. subsidiary, the Coast Line Railway, has incorporated among other things to build a branch from Pescadero to Boulder Creek.

May 18th, 1905: Ocean Shore Electric Railway incorporates to build a railroad from San Francisco to Santa Cruz via the coast and a branch line from Pescadero to Boulder Creek.

June 17th, 1905: Ocean Shore Chief Engineer Rogers is surveying an electric right-of-way from Pescadero to Boulder Creek.

August 4th, 1905: Mission Hill tunnel completed this day.

August 15th, 1905: Ocean Shore Electric Railway begins construction out of Santa Cruz.

August 26th, 1905: Tunnel No. 6 near concrete arch site to be moved inward eight feet to allow for the lessening of the curve.

September 2nd, 1905: Temporary narrow gauge

Right: Several railroad employees pose for the camera after just inspecting the damage to tunnel #3 from the Glenwood side.— Courtesy: Bill Harry Collection

Below: The broad gauge local arrives from Boulder Creek yet the line over the mountains is still not open. Note the abundance of 3-rail track. — Courtesy: Bruce MacGregor from the Vernon Sappers Collection

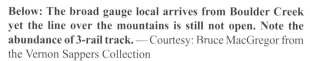

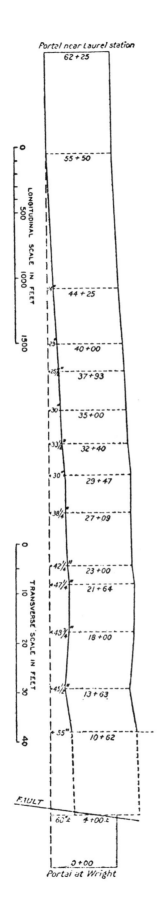

Portal near Laurel station

62 + 25

0

LONGITUDINAL SCALE IN FEET

500

55 + 50

1000

44 + 25

1500

40 + 00

37 + 93

35 + 00

32 + 40

29 + 47

27 + 09

0

TRANSVERSE SCALE IN FEET

10

23 + 00

21 + 64

20

18 + 00

30

13 + 63

40

10 + 62

FAULT

4 + 00

0 + 00

Portal at Wright

Summit tunnel alignment after Earthquake, figure 42 —
Courtesy: U.S. Geological Survey, Menlo Park, California

tracks laid around tunnel No. 6 on the old Santa Cruz and Felton right-of-way until the tunnel work is completed.

November l6th, 1905: Tunnel No. 6 has been completed.

November 25th, 1905: Western Shore Lumber Company incorporates for $1,000,000 to go after the timber in Butano Basin once Southern Pacific or Ocean Shore reaches Pescadero. President, Timothy Hopkins.

December 2nd, 1905: Work has begun on straightening the right-of-way and lessening the curves from Felton to Boulder Creek.

February 17th, 1906: 400 men are at work broad gauging the system from Santa Clara to Alameda.

March 1st, 1906: The only through narrow gauge trains are passenger trains.

April 15th, 1906: The third rail has been thrown over and the broad gauge has begun from Alameda to Santa Clara.

By April 17th, of 1906, the South Pacific Coast had been broad gauged from Alameda to Wright's, work was progressing well on the Santa Cruz to Boulder Creek portion, and the widening of the two mile-long-plus Summit and Laurel tunnels was about to commence. If all went according to predictions, broad gauge trains would be riding the rails from Santa Cruz and Boulder Creek to Los Gatos by Christmas. At the same time, judging from the apparent race between the Southern Pacific and the Ocean Shore Electric Railway, Mr. Timothy Hopkins and Company would soon have their Pescadero timberlands on the mainline of a broad gauge railroad, and the California Redwood Park via Boulder Creek would be serviced by up-to-date passenger equipment. In fact, there was even talk of running an electric line from Boulder Creek to the park.

5:12 a.m., Wednesday, April 18th, 1906: It was a cold, calm, and quiet predawn morning. Most of the people in the mountains were up, yawning, stretching, wiping their eyes, scratching their heads, and in general trying to go from a state of sleepiness to a state of being awake. Fireplaces were burning, trying to

Roger's Manifold and Carbon Paper Co., 75 Maiden Lane, N. Y.   Printed Train Order Books, Patent No. 105,250.

FORM
31

TRAIN ORDER NO. *204*

FORM
31

Nov 28 190*6*

To *C&E Eng 9*   At *Wright*

X _____ *Opr.;* _____ *M.*

1 Eng 9 will run extra
Wright to San Jose
and will meet no 806
eng 2007 at Los Gatos
No 806 gets this at Los
Gatos

J.C.W.

CONDUCTOR AND ENGINEMAN MUST EACH HAVE A COPY OF THIS ORDER.

Repeated   at   *10:34 a.* M.

CONDUCTOR.	TRAIN.	MADE.	TIME.	OPR.
Cattrviie X	*9*	*Com*	*1034am*	*Crichton*

For some time after the earthquake there was 3-rail track from Wright's to San Jose as this dual train order for both narrow gauge No. 9 and broad gauge No. 2007 attests to. — Courtesy: Gene O'Lague Collection

knock the predawn chill off of the cold night air; stove tops were warm; boiler pressure in the steam locomotives at the Boulder Creek yards and in the stationary steam engines at the various mills was coming up to operating conditions; kerosene lamps had been lit; bodily functions had been attended to, and now the coming of another Spring sunrise was about to occur.

Suddenly, ripples began to appear on millponds; a creaking sound started coming from the bases of many of the oak, madrone, and redwood trees; windows proceeded to quiver and roll; harnesses rubbed against barn walls as they pivoted about the nails on which they were hung; railroad cars commenced to sway back and forth from their trucks. Within 15 seconds, a thundering series of shock waves came from beneath the ground that put everyone on the floor whether they were up or not. What was occurring, of course, was the largest recorded and remembered earthquake ever experienced along the San Andreas Fault. Before it was through it would level almost every single fireplace and chimney in the Santa Cruz Mountains, fell hundreds of standing trees, do inestimable amounts of damage in many forms, and remind the grim and serious-faced people who lived in these mountains of their very tangible lives here on earth. Miraculously, however, only two local deaths would be attributed to this earthquake.

Of all the devastation and destruction to occur in the San Lorenzo Valley, it would be the movement of the San Andreas earthquake fault across the Summit Tunnel between Wright's and Laurel which would cause the greatest damage. Approximately 400 feet in from the Wright's side, the entire mountain took a fivefoot lateral shift to the northwest. The most noticeable and immediate effect this had was to completely destroy the 6,200-foot Summit Tunnel. Just a few days later, Engineer Everett P. Carey, after having surveyed the damage, filed the following report:

> The damage to the tunnel itself consisted in the caving in of overhead rock; the crushing in toward the center of the tunnel of the lateral upright timbers, and the heaving upward of the rails, due to the upward displacement of the underlying ties. In some instances, these ties were broken in the middle. In general the top of the tunnel was carried north or northwest with reference to the bottom.

With the Summit Tunnel in a state of collapse, the plans of a few days ago to open the broad gauge over the hill, or any railroad for that matter, would have to be shelved for a while. What was about to be a broad gauge railroad to Los Gatos, San Francisco, Alameda, and San Jose was now just a narrow gauge shortline from Laurel to Santa Cruz and from Boulder Creek to Felton, cut off from the rest of the system.

For the first three or four days after the earthquake, the people of the San Lorenzo Basin were probably more in a state of shock than anyone else. All lines of communication had been cut. There was no telephone, no telegraph, no newspaper, no railroad, and no informed traveler from whom to glean any information. All anyone knew for sure was that something cataclysmic had happened because every day the air was filled with a foul-smelling, dark, ugly haze, and at night an orange glow filled the sky from the direction of Palo Alto and San Francisco. No matter how horrible the thought, for all anyone knew, the outside world didn't exist anymore.

As the days progressed, the unknowing horror of it all disappeared. One by one, people drifted into the mountain communities, relating what they had seen and heard until a composite picture of the unbelievable events began to take shape. San Francisco burned to the ground, San Jose in ruins, Stanford University in rubble, and Santa Cruz a city of fallen bricks and broken windows. "Impossible," said many, no matter how true it was.

As days turned into weeks, the shock and disbelief gave way to the realization that there was a lot of rebuilding to do. One of the prime suppliers of muchneeded building materials was obviously going to be the San Lorenzo Basin due to its proximity to the disaster. Within a matter of days, the railroad had been checked out, cleaned up, and put back in operation between Boulder Creek and Santa Cruz. With the small amount of equipment that was left on this side of the mountain, including that which was borrowed from the Dougherty Extension Railroad, service resumed. Soon, anyone who had any kind of timber to cut and a milling operation to do it with, was working to the limits of his equipment. In addition, the lime kilns and sand plants were also running at capacity.

Among those mills involved in furnishing materials for the reconstruction of San Francisco after the earthquake were F.A. Hihn's operations. Originally in 1900, Hihn's mill on Gold Gulch had been torn down and moved to Laurel. Here, he set up a mammoth operation in 1902 to begin the logging of the upper headwaters of Soquel Creek. On September I st, shortly after the new mill began its first season, a fire befell the operation and totally destroyed it and over 1,000,000 board feet of cut lumber in the drying yard. After the salvage crews were through, it was estimated that over $85,000 worth of damage had been sustained by the mill. As with most mill fires, Hihn accepted it as a chance you take in getting out lumber. With new ambitions and higher goals, he started reconstruction on the mill in 1903. At the same time, he laid out a complicated network of skid roads and cable roads in just about every gulch and gulley along Soquel Creek. In addition, he constructed a two-

Narrow gauge engine #20 with train leaves the Sunset spur near the Wright's reconstruction area. — Courtesy: Gene O'Lague Collection

mile-long main cable road along Soquel Creek to drag the cut saw logs to the mill. Although the mill and the skid road operation was ready to go with the 1905 season, Hihn decided not to commence operations until 1906 when broad gauge service to Laurel was scheduled to be provided late in the year.

As a result of the earthquake cutting off the railroad and leaving only a few narrow gauge freight cars on the Santa Cruz side of Summit tunnel, F.A. Hihn opted to leave the Laurel sawmill closed for the time being. He did, however, due to the large demand for shingles, purchase and move the old S.H. Rambo 50,000-unit capacity shingle mill to Laurel and commence its operation. In addition, he set up a sawmill on Kings Creek on the Newman property above Boulder Creek in order to meet the reconstruction needs of San Francisco. This was easier than Laurel because Kings Creek was already serviced by the Dougherty Extension Railroad, and Hihn anticipated that soon the broad gauge might be extended this far, also.

With the need for reconstruction materials at a premium and the impossible freight conditions brought on by the lack of narrow gauge equipment between Santa Cruz and Boulder Creek, the Southern Pacific began an all-out effort to broad gauge at least that portion of the line as soon as possible. By November of 1906, broad gauging had been completed as far as the steel bridge at Big Trees, and work was steadily continuing toward Boulder Creek. Fortunately, the 5,800-foot Glenwood to Laurel tunnel had only sustained minor damage, and as a result, narrow gauge service as far as Laurel had resumed in early July. As for the Summit tunnel, that was another story. It was estimated that it wouldn't be repaired and reopened until at least the early spring of 1907.

By May of 1907, the Summit tunnel was still unopened. As most people had expected, the damage was so significant that a new tunnel, in effect, had had to be dug. As of now, only a four-foot by six-foot hole connected the two crews that were reworking the tunnel from each side. At the same time, however, broad gauging to Boulder Creek, including a branch spur from Shingle Springs to the Newell Creek Mill, was about completed. It was predicted that by the end of the month broad gauge trains would soon be running to Santa Cruz. It was also about this time the S.P. put out the word that due to the discontinuity of the rail service over the hill, the line would not be reopened until broad gauge trains could run the entire distance. This meant there would be no through service until at least January of 1908.

On June 8th, 1907, at 6:50 a.m., the last narrow gauge train left Boulder Creek for Santa Cruz. Before the day was through, the third rail had been thrown over, and broad gauge trains were making the run to Felton and beyond instead. In order to expedite matters, soon all freight and passenger trains were run through to Pajaro from Boulder Creek, and the importance of Santa Cruz as a transfer point was lessened. This, however, did not end the narrow gauge operations totally. Because of the extensive amount of time and work involved in widening the Glenwood to Laurel tunnel, the line from Laurel to Felton was still narrow gauge. Also, due to the light-weight bridges on the Old Felton branch, the line was three rail from Felton to Felton Junction and then narrow gauge into Old Felton. This meant that Felton was now the point where all narrow gauge freight was transferred to broad gauge cars. This freight consisted primarily of oil for the limekilns and lime kegs from the limeworks along with shingles from Hihn's mill at Laurel.

When the third rail was thrown over from Boulder Creek to Felton, the California Timber Company narrow gauge operations on the Dougherty Extension Railroad and above the Newell Creek Mill were land locked. In order for both operations to continue simultaneously, two separate railroads would have to be maintained. On the Dougherty Extension Railroad, the "Dinkey" and 31 flatcars were assigned to take care of the Waterman Creek Mill. On the Newell Creek Railroad, a new 0-4-0 saddletank engine named the "Kitty" was brought in to bring the saw logs from the woods. As conditions warranted, locomotives and other equipment were swapped via S.P. broad gauge flatcars between the two operations.

When broad gauge plans were first laid out in 1902, they included a lot more than just the widening of the line over the hill. At the same time, the southern Pacific began broad gauging between Santa Cruz and Los Gatos, they also started to construct a straight line cutoff from Los Gatos to Mayfield (South Palo Alto). It was their intention that once the line from Pajaro to Santa Cruz had been upgraded, the branch from Santa Cruz to Los Gatos widened, and the route from Los Gatos to Mayfield constructed, many if not most of the S.P.'s crack Los Angeles to San Francisco

passenger trains would be rerouted over this new track. In addition to the long-distance trains, once the new cutoff and broad gauge mountain right-of-way was opened, a much more direct route would become possible for all of the heavy excursion trains and the scenic locals between San Francisco and Santa Cruz. To that end, construction had continued after the earthquake and the Mayfield-Los Gatos Cutoff was officially opened for business on November 5th, 1907. Hopefully, the mountain route would also be opening up very shortly.

While work had definitely progressed on the Summit tunnel, it still was a long way from being complete. Although a broad gauge right-of-way had now been run all the way through from Wright's to Laurel, the tunnel itself still had to be concreted in many places and shorn up in others. In addition, nothing had been started on the Laurel to Glenwood tunnel, and no three-rail track had been run from beyond Felton. Unfortunately, as luck would have it, this was not to be the worst part of the delay.

It was just about this time when the financial panic of 1907 hit. The lumber business went sour, lime production almost died, and any thought to broad gauging the Dougherty Extension Railroad and extending it to Pescadero, or just as far as Kings Creek to service Hihn's mill, was purely a dream at this point in time. Also, the Southern Pacific was dragging its feet due to the uncertainty of the financial market. In December of 1907, they stopped all construction and rework over the hill until such time as better financial conditions would arise. Consequently, for the San Lorenzo Valley and the Santa Cruz area's, this "temporary" delay meant they would have to depend on their rail service to be provided via Pajaro. While this didn't have too much effect on the freight business, it certainly slowed the tourist market for the parks and summer resorts in the San Lorenzo River Basin.

On December 5th, 1908, after over a year of no action on reopening the hill, the Southern Pacific announced that work would begin at once to complete the broad gauging between Wright's and Felton. They further stated they expected to have the road in full operation by next June. Obviously the passenger traffic was about to boom, and the possibility of the Ocean Shore Electric Railway completing their line to Santa Cruz spurred the Southern Pacific on.

By the end of March 1909, the work of enlarging and timbering the Laurel to Glenwood tunnel was about complete. Also, the work of concreting the Summit tunnel was about finished. All along the line from Glenwood to Felton, hundreds of Italian, Greek, and Japanese laborers were at work grading the right-of-way, laying down broad gauge ties, and spiking heavy steel rails into place. At the same time, the new broad gauge spur from Felton across the San Lorenzo River

RECEIVED at No. 318 Fillmore St., San Francisco.
TELEPHONE: PARK 1148.

102 SF cH KC 13 Paid   Via SanJose

Wright Cal. jan. 1st 09

Mr Roy Andrus

                1608 48th Ave.   Ocean Beach SF

Will meet you on noon   train saturday

          at Wright Cant get to SantaCruz

                                        Jeannette

                                        514p

MONEY TRANSFERRED BY TELEGRAPH.   **CABLE OFFICE.**

Even as late as January 1, 1909 the track to Santa Cruz was not open; so shows this Wright's telegram from Jeannette King to her husband of the future, Roy Andrus. — Courtesy: Jean Andrus Collection

to old Felton had been completed, and the antique narrow gauge from the Junction via the original Santa Cruz and Felton route was being taken up. Barring another earthquake or a financial turnaround, it looked like the San Lorenzo Valley and the City of Santa Cruz were soon going to be on the mainline of a modern broad gauge railroad to San Francisco.

1909-1915 The Golden Era

On May 29th, 1909, the first broad gauge train made the run over the mountain from Los Gatos to Santa Cruz. It was No. 84, the brand new Scenic Local, which had just been put on from San Francisco, via the Mayfield-Los Gatos Cutoff, over the mountain to Santa Cruz, and then on to Monterey. All along the way, this double-header special was greeted by hundreds of people who had turned out to get a glimpse of the first real sign of prosperity since the 1907 panic. If the Southern Pacific could do this, obviously the country was on the road to recovery, and the local future was bright with promise.

It was estimated the Southern Pacific had spent over $600,000 in widening the six tunnels and another $400,000 in lessening curves, regrading the right-of-way, and laying broad gauge track. In addition, as soon as the 1909 Summer season was over, management was planning to invest another $500,000 in ballast and more track work such that the roadbed would be in the best condition possible for heavy mainline trains next year. The mainline over the mountain was not the only upgrading the S.P. had planned. All along the Boulder Creek right-of-way, heavy steel rail had been set down, bridges had been replaced or strengthened, and the roadbed had been upgraded. One by one, the small S.P.C. depots were being replaced by larger structures. Already, a new station had been established at Brookdale; by August of 1909, the Ben Lomond depot had been replaced; before the 1910 season would begin, Boulder Creek would also have a modern facility.

In many ways, this particular time in history for the San Lorenzo Valley and for the City of Santa Cruz could genuinely be known as its golden era of

Thousands of people line the Santa Cruz platform to greet the first broad gauge train over the mountains after three years of line closure. — Courtesy: Bruce MacGregor from the Bill Wulf Collection

railroading. The route over the mountain by early 1912 had definitely become a mainline operation. Each day, name trains such as the San Francisco Limited, the Santa Cruz Limited, The Scenic Local, and the Sacramento Express traveled the mountain route. Also, unnamed trains with unofficial titles like the Daisy flyer and the Cannonball Vestibule made local runs to San Jose and Oakland. In addition, with the Waterman Creek Mill, the F.A. Hihn Mill on Kings Creek, the Newell Creek Mill, the California Powder Works, the Union Lumber Company, and other concerns producing at capacity, freight trains were a big item in the mountains. Also, on the Boulder Creek branch, there were as many as ten passenger trains and two freight trains a day each way. Besides scheduled trains, excursion trains roamed the Santa Cruz Mountains, sometimes pulled by triple-headed steam power, to such places as the beach at Santa Cruz or the tranquil forest retreats at Mount Hermon and Henry Cowell Big Trees.

As of now, automobiles and trucks, while present to some degree, were a contrivance of the future. If you really needed to get from here to there in any time at all, first-class rail service was the only way to go. To that end, the Southern Pacific had

generously provided day and evening schedules to meet those needs.

This golden era from 1909 to 1915 closely resembled the crest of a wave, constantly gaining and losing momentum as it swept toward its final transition downward. It would be during this period that most of the large lumber companies would cease operations in the San Lorenzo Valley. The Waterman Creek Mill would close down after 1913; the Newell Creek Mill would extend its railroad into the woods for another mile and a half in 1912 and then close down entirely after the 1913 season; in late 1909, F.A. Hihn would sell all of his lumber interests to the A.P. Hammond Company; and by 1910, the Kings Creek Mill would be an operation of the past. Besides the lumber companies, the California Powder Works would stop running after almost 50 years of continuous operations, and the Cowell Lime Works on High Street in Santa Cruz would finish. On the plus side of the ledger however, the Hammond interests, under Hihn's name, would reopen the sawmill at Laurel in 1913. For several years, they would log the upper Soquel Basin. Also, the Cowell Lime Works would establish a large new facility near the railroad at Rincon. Likewise, the sand business around Olympia and the clay business

Typical of the many early broad gauge trains which roamed the Santa Cruz Mountain Division was this local passenger, crossing the concrete arch in the San Lorenzo Gorge below Inspiration Point. — Jean Andrus

The slope of the mountain above the southern entrance to tunnel No. 5, below Inspiration Point, was such that during severe winter storms rocks and debris would continually fall from the hill and block its face. To alleviate this problem, 75 feet of tunnel was added to the face and then the mountain was groomed down on top of it. This is typical of the many winter problems with which the railroad crews on the mountain division had to deal. — Courtesy: U.C. Santa Cruz, Special Collections

near Tank Siding would increase. At the same time, much of the logged-over San Lorenzo Valley timberland would be subdivided into recreational lots, and tourists would swarm by the thousands to the various spots to examine these choice pieces of property.

On April 25th, 1914, the Dougherty Extension Railroad, also known as the Boulder Creek and Pescadero Railroad, the Dinkey Line, and the Northern Extension Railroad, would be leased from the California Timber Company and would formally become the "Wildwood, Boulder Creek, and Northern Railroad" for the next two years. Its stated purpose was to service the Wildwood No. 1 and No. 2 development areas. Mr. E.S. Cheney, a photographer and developer from Oakland, was responsible for this operation. Each Saturday and Sunday during the Summer, the Dinkey with some makeshift cars or a newly purchased eight-passenger rail car would meet the arriving trains and transport the unsuspecting tourist from Boulder Creek up to the Wildwood area near the old Cunningham & Company Mill. Once there, Mr. Cheney would wine and dine and soft-sell property to the interested parties. Lots went for the unbelievable price of $125.00 each, and houses were a mere $250.00 to $600.00, depending on what conveniences were desired.

While real estate sales and developments contributed greatly to the influx of tourists by train into Boulder Creek, this was not the prime drawing card. The main interest was the California Redwood Park. The Park, especially during the 1915 Exposition when Andrew P. Hill displayed its photographic beauties in San Francisco, was deluged with visitors. Here was a place where people could go and get away from the trial and the torment of city life. Here was a place where people could touch and smell this spirit of life that had existed hundreds of years before the first white man had come to California. Here was a place where people, if they really wanted to, could get in contact with themselves, their origin, and their God. To that end, Moody and Cress operated daily stages from the Boulder Creek Depot to Big Basin and back. They also ran a livery business to take care of any individual traveler's need.

The Summer seasons of 1913 through 1915 were the years during which the mountain division would reach its quality point of operations. The broad gauge passenger trains were of the most modern design and best equipped for the times. The right-of-way was well taken care of. In addition to a new automatic block system, a wand or staff system had been established between Glenwood and Alma. Its purpose was to prevent the possibilities of head-on collisions in the two, mile-long plus, tunnels and for extra safety due to the heavy amount of traffic on the line.

The morning train down from Boulder Creek makes the final curve across the Zayante Creek trestle just before it will have to apply the brakes for Felton. — Courtesy: Boulder Creek Historical Society

Basically, the system worked as follows: There were two switches, one at Alma and one at Glenwood. Each of these switches shared a common key that was carried on a wooden wand. When one switch was opened, the other would be closed. Thus, two trains traveling in opposing directions could not be on the track between the two switches at the same time. The wand would first be picked up at Glenwood by the Alma-bound train. The switch would be closed, and the train would proceed on to Alma. Once there, the train would clear the second switch, and then the wand would be passed to the crew of the waiting Glenwood train. The same procedure would then occur all over again, only in reverse. When there was no waiting train, the wand would be left hanging on either switchstand. Logistically, the schedule was such that the wand was always in the right place at the right time. All during the many years this wand system would be used, there would never be an accident between points.

Lingering morning shadows and passengers off the Hotel Rowardennan carriage greet the 11:50 a.m. Santa Cruz Local at Ben Lomond. — Courtesy: Roy Graves Collection, U.C. Berkeley, Bancroft Library.

The Coming of the Automobile and the Decline of the Steel Wheel

By the end of 1915, a new conveyance known as the automobile had made its appearance on the transportation scene. Soon, concrete and macadam streets and highways were being built everywhere to replace their dirt-rutted counterparts. As could be expected, the demand for a better quality road over the Santa Cruz Mountains wasn't long in coming. By 1915, bonds had been issued to build a 15-foot-wide Portland Cement highway between Los Gatos and Santa Cruz.

Soon, the horse and buggy would not be the only form of transportation affected by the automobile. With a modern two-lane highway completed over the mountains and better quality intracounty roads established, railroad passenger ridership and freight service, due to the auto and the truck, began to decline. After all, why ride the train when you could be out enjoying the panoramic views and exhilarating ride in the privacy and convenience of your own automobile? Likewise, why haul fruit and produce bound for San Francisco all the way to the railroad and then have to load the cars, when a truck could pick it up at your ranch or farm? Thus, the stage was set. With most of the lumbering over, the story of the decline and eventual death of railroading in the San Lorenzo river Basin had begun.

As with most changes and transitions, they take place gradually. As people live their day-to-day lives, they barely realize they're happening. Yet, when viewed over a 25-year span, change has occurred. The old has grudgingly given way to the new. To illustrate this process, we will do away with the text at this point and instead look at an outline of events as they happened in the San Lorenzo River Basin during the 25-year period from 1915-1939.

June, 1915: An automobile replaced the Wildwood, Boulder Creek and Northern Railroad between town and developments No. 1 and 2.

May-September, 1916: Boulder Creek passenger train arrivals and departures remain at four trains a day each way. No additional service is to be added during the summer.

January, 1917: Brookdale agency closed during winter months.

Beginning WWI, 1917: Dougherty Extension Railroad and Newell Creek Railroad are taken up.

Summer, 1919: New Los Gatos to Santa Cruz Highway Route 5 opens. 12,000 cars a day make the trip during the weekends.

Winter, 1920: Laurel station agency closed.

September, 1921: Two passenger trains, the Limiteds and the Scenic locals, and one freight train a day each way between Los Gatos and Santa Cruz. There is only one freight train three times a week between Boulder Creek and Felton. Also, there is no more evening freight. Now, most freight is routed via Pajaro.

September, 1925: Mount Hermon agency to be open only during the summer months from here on.

June, 1926: Old Felton freight depot abandoned.

February, 1927: Glenwood station agency closed.

Summer, 1927: Three passenger trains a day

Right: The "Wildwood" gas car takes prospective buyers up the old Dougherty line to the real estate development of the same name. — Courtesy: Roy Graves Collection, U.C. Berkeley, Bancroft Library

Below: During 1910 McKeen motor cars were put on between Santa Cruz and Boulder Creek in addition to the regular trains to help handle a heavy summer passenger business. After a very short time, however, they were taken off because they couldn't handle the grade in the San Lorenzo Gorge. Many's the time that Senior Felton Resident, Ted Toft, remembers everyone having to get off the car and help push it over one particular steep portion of track near town. — Courtesy: Harold Van Gorder Collection

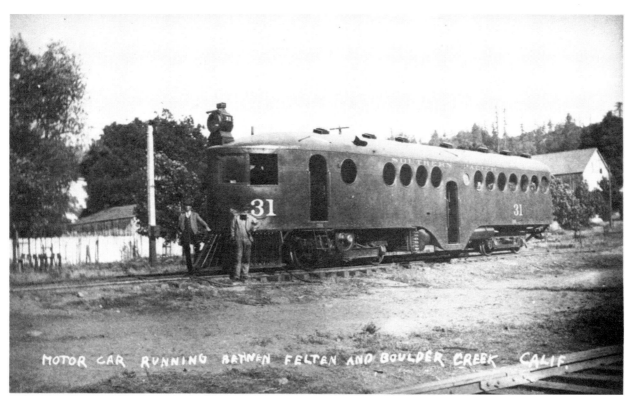

each way between Los Gatos and Santa Cruz, two to San Francisco and one to Oakland.

December, 1927: Passenger trains from Boulder Creek to Santa Cruz reduced to one a day each way. The other three trains were replaced by S.P. transportation company buses.

Summer, 1928: Service on the Boulder Creek branch reinstated to four trains a day each way.

Summer, 1929: Only one passenger train a day between Boulder Creek and Santa Cruz.

October, 1929: Boulder Creek train only makes trip as far as Felton to meet mountain trains. All trips to Santa Cruz are accomplished by bus. Ben Lomond and Brookdale agencies are closed permanently.

Summer, 1930: All passenger trains have been discontinued to and from Boulder Creek and have been replaced by bus. Freight service limited to once a week or when necessary.

January, 1933: Mount Hermon station agency closed for good.

June, 1933: "Clems" station point and "Call of the Wild" station point are abandoned as flag stops.

December, 1933: The Limiteds and the Scenic Locals are gone. There is now only one passenger train a day over the mountains during the winter.

February, 1934: Boulder Creek branch from Felton abandoned. All future service to be provided by bus and truck.

July, 1934: Work begins on a new modern three-lane highway with 500-foot-radius curves over the mountain. The new highway will eliminate 130 curves.

Fall, 1934: Wright's station agency closed.

May, 1939: Big Trees abandoned as a flag stop.

As with all drowning victims, there is always that last and final gasp before the long descent to eternity. So it was with the Southern Pacific's Mountain divison.

During the Summer of 1939, the passenger schedule was upgraded such that two trains made the run from San Francisco to Santa Cruz, and three trains made the return run from Santa Cruz to San Francisco. In addition, connecting service was provided with San Jose and Oakland trains at Los Gatos. While the trains were anything but long, the S.P. did make an attempt at providing good service over the hill.

Also during the summer of 1939, the new one and a quarter million dollar Route 5 (later Highway 17) was to open. One of the few things which had continued to provide the S.P. with passenger ridership over the years was the fact that the old Route 5 was a twisting, winding road that took up to three hours to travel point to point. Now, with the new highway completed, traveling time was ideally cut to under one hour, and what little ridership the S.P. had had was quickly reduced to almost nothing. With the end of December, the S.P. reported that only $11,034 in yearly passenger revenues had been received from the mountain division. Also, while there was some revenue received from freight, mail, and express, it in no way offset the $29,210 yearly maintenance costs. It didn't take a mathematician to figure out some complicated economic formula for this situation. Basically, the S.P. run over the hill was going broke, and the way things were shaping up, it could only get worse.

On February 25th, 1940, it began to rain in Santa Cruz County. By the evening of February 26th, it had rained so hard and so long that many slides began to occur along the S.P. right-of-way. When it came time for the evening train to Los Gatos, orders were given to route it via Watsonville Junction, as conditions over the mountain were hazardous. On February 27th, the rain continued to pound Santa Cruz County. All trains were routed via the Junction until further notice. By the time February 28th had come and gone, the State had suffered millions of dollars in losses from what many would say was the worst storm ever to hit California. Locally, Santa Cruz County, and especially the San Lorenzo River Basin area, was a disaster. In particular, the Southern Pacific right-of-way over the hill was buried in many places and fallen away in others. On February 29th, temporary bus service was started from Los Gatos to Santa Cruz, and all freight

Above: Hundreds of people line the Glen Arbor platform waiting for the train from Boulder Creek which will return them to Santa Cruz and beyond. Glen Arbor was a large real estate development started by Mr. Coffee (Senior) which generated much traffic for the railroad, especially during the summer months. — Courtesy: Lawrence Coffee Collection

Below: The Scenic Local emerges from the dark of tunnel #4 into the bright midday sunlight at Clems. — Courtesy: Santa Cruz County Octagon Museum

An early afternoon train bound for Santa Cruz makes the stop at Laurel just before entering the Laurel-Glenwood tunnel. — Courtesy: Bruce MacGregor Collection

Above: Clarence Draper, Postmaster and owner of the general store, poses in the noontime sun at Glenwood. — Courtesy: Muriel Ann Bently Collection

Below: the town of Wrights as it looked about 1915. — Courtesy: Bill Wulf Collection

The Los Gatos passenger and freight depots as they appeared around 1910. — Courtesy: Vernon J. Sappers Collection

trains were routed via Watsonville Junction until such time as the mountain right-of-way could be reopened.

As had been the case so many times in the past railroading history of Santa Cruz County, the natural elements would once again be the executioners. After a thorough examination of the damage sustained by the railroad and after a careful cost review, it was announced that the S.P. could not reopen the hill for less than $54,375. Based on recent income figures and all possible revenues from the foreseeable future, the Southern Pacific management decided reopening the line would be like dumping good money after bad. Accordingly, they petitioned the Interstate Commerce Commission to abandon the line from Olympia, where heavy amounts of sand were still being shipped, to Los Gatos. In place of the rail passenger service, they would continue buses over the hill, and all freight would now be routed via Watsonville Junction.

During the I.C.C. hearing, the Santa Cruz City Council, the Chamber of Commerce, and the County Board of Supervisors all vigorously opposed the abandonment. Their arguments, however, when weighed against the facts that the S.P. was losing $30,000 a year on the passenger service alone and that as few as five people were riding each train, had little impact. On June 4th, 1940, much to the displeasure of many Santa Cruz City and County officials and residents, the I.C.C. granted the abandonment, and the once great link to Los Gatos and San Francisco was no more.

As with most sacred institutions that fade into history, no one really wants to let them go. Yet, the pendulum on the clock of eternity must continue to swing through transition. Thus, the time for the railroad over the hill had come. It had been born of the expanding dream; it had grown to adulthood during one of the greatest growth periods in the history of railroads; it had approached old age from its golden era with grace and with dignity; and finally, it had accepted its fate as a dream of the past living in the reality of the future. Soon, the only railroading left in the San Lorenzo River Basin would be the sand train operation from Santa Cruz to Olympia.

154

It's 6:55 p.m.; evening train #32 pulled by Pacific locomotive #3108 has just arrived in Santa Cruz from San Francisco. This engine was typical of its sister locomotives 3101-3109, all of which worked the Santa Cruz Mountains in the 1930's. — Courtesy: Bill Harry Collection

The Santa Cruz passenger train #34 bursts forth from tunnel No. 5 (formerly No. 6 during narrow gauge days) to break the silence of a 1937 morning in the San Lorenzo Gorge.
— Courtesy: Fred Stoes

In later years most freight for the Rincon-Felton-Olympia area was shipped via Watsonville Junction rather than over the mountains because of the grades involved. Shown here at the concrete arch, #2921 brings the morning freight up from Santa Cruz. — Courtesy: Fred Stoes

Felton, May 1938: when trains still ran through to Los Gatos. — Courtesy: Fred Stoes

Typical of the many wayside flagstops found along the Felton-Boulder Creek branch was this one at Brackney. — Courtesy: The Valley Press from the Jack Bettencourt Collection

Above: The Felton Train has just made the stop at Glen Arbor as viewed from the Coffee residence front yard.
— Courtesy: Lawrence Coffee

Below: Locomotives Nos. 2937 and 2179 sit at the ready in Boulder Creek waiting to take on the duties of their respective trains per the number boards. — Courtesy: Harold Van Gorder Collection

The afternoon train for Boulder Creek has just arrived in Ben Lomond. — Courtesy: Vernon J. Sappers Collection

Although not shown here, Mrs. Thomas Aram tells of the children who used to sit on the roof of the Brookdale depot and greet the arriving passengers with: "Soda Water, Soda Water, Ginger ale pop, Brookdale, Brookdale, always on top." — Courtesy: U.C. Santa Cruz, Special Collections

The S.P. Transportation Co. Felton-Boulder Creek bus of the 1920's and 1930's takes on a single passenger at Big Trees. — Courtesy: California State Library Collection

Train #119 charges the grade just outside of Santa Cruz as it begins its slow climb to Felton. This train in the late 1920's ran from Watsonville Junction to Felton, where it made connections with a bus for Boulder Creek because there was no longer sufficient ridership to warrant the train going any further. — Courtesy: Bob Willey Collection

The afternoon local is about to depart Boulder Creek for such far away places as the Fish Hatchery, Newell Junction, Golf Links, and finally, Santa Cruz. — Courtesy: Vernon I Sappers Collection

Left: In later years, rather than overload the single main between San Jose and Watsonville Junction, special trains were run over the mountains. Shown here a Nurse's Special charges the grade near Olympia in 1937. — Fred C. Stoes

Right: Train 185 making the 3:00 p.m. run from Los Gatos to San Jose passes the camera of photographer Will Whittaker at Vasona Junction in March of 1939.

Left: For over 48 years the San Lorenzo Valley was serviced by the railroad. Then on Thursday, January 18th, 1934, the era ended when the last train left Boulder Creek. Its consist included two empty gondolas and nine loaded boxcars carrying ties to the Sacramento Northern Railroad for G. M. Locatelli. Its crew: Engineer, Bill Bohrmeister; Fireman, A.G. Bryan; Brakemen, Jack Ryder and Al Ashley; and Conductor F.E. Page. — Courtesy: Harold Van Gorder Collectio

Right: One of the best tourist drawing cards for the Santa Cruz Mountains has always been the State Park at "Big Basin." Shown here a family of campers partake of the area. In the early days of the park, tourists came by train to Boulder Creek and then by the Moody & Cress Stage Line the rest of the way. Later, as the roads became better, the auto replaced both the train and the stage line. — Courtesy: San Jose Historical Museum

The year is 1938. The daily mountain local draws its three car freight across the first Los Gatos Creek crossing just west of town. — Courtesy: W.C. Whittaker

Perhaps the last photograph ever taken of a train to Santa Cruz, morning local #34 is seen leaving San Jose just before 1940. — Courtesy: W.C. Whittaker

These three twilight views of Olympia — Bob Willey, Laurel — Fred Stoes, and Wright's — Malcolm Gaddis, taken shortly before the line was abandoned depicts points which were at one time major stops along the mountain run.

March 11, 1941. The morning train #31 waits for the connecting bus from Santa Cruz to Los Gatos shortly before it is about to leave for San Francisco. Los Gatos was now the end of the once famous South Pacific Coast dream. — Malcolm Gaddis

After over 60 years of operation the mountain branch fell prey to time and the elements, and died. Shown here Bill Harry photographed the last piece of railroad equipment ever to cross the first Los Gatos Creek Bridge just west of town. June 21, 1940.

	EASTWARD						SAN FRANCISCO SUBDIVISION			WESTWARD				
	FIRST CLASS						Time Table No. 147				**FIRST CLASS**			
Capacity of sidings and spurs in car lengths	138	32	168	34	46	Distance from San Francisco	March 30, 1940	Distance from Santa Cruz		123	31	185	45	33
	Passenger	Santa Cruz	Passenger	Passenger	Passenger		San Jose-Santa Cruz Branch			Passenger	Santa Cruz	Passenger	Passenger	Passenger
	Leave Daily EX.SAT.,SUN & HOLIDAYS	Leave Daily EX. SUNDAY	Leave SATURDAY ONLY	Leave Daily	Leave Daily EX. SUNDAY & HOLIDAYS		**STATIONS**			Arrive Daily EX. SUNDAY & HOLIDAYS	Arrive Daily EX. SUNDAY	Arrive SATURDAY ONLY	Arrive Daily EX.SAT.,SUN & HOLIDAYS	Arrive Daily
BKWO TYP		5.18 PM		9.45 AM	5.55 AM	46.9	TO R SAN JOSE	33.8		s 8.34 AM	s 3.21 PM	s 7.27 PM	s 8.37 PM	
		Via Los Altos		Via Los Altos			0.7				Via Los Altos			
16 W				9.53	6.07	47.6	W. P. R. R. Crossing	33.1						
P						50.7	3.1 CAMPBELL	30.0			f	3.09	7.15	f 8.29
65 Yard W P 18	6.37 PM	s 5.28	2.30 PM	s 9.58	6.15	53.3	2.6 R VASONA JUNCTION	27.4		s 6.55 AM	s 8.24	3.00	7.06	f 8.24
	s 6.46 PM	s 5.36	s 2.40 PM	s 10.06	s 6.25 AM	51.8 54.3	2.5 TO R LOS GATOS	24.9		6.49 AM	s 8.18	2.50 PM	6.56 PM	s 8.18
29 P			f 5.45		f 10.15	57.0	ALMA	22.2			f 8.07			f 8.07
13 W			f 5.58		f 10.28	61.3	4.3 WRIGHT	17.9			f 7.54			f 7.55
7 P						63.4	2.1 LAUREL	15.8			f			f
23 P			f 6.13		f 10.43	64.8	1.4 GLENWOOD	14.4			f 7.39			f 7.41
12 P						66.6	1.8 TANK SIDING	12.6			f			f
9 P			f 6.23		f 10.53	68.6	2.0 MEEHAN	10.6			f 7.29			f 7.31
34 P			f 6.27		f 10.57	70.4	1.8 OLYMPIA	8.8			f 7.25			f 7.27
			f		f	72.1	1.7 MT. HERMON	7.1			f			f
9 Yard W P 33			s 6.34		s 11.04	72.4	0.3 TO FELTON	6.8			s 7.18			7.21
			f		f	73.3	0.9 BIG TREES	5.9			f			f
23 P			f 6.42		f 11.12	75.4	2.1 RINCON	3.8			f			f 7.10
17 BKWO TYP			f		f	78.0	2.6 EBLIS	1.2			f			f
			s 6.53 PM		s 11.26 AM	79.2	1.2 TO R SANTA CRUZ	0.0			7.00 AM			7.00 PM
		Arrive Daily EX.SAT.,SUN & HOLIDAYS	Arrive Daily EX. SUNDAY	Arrive SATURDAY ONLY	Arrive Daily	Arrive Daily EX. SUNDAY & HOLIDAYS		(33.8)			Leave Daily EX. SUNDAY & HOLIDAYS	Leave Daily EX. SUNDAY	Leave SATURDAY ONLY	Leave Daily EX.SAT.,SUN & HOLIDAYS	Leave Daily
		(0.09) 16.67	(1.35) 21.35	(0.10) 15.00	(1.41) 20.08	(0.30) 17.80	Time over District Average Speed per Hour			(0.06) 25.00	(1.34) 21.57	(0.31) 17.23	(0.31) 17.23	(1.37) 20.91

In anticipation of the mountain line being reopened, in March of 1940 this timetable appeared for the San Jose to Santa Cruz branch. Ironically, it never happened. — Courtesy: Harold Soper Collection

The Santa Cruz Lumber Company

During 1931 when times were hard and most men were out of work because of the depression, a concern known as the Santa Cruz Lumber Company, under the careful guidance of George Ley, was able to organize to finally go after all of the large timber in the upper Pescadero Creek Canyon. Although the woods operation actually took place in San Mateo County, the company's 50,000-board-foot capacity sawmill was on the headwaters of Pescadero Creek in Santa Cruz County.

To get the saw logs from the woods to the mill, a seven-mile broad gauge railroad was built much along the survey line of the original Boulder Creek and Pescadero planned right-of-way. A second-hand shay locomotive from the San Joaquin and Eastern Railroad and five ex-Yosemite Valley flatcars were purchased to fill the railway's transport needs.

By 1932, the railroad and the mill were in full operation. Hank Humphrey, ex-San Vicente Lumber Company Engineer, was now Engineer on the Shay.

For the next two decades, the operation flourished, and most of the big trees in the Pescadero Canyon were removed via the railroad and then cut into finished lumber at the mill. The only accident of any consequence occurred when a flatcar broke loose on a 200-foot cable incline about two miles below the mill. The car went all the way to the bottom, crashed into another loaded flatcar, and the two were demolished. From then on, the railroad operated with three flatcars, using the other two for parts.

In the early 1950's, the company acquired much of the Butano property from the Pacific Lumber Company. Unable to build the railroad over the steep Pescadero Ridge into Butano Forest, a truck road was cut, and the last lumber company railway came to an end in the Santa Cruz Mountains.

For the next twenty or so years, the Santa Cruz Lumber Company logged the Butano. Finally, on February 29th, 1972, with all the large first-growth trees gone, and over forty years of successful operations behind them, the company cut their last board foot of lumber. After almost 100 years of logging in the San Lorenzo, Pescadero, and Butano Basins, the forests had been harvested. From this day forth, the Santa Cruz logging industry would be cutting second-growth trees.

Right: When photographer, and then company employee, Fred Stoes went to take this picture, the Santa Cruz Lumber Co. Shay had no identifying markings on it. To rectify this, he made same out of paper and taped them to the side of the locomotive. Voila! Logs are being off loaded into the Pescadero pond by S.C. LBR Co. #2.

Left: The Santa Cruz Lumber Company mill in Pescadero Canyon. — Courtesy: Fred Stoes

Right: Engineer John F. (Hank) Humphrey stops the Santa Cruz Lumber Co. train in a clearing along Pescadero Creek; Brakeman, Henry (Hank) Johnson positions himself on a saw log; the shutter clicks, and a last view for this chapter of the once great Santa Cruz Mountain lumbering industry is preserved for the annals of history. —Courtesy: Henry Johnson Collection

Ocean Shore/Southern Pacific/San Vicente Lumber Co. Railroads

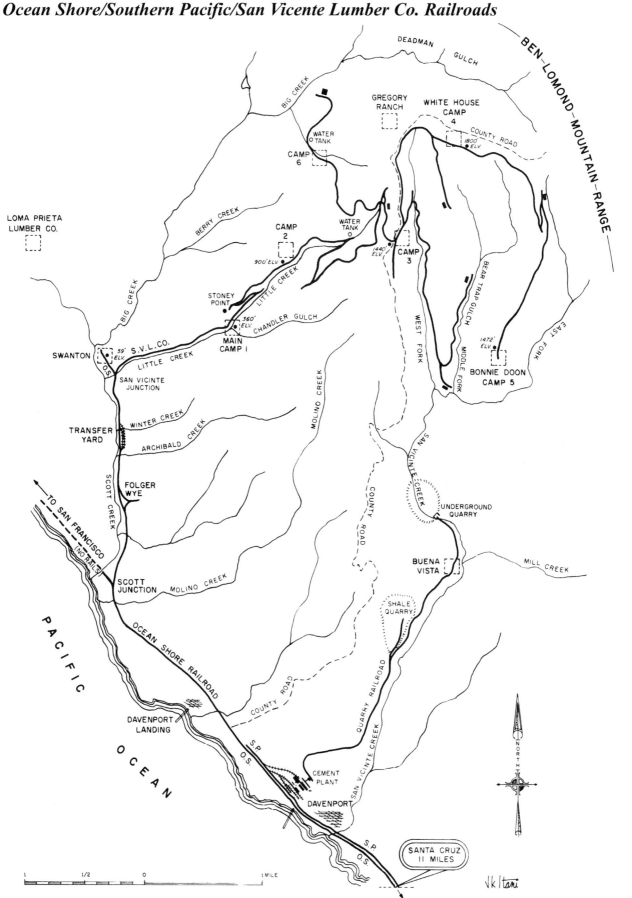

DEADMAN GULCH

BEN-LOMOND-MOUNTAIN-RANGE

BIG CREEK

GREGORY RANCH

WHITE HOUSE CAMP 4

COUNTY ROAD

1800' ELV.

WATER TANK

CAMP 6

BERRY CREEK

LOMA PRIETA LUMBER CO.

CAMP 2

WATER TANK

900' ELV.

1440' ELV.

CAMP 3

BEAR TRAP GULCH

LITTLE CREEK

STONEY POINT

360' ELV.

CHANDLER GULCH

MAIN CAMP 1

MIDDLE FORK

WEST FORK

EAST FORK

1472' ELV.

BONNIE DOON CAMP 5

SWANTON

59' ELV.

S.V.L.CO.

O.S.

LITTLE CREEK

SAN VICINTE JUNCTION

WINTER CREEK

ARCHIBALD CREEK

MOLINO CREEK

TRANSFER YARD

SAN VICINTE CREEK

UNDERGROUND QUARRY

SCOTT CREEK

FOLGER WYE

TO SAN FRANCISCO (NO RAILS)

COUNTY ROAD

BUENA VISTA

MILL CREEK

SCOTT JUNCTION

MOLINO CREEK

SHALE QUARRY

PACIFIC OCEAN

OCEAN SHORE RAILROAD

COUNTY ROAD

QUARRY RAILROAD

DAVENPORT LANDING

S.P.

O.S.

CEMENT PLANT

SAN VICINTE CREEK

NORTH

DAVENPORT

S.P. O.S.

SANTA CRUZ 11 MILES

JK Itani

1   1/2   0   1 MILE

168

4

The North Coast

Let the sawmills rip, and the lime kilns rage;
Santa Cruz County has come of age ...

I.T. Bloom stood high atop Ben Lomond Mountain overlooking the vast uncut pine and redwood forests that stretched to the sea. "If only there was an economical way to harvest and transport this untold wealth of prime forest products," thought the pioneer lumberman. In Pescadero Canyon alone, there was over 800,000,000 board feet of timber just waiting to be felled. Over the ridge in Butano Canyon, another 400,000,000 board feet had yet to feel the weight of the lumberjack's heavy axe. Down in Gazos Creek, there was still 300,000,000 board feet of lumber which had not been cut. South of the Gazos, along the coastline, lay the canyons of Scott Creek, Mill Creek, Little Creek, and San Vicente Creek, where another 615,000,000 board feet of timber stood in its natural state. The only reason that all of this lumber remained untouched was because most of the lumber companies, including those owned and operated by I.T. Bloom, were waiting for a railroad along the coast from Santa Cruz to San Francisco.

From all indications, it looked as though a railroad along the coast was a sure thing. Already, several different companies had incorporated over the last 20 years to try to build such a road, and many more companies were on the financial horizon. All who were waiting for such a rail line knew it would only be a matter of time before one of the many such companies would step forth with the wherewithal to do it.

In February of 1901, a new company, the Bay and Coast Railway, applied to the Santa Cruz Board of Supervisors for a franchise to build an electric line up the coast. The line was to run from Redwood City to Woodside, to La Honda, to Davenport Landing, and on to Santa Cruz. In addition, there was to be a branch line from Pescadero to Big Basin, to Boulder Creek. It was estimated that the $450,000.00 freight and passenger line could be completed, and in operation, within two years of the franchise approval. In January of 1902, the predecessor to the San Francisco and San Mateo Electric Railway proposed essentially the same project with the extension of the line to San Francisco. On October 3rd, 1903, the San Francisco and Southern Railroad went one step further and incorporated to build the line down the coast at a cost of $5,000,000.00. As with all of the previous expansionary proposals, nothing went further than the talk stage.

The Coast Line Railway and The Ocean Shore Electric Railway

It was early in the month of April 1905. For the first time, the local residents along the coast, and those in Santa Cruz, began to seriously watch the everchanging railroad events with increased interest. Somebody knew something about the local events that were taking place and somebody wasn't telling. Recently, during the months of January and February, several people reported seeing a group of Southern Pacific surveyors and engineers at different points along the coast between Santa Cruz and San Francisco.[7] When interviewed by the local press, Chief Engineer William Hood stated that the survey was strictly preliminary in nature, conducted for the purpose of getting an estimate of what it would cost to bring a branch line up the coast to open up the timber, lime, and other resources of the area. In March, a similar group of surveyors and engineers were again

[7]Note: this narrative deals primarily with the operation of the Ocean Shore Railway as it took place within Santa Cruz County. For those who desire more information concerning the complete history of the Ocean Shore, there are two fine publications currently in print. The first is a book by Jack Wagner entitled *The Last Whistle,* and the second is a *Western Railroader* magazine article by Rudolph Brandt entitled *Ocean Shore Railroad.*

Lumber companies and lime operations were not the only concerns which operated private railroads in the Ben Lomond Range of the Santa Cruz Mountains. Shown here a Big Creek Power Co. flume inspector stops at an unknown location somewhere along the Company's many miles of wooden railroad to pose for an 1896 photograph. — Courtesy: Rita Mattei-Lena Sonognini Collection

seen. This time, however, according to their Chief Engineer, John B. Rogers, they were taking a survey for a new company to be known as the Ocean Shore Electric Railway. Now, with eastern cement entrepreneur William J. Dingee's announcement that one of the largest cement plants ever to be built in the United States was soon to be constructed near Davenport Landing, rumors were flying.

On April 15, 1905, all speculation was temporarily cast aside when the following news story appeared in the local newspapers:

Articles of Incorporation for the Coast Line Railway Company were filed in the County Clerk's office in Santa Cruz today. The Southern Pacific has finally incorporated a company to build a road north along the coast via Pescadero, between Santa Cruz and San Francisco. The road will be eighty miles long with a twenty mile branch line between Pescadero and Boulder Creek . . . The Company was incorporated for $3,000,000. The directors are all S.P. officials ... Several electric and steam road promoters have within the past two or three years figured on building lines into the county. The S.P. people have, therefore, incorporated to build and thus get rid of a competing line to Santa Cruz.

In July of 1890, Chief Engineer Hood had conducted a preliminary survey for the S.P. along the coast. Five years later, he did it all over again. Now in 1905, after having completed a third survey, Hood's work was about to pay off. At last, the long-awaited railroad along the coast that would open up all the lime, lumber, and farming areas, was going to be built. At least it was going to be started. Initially, the S.P. was going to build its line to Davenport Landing where it had secured a contract with Mr. Dingee to handle all of the Santa Cruz and Portland Cement Company business. Later, it was predicted, the line would be extended on to Pescadero and San Francisco as soon as the proper financing could be secured.

On May 18th, 1905, undaunted by the Southern Pacific's incorporation, the Ocean Shore Electric Railway filed its own articles of incorporation with the County Clerk's office in Santa Cruz. Who was this upstart that thought it could take on the vested interests of the Southern Pacific when so many companies which had gone before it had failed? The Ocean Shore Electric Railway was a corporation organized by a group of prominent San Francisco businessmen who had a dream that one day, perhaps, their railroad would be part of a transcontinental line known as the "Western Pacific." With that in mind, J. Downey Harvey, a well-known western financier; J.A. Folger, noted coffee baron; P.D. Martin, a young energetic land speculator; C.C. Moore, president of one of the largest engineering firms on the west coast; and H.D. Pillsbury, an experienced San Francisco Railroad attorney; all came together to make their dream a reality.

The reason the Ocean Shore didn't pay much attention to the Southern Pacific's incorporation to build up the coast was because they knew it was a bluff. Obviously, Mr. Dingee of the Santa Cruz and Portland Cement Company had approached the Southern Pacific prior to the Ocean Shore incorporation with a proposal to build a spur from Santa Cruz to the cement plant. The Southern Pacific

had gone one step further and made it look like they were building to San Francisco. In truth, the S.P. already had over twenty million dollars of its capital tied up in the recently completed Lucin Cut-Off and San Francisco to Los Angeles coastline branch, and the construction currently underway on the Bayshore Cut-Off. At this particular time, the S.P. was not about to invest another five million dollars for a line up the coast. Besides, the S.P. management knew that if they could keep the Ocean Shore bottled up on the coast, most of its freight would be coming over Southern Pacific tracks anyway.

All during the months of May and June, right-of-way agents, representing both companies, were hard at work purchasing the necessary properties so that each company could begin its construction. By the middle of July, the Ocean Shore announced that their line had been secured through to San Francisco with the exception of those properties currently under condemnation proceedings. By early August, the Southern Pacific had secured their own 11.88 mile right-of-way out of Santa Cruz as far as the cement plant site. Ironically, once construction would begin, both railroad companies would be starting out to build the same "competing" line, at about the same time, within 20 feet of each other in most places.

By the 15th of August, all of the grade stakes had

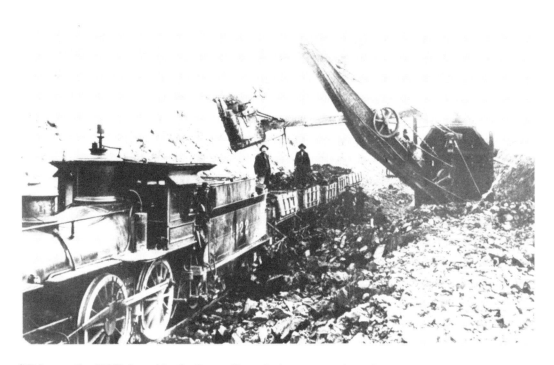

S.P. locomotive #1222, leased by the Ocean Shore during construction, of the south end, is seen working in a cut near Davenport. — Courtesy: Francis J. Carney Collection

The long Ocean Shore trestle at Davenport is being filled in this rare view, circa 1906. — Courtesy: John Schmale Collection

been driven into position, and Shattuck and Desmond, who had won the Ocean Shore contract from Santa Cruz to Scott Creek, were about ready to begin construction. In order for the Ocean Shore to meet its scheduled right-of-way completion in just a short 18 months, hundreds of men had been employed at various points along the line to speed up construction. In addition, as a further time saver, C.E. Loss and Company had been awarded a parallel contract to build the railroad south from San Francisco toward Scott Creek. If all went according to plan, the Ocean Shore would announce the grand opening of its double-tracked, electrified, San Francisco to Santa Cruz mainline on February 1st, 1907.

Unfortunately, the Southern Pacific had most of their capital and manpower tied up in other ongoing construction. As a result, the Coast Line Railway construction efforts in no way resembled those of the energetic Ocean Shore Electric Railway.

With the arrival of Ocean Shore engine No. 1 on October 21st, 1905, the work of building the line north was begun in earnest. As railroads go, there really wasn't much to the actual construction of the Ocean Shore between Santa Cruz and Scott Creek. About the only real engineering difficulties encountered were the erection of some rather substantial trestles across Majors and Laguna creeks, and the high gulch near the Yellow Bank Dairy. As to the grade and curvature of the line, it was kept essentially level and straight through the use of extensive cutting-and-filling operations. Altogether only 16 curves would be required to reach Scott Creek. As a result, in just a short four months the Ocean Shore was able to Jay track within two miles of Davenport Landing and continue on with the grading considerably farther.

By the 20th of January in 1906, activities around the Santa Cruz and Portland Cement plant site were in high gear. Already, there were over 300 construction men working at the plant site and up San Vicente Creek on the broad gauge quarry railroad. In addition, a village known as Davenport, complete with hotels, stores, and family dwellings, had been laid out just south of the plant. For months, Davenport Landing had been the scene of ship after ship off-loading their valuable cargos of railroad ties, steel rail, steam donkeys, and grading equipment to and in the construction of both railroads. Now, the Ocean Shore had begun freight operations to Davenport, bringing in most of the massive machinery and building materials that would be used to erect the cement plant. At the same time, it was continuing to push its line north toward Scott Creek with most of the grading having progressed that far. Ideally, if all progress continued at its projected rate, Engineer Rogers was predicting there would be at least one electrified track completed the entire 80-mile distance by October.

Things were obviously going favorably for the Ocean Shore Electric Railroad. In September of 1905, they had upped their capital stock issue from three million to five million dollars. By February of 1906, the new bonds had been mostly sold. In July of 1905, they had purchased 2,000 acres of property at the mouth of Scott Creek where they planned to erect a fine new summer resort. In September of 1905, the Ocean Shore had finally secured a right-of-way across Ernest V. Cowell's strip of land at the beach in Santa Cruz such that they soon would be able to build a deep water wharf. In February of 1906, they purchased the Santa Cruz Street Railroad system with an eye on expansion to Watsonville and a large station complex in Downtown Santa Cruz. By April 17th, 1906, the O.S. had laid track about a mile beyond Davenport and all of the right-of-way to Scott Creek had been graded. At the same time, C.E. Loss and Company had tracked as far south as Mussel Rock from San Francisco, and the grading of the right-of-way had been completed for several miles beyond that.

As had happened so many times before in the brief history of Santa Cruz County, the awesome force of the Earth's time clock was once again to deal a deadly blow to the unimportant plans of mankind. No one needs to be told what happened on that fateful morning of April 18th, 1906, when the dreams of development and expansion dissolved in the fiery ashes of disaster. While everywhere chaos and devastation reigned supreme, nowhere was it more

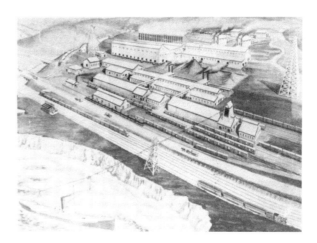

The future was to be grand and glorious according to this artist's concept of the completed Santa Cruz & Portland Cement Co. Plant and its supporting industries such as the railroads and the shipping industry. — Courtesy: Alverda Orlando Collection

felt than on the Ocean Shore Railway. By the time the Earth had stopped adjusting to the unknown forces within it, major amounts of the Ocean Shore's right-of-way and its construction equipment had been claimed by the sea at Devil's Slide. In addition, the financial assets of most of the directors and major stockholders had been reduced to rubble. As of April l9th, the previously rosey future of the Ocean Shore Electric Railway was in serious doubt. As with all major calamities, the only thing the Ocean Shore could do was pick itself up and begin again. Management wasn't entirely sure where the money to do so was coming from, but they figured it would and so cleanup and construction continued.

As luck would have it, not much damage had been sustained by the south end. As a result, Shattuck and Desmond were able to continue on with the grading and track-laying to Scott Creek. By the 15th of June, regular passenger train service had begun from Santa Cruz to San Vicente Creek near the cement plant. Two roundtrips were made a day, one in the forenoon and one in the afternoon. At the same time, the Ocean Shore was doing quite a lucrative freight business to the cement plant, because the Coast Line Railway had only progressed three miles out of Santa Cruz. By the first of October, Shattuck and Desmond had lived up to the terms and conditions of their construction contract. The O.S. right-of-way had been graded and tracked 14.04 miles to Scott Creek.

It was at this point that rumors began to circulate concerning the solvent future of the Ocean Shore Electric Railway. During the earthquake, most of the Ocean Shore's construction equipment and over 4,000

Ocean Shore 4-4-0's No's 1 & 2 are seen in these two views circa 1908. — Courtesy: John Schmale Collection, Ted Wurm Collection

The Davenport cement facility operated a steam powered broad gauge railroad from the plant to the quarry in the early years. Shown here in 1913, with Harvey Williams in the cab, was #1, one of two Porters owned by the company. — Courtesy: Alverda Orlando from the Harvey Williams Collection

Southern Pacific freight and passenger crews pose in front of switcher #1023 at Davenport. — Courtesy: Mrs. William Sinnott Collection

In 1922 the entire company broad and narrow gauge system was converted to narrow gauge electric. As seen here, one of the two Baldwin electric engines poses at the plant. — Courtesy: Bruce MacGregor Collection

feet of its right-of-way, on the north end, had been destroyed. It had taken a considerable amount of money and manpower to recover, repair, and replace the losses. Also, many of the Railroad's financial backers had been ruined. and the O.S. management had not been too successful at finding new sources of capital. As a result, most onlookers were becoming aware that the Ocean Shore Electric Railway was operating on a shoestring budget at best.

To offset this speculation, President J. Downey Harvey took an all-or-nothing gamble and announced that the line would be in operation from San Francisco to Half Moon Bay by July of 1907, and as far as Santa Cruz by the middle of next summer. By March the contracts for construction from San Francisco to Half Moon Bay had been let, and over 4,000 men were at work pushing the O.S. onward. At the same time, Shattuck and Desmond had received a new contract for the construction of the line north from Scott Creek to the Waddell Bluffs. Once again, on the surface anyway, it looked as though the Ocean Shore meant business.

While the Ocean Shore had recently been the object of most of the public's attention, the S.P.-Coast Line Railway cooperative had not been sitting idle. By May of 1907, nine miles of right-of-way had been completed out of Santa Cruz, and the S.P. was predicting the line would be in operation to Davenport before the summer was over. Once this happened, it meant the Ocean Shore would soon be losing almost all of its freight and passenger business on the south end. As if this wasn't bad enough, after the Ocean Shore had finally come to an agreement with Ernest Cowell for access across his shoreline property such that they could erect a railroad wharf, the S.P. effectively blocked the plan by building a spur track right across its projected path. To make matters worse, when the City of Santa Cruz passed Ordinance No. 638 on September 7th, 1907, allowing the O.S. to extend their line from its present terminal to the Company's proposed terminal in the center of town, no one had counted on the Southern Pacific not allowing access across its property. As a result, there sat the Ocean Shore bottled up on a small bluff overlooking the unreachable Monterey Bay and the unattainable downtown Santa Cruz.

By September of 1907, the Ocean Shore was experiencing serious economic difficulties. Because of the financial after-effects of the 1906 earthquake and fire, the railroad had not been able to sell all of its 5% interest carrying bonds which had been voted upon. Therefore, construction work could only be continued with money realized from assessments against the railroad's current stockholders. This burden was proving heavier than some of these could bear or cared to continue. Many of the minority

stockholders had no more cash at their command and were, therefore, forced to dispose of their holdings. This, due to the current money market, proved to be an extremely difficult thing to do. Because of this increasing crisis, work on the completion of the line began to slow down, and the projected opening of the completed line slipped farther into the future.

About this time, directors Harvey and Folger, who jointly owned over 51% of all of the outstanding stock, and who, therefore, had the ability to sell a controlling interest in the railroad, went looking for some financial assistance from Gould of the Western Pacific. No one knows what agreements, if any, were made, but shortly after the meeting took place, the ultra-conservative Hibernia Bank of San Francisco purchased $80,000.00 worth of Ocean Shore Bonds. As to whether the bank was joining Gould or whether they did so on his guarantee, no one knows. The important thing was the Ocean Shore received a public shot in the arm which increased its sale of bonds and allowed construction to continue.

Toward the end of 1907, a financial panic gripped the nation for a short time that had serious after-effects on the Ocean Shore Railway. As a result, whatever help eastern capital had been in the past in continuing the construction of the line had now come to an end. From here on out, if the railroad was ever to be completed it would have to be done with local investors. To that end, in early 1908, bond rallies were held, first in Santa Cruz, and then in San Francisco. While most realized the meager financial situation of the Ocean Shore, many thought the condition was only temporary. Based on the sales pitch that once the line was completed financial utopia would be at hand, enough bonds were sold to allow construction to continue.

It was at this point in time that the future of the Ocean Shore looked most promising. Real estate sales up and down the coast were booming. Growers were looking forward to the day when all of the produce raised on the coast could be shipped by rail. Also, tourist attractions, hotels, restaurants, and merchandising stores were going up at a phenomenal rate. Likewise, rock and lime quarries were impatiently waiting for the Ocean Shore. Finally, all that uncut timber along the Ocean Shore right-of-way stood waiting for the railroad that would ship it all out once it had been cut.

By the time May of 1908 had rolled around, the Ocean Shore was beginning to look more and more like the 80-mile coastline railroad it was supposed to be. Track had been laid as far south as Princeton, and rumor had it that by October passenger trains would finally be in service to Half Moon Bay. In addition, grading had continued on as far as Tunitas Creek where a giant trestle 515 feet long and 88 feet high was

A string of wooden reefers lines the freight platform of the Southern Pacific's depot at Davenport, circa 1910. — Courtesy: Southern Pacific Company Collection

currently under construction. From there to Scott Creek, it was only 26 miles, and even this section was being worked in places.

While the Ocean Shore's future looked promising, especially on the north end, as long as the line remained incomplete, the south end would be a different story. By now the S.P.-Coast Line Railway had begun freight and passenger operations to Davenport. As a consequence, the Ocean Shore's two mixed trains, which daily operated between Santa Cruz and the wye at Scott Creek, were both short and empty. Altogether, this hapless operation had only been able to generate a little over $ 10,000 gross income for the first six months of 1908. To put it bluntly, this wasn't even enough to meet the payroll. If things didn't start to get better, and soon, the south end would temporarily have to shut down service.

On May 8th, 1908, the San Vicente Lumber Company was incorporated to go after all of the timber from Scott Creek near the community of Swanton to the top of Ben Lomond mountain. It was rumored that the company had over $10,000,000 behind it, and that it was to be one of the largest lumbering operations Santa Cruz County would ever see.

In order for the San Vicente Lumber Company operation to be competitive with the other ongoing lumber concerns in the area, the company had decided to build their sawmill and distribution yard near downtown Santa Cruz. Also, because of the massive scale of the operation, the company made plans to build a nine-mile broad gauge railroad from Swanton up Little Creek to their main logging camp. This, of course, posed the logistical question, how do you get the cut logs from Swanton to Santa Cruz, 16 miles away? Obviously, with the Ocean Shore Railway only two miles from Swanton, the answer was simple.

Shortly after the incorporation announcement, the San Vicente Lumber Company was to enter into a long-term contract with the Ocean Shore. In the contract, the San Vicente Lumber Company agreed to advance the necessary funds for the Ocean Shore to build a branch line from their wye at Folger on Scott Creek to the company's broad gauge line at Little Creek. In addition, a small spur, approximately 300 yards in length, would be built from the Little Creek Junction to the center of Swanton. In return for the advancement of funds, the Ocean Shore was to reduce each month's San Vicente Lumber Company freight

At the quarry the company used narrow rather than broad gauge equipment because it was easier to lay down and take up. Shown here in these two views are a narrow gauge Davenport and Vulcan respectively at work. — Courtesy: Alverda Orlando from the Lone Star Industries collections and the John D. Schmale collection

University of California engineering students aboard a special Swanton bound Ocean Shore train are shown leaving Santa Cruz. Just south of Swanton in a meadow to the west of Little Creek Switch the college used to have an engineering surveyor's camp for students. — Courtesy: Louis Stein Jr. Collection

bill by 25% until such time as the advancement was repaid. In addition to the financial arrangement, the companies also agreed that a two-track transfer yard would be laid out about a half a mile below Little Creek Junction. As part of this arrangement, each company would be allowed to use that portion of the branch line between Little Creek Junction and the transfer yard.

Soon after the branch line had been completed, another lumbering concern, the Loma Prieta Lumber Company, announced plans to commence timbering operations in the area. Recently, the company had purchased a tract of land on Mill Creek, about a mile above Swanton, where they now were in the process of constructing a 30,000-board-foot capacity sawmill. While the operation, when begun, would be much smaller in scope than the San Vicente Lumber Company, it would no doubt add additional revenues

to the Ocean Shore's coffer. To that end, a short thousand-foot spur was laid down at Swanton to service the needs of the Loma Prieta Lumber Company and additional freight revenue looked forward to.

By the end of 1908, the Ocean Shore had been able to begin freight and passenger service on both ends of the line. On the north end, two passenger trains a day were operating between San Francisco and the end-of-track at Tunitas Glen. In addition, wellpatronized weekend excursion trains were operating to the many beach resorts that had been recently established along the coast. Likewise, on the sound end, freight and passenger service had been extended to Swanton, and large quantities of logs and finished lumber were now coming over the "division" from the San Vicente Lumber Company and the Loma Prieta Lumber Company.

Right: An unknown lady poses aboard an Ocean Shore flatcar in the San Vicente Transfer Yard.
— Courtesy: Rita Mattei-Lena Sonognini Collection

Below: Ocean Shore engine #6 sits idle at Santa Cruz. — Courtesy: Roy Graves Collection, U.C. Berkeley, Bancroft Library

Little Creek Switch, straight ahead: Ocean Shore main into Swanton, to the left. — Courtesy: Stanford University Library

Laurel Grove Inn at end of track in Swanton. The Inn was owned and operated by the Matteis. It served as a residence for boarders and the local Swanton Post Office. Mrs. Mattei was the Post Mistress. — Courtesy: Rita Mattei-Lena Sonognini Collection

Ocean Shore locomotive #4 at Swanton. — Courtesy: Roy Graves Collection, U.C. Berkeley, Bancroft Library

Passengers await the departure of the Ocean Shore Train for Swanton in this well known Santa Cruz view. — Courtesy: Louis Stein Jr. Collection

The term "division" had been given to the northern and southern sections of the Ocean Shore right-of-way when construction work on the 26-mile uncompleted portion of the line had been halted due to the unsettled financial conditions of the road. While this caused great concern locally, management was not too alarmed, as the line, even in its uncompleted condition, had been able to show a net profit of $270,000 for fiscal year 1908.

The year 1909, although looked forward to with bright promise, was to be a rather disappointing time in the short history of the Ocean Shore Electric Railway. Whatever meager gains had been made in 1908 would be wiped out in the month of January.

Severe rainstorms pounding the coast caused so much damage to both ends of the Ocean Shore right-of-way that the line was not able to reopen for over three months.

In addition, the Southern Pacific, with the completion of the Bayshore and Los Gatos cutoffs and the broad gauging of the line over the Santa Cruz mountains, was able to reduce the San Francisco to Santa Cruz travel time to only two hours and thirty minutes. This was an unmatchable time as far as the Ocean Shore was concerned, even if their road would have been in full operation. To make matters worse, creditors were starting to hound the railroad for overdue accounts, the existing right-of-way was in a state of disrepair, and the Ocean Shore, with no operational funds for almost four months, was about busted. Obviously, what was needed was a great deal more money, not only to upgrade the line and continue operations but also to complete it. More money, however, based on previous precedents, was now only a pie in the sky pipedream.

With the approach of the Winter Solstice of 1909, the Ocean had spent its last farthing. Now, there was nothing left in the cash drawer except cobwebbed I.O.U.'s. In addition, there were no more open credit accounts upon which to draw. At last, the final economic card had been played and fate was to be the winner. The financial game of RAILROAD was over for the Ocean Shore. As with all time sacred dreams of greatness which end in failure, the only course left open to the management of the Ocean Shore was bankruptcy.

On December 6th, the company fell into the hands of the court-appointed receivers. In July of 1910, receiver Frederick S. Stratton filed a petition with the court requesting that the line be sold at public auction to cover claims against the Ocean Shore totaling more than $2,300,000. On January 17th, 1911, the public auction was held and the line was sold to a group of men comprised of previous bondholders for $1,136,000. By February 2, 1911, the new management had taken control, and in a short while the Ocean Shore Electric Railway would be a dream of the past.

The Ocean Shore Railroad Company

On October 9, 1911, a new company, the Ocean Shore Railroad Company, was incorporated. Interestingly enough, the word "Electric" had been dropped from the company's name. It was the stated plan of the new management, C.C. Moore, R.B. Robbins, F.W. Bradley, and A.C. Kains, to pick up where the old Ocean Shore had left off. This, however, with the cards stacked against the Ocean Shore as they were, was going to be easier said than done. While once again, grandiose schemes and optimistic promises would be put forth regarding the completion and operation of the line, it would be its financial reality that would determine its future. From the beginning of 1912 until the final demise of the Ocean Shore, it would remain an uncompleted road, operating two separate divisions.

The Southern Division

With the passing of the Summer of 1912, most of the plans and statements previously made concerning the completion and expansion of the Ocean Shore Railroad had faded into the forgotten past. By now, the Company's Southern Division had digressed into the quaint little down home short line

that it was forever destined to be. The line was 15.55 miles in length from Santa Cruz to Swanton. Its only depot facility consisted of a small ticket office and waiting room sitting perched on a hill, overlooking the mammoth operations of the Southern Pacific, in downtown Santa Cruz. Its rolling stock, while varying from time to time and season to season, was generally comprised of 42 flatcars, two boxcars, one maintenance-of-way boxcar, one baggage-passenger coach combine, and two second-class passenger coaches. Its primary motive power was furnished by locomotives No. I through No. 6, although only two such locomotives were assigned to the Southern Division at any one time. The main function of the Southern Division was to furnish the San Vicinte Lumber Company with freight service from their timber holdings to their mill in Santa Cruz, 14 miles away. Over and above this, the parallel Southern Pacific Davenport branch usually took care of most everything else.

From 1912 until 1920, the basic operation of the Southern Division would remain about as it was. Each day would see two trains, usually mixed, making their way from the small depot near the beach in Santa Cruz to the Mattei's hotel at Swanton and back again. The trip took approximately 45 minutes each way, and except for a few unscheduled flag stops, there was never much change in this day-to-day routine.

To write the short history of the Ocean Shore Southern Division off in such an abbreviated manner would be to do it a disservice. There was more to this story than just the facts and figures corporate history of a short-duration railroad. This line also involved the lives of the local people who worked on it and were served by it. Fortunately for this author, I was able to interview 87-year-old Tom Wilson who worked as a brakeman and conductor on the Ocean Shore for over ten years. We will depart from the narrative at this time and present a paraphrased review of that interview.

Question: What was a typical day's routine like?
Answer: We started out right from the point where the bridge on West Cliff Drive crosses the S.P. tracks today in Santa Cruz. There used to be a passenger walkway from the bridge to our little depot. From the depot, the train would go to Rapetti where the San Vicente Lumber Co. had their mill down on Delaware Ave. and West Cliff Drive. Here, we would pick up the empty flatcars on their way back to Swanton. From Rapetti to Swanton, there weren't many stops. At Scott Junction, the railroad took a hard right turn down a steep grade into the flats along Scott Creek. At the bottom of the grade, we had our wye where the train would be turned around and then backed into Swanton. About a half a mile out of

Believing that the second Ocean Shore Company would surely complete the line, several small businessmen, such as Isaiah Hartman of Boulder Creek shown here, once again invested in the railroad.
— Courtesy: Doug Sarmento from the Jimmy Hartman Collection

Swanton, we would come to the transfer yard. Here, we would cut off the empty flatcars for the San Vicinte timbering operations up Little Creek and then back the rest of the train into Swanton. The Little Creek switch was always in position for the Ocean Shore train. Upon leaving Swanton, the train would stop at the transfer yard and pick up the loaded flatcars bound for the mill in Santa Cruz. From there it was back to the mill at Rapetti where the flatcars would be cut out and then over to the Santa Cruz depot.

Question: Where exactly was the transfer yard and how big was it?

Answer: The transfer yard lay parallel to Scott Creek between Archibald Creek on the south and Chandler Creek on the north. It had only two tracks, one for holding empties and one for holding loaded cars. Sometimes the San Vicinte boys would try to slip by a flatcar that wasn't loaded properly, but, I'd always hold my ground and tell them we wouldn't accept it.

Question: At what points did the Ocean Shore have stations on the South end?

Answer: The only station the company had was at Santa Cruz. All the rest of the stops along the right-of-way were usually at points where we had spur tracks. The only exception to this was at Swanton where we used the hotel. Mrs. Mattei ran the post office and occasionally took care of passengers.

Question: Did you share any stops with the Southern Pacific?

Answer: The only common S.P.-Ocean Shore stopping point was at Gordola. There, the S.P. used to haul out asphalt. We also stopped at the school house at Majors where we used to pick up a school teacher who was a regular passenger.

Question: What other freight customers did the Ocean Shore have besides the San Vicente Lumber Co. and the Loma Prieta Lumber Co.?

Answer: We didn't have the Loma Prieta Lumber

Conductor Brown originally came from the Santa Fe where after holding second in seniority he had been wrongly fired. After fighting the A.T. & S.F. for over two years about it, he was finally reinstated with full back pay and No. 1 seniority — -Courtesy: Tom Wilson

The local folks pose for a group photo in front of Ocean Shore No. 5 at Swanton. Left to right: Conductor, O.S. Smith; Lena Sonognini, and Engineer Harry Delmas. — Courtesy: Rita Mattei-Lena Sonognini Collection

Jim Gray (in overcoat) poses with his northend-southend connecting auto stages and passengers in front of the Swanton House in Pescadero. — Courtesy: Bob Gray Collection

Co. for very long. We hauled out split stuff, posts, pickets, shakes, and ties for Mr. Woods who had a small operation at Swanton. Also, we hauled scrap wood from the San Vicinte sawmill and planing mill to a downtown woodyard where it was sold for $5.00 a bundle. In addition, we hauled artichokes from three Wilder ranches which were leased by the San Mateo Produce Company. Once in a while, we even hauled groceries from the store at Davenport up to the various folks at Swanton. Likewise, during the season we hauled large amounts of brussel sprouts.

Question: When did the Autobus start?
Answer: On April 18, 1914, Jim Gray, who used to be an Ocean Shore brakeman on the north end, started running two Stanley steamers between Tunitas Glen and Swanton. He worked out a deal where the Ocean Shore charged $4.50 for the fare from San Francisco to Santa Cruz, and he in turn was handsomely reimbursed by the company for his connecting stage service. Later he married one of the Mattei girls.

Question: Who made up most of your ridership?
Answer: Most of our riders were San

Vicente Lumber Co. employees. At one time, we carried a lot of the cement plant employees, but due to a bad change in the time schedule by an ex-S.P. employee, they all went over to the S.P. Sometimes when the weather was bad and the dirt road into Santa Cruz was nothing but mud, the local people would park their cars and buggies at Swanton and ride the train into town. We also carried many fishermen and hunters who we would let off at various points along the right-of-way.

Question: When was your busiest time?
Answer: Payday at the lumber camp usually generated a lot of ridership for us. There was this lady in Davenport Landing who ran an establishment that catered to men. For some reason or other, she always needed extra female help come payday. Thus, on the afternoon train to Swanton, we would always be carrying extra ladies from Santa Cruz. At our last stop before Davenport Landing, I'd motion the engineer with a special hand signal to let him know we had to make a flag stop. Once at Davenport Landing, all of the ladies would get off the train. Upon returning from Swanton the train would be loaded with men eager to part with their hard-earned cash. After the stop at

Ocean Shore No. 6 meets No. 9 on a typical summer's outing along the north end. — Courtesy: Bob Gray Collection

the Transfer Yard I'd again give the engineer the appropriate hand signal for the flag stop at Davenport Landing. Once there, about half of the train would unload. On the next morning train from Santa Cruz, the same rigmarole would take place all over again, only this time in reverse. The men would go back to the Little Creek timbering operation, and the ladies would accompany us on the return trip to Santa Cruz. This went on for many, many paydays.

Question: Who was in charge of the Southern Division?

Answer: The superintendent of the Southern Division was K.K. Jordan. He was a fine man if you did your work. He never bothered you. He got me my first job on the Ocean Shore as an extra brakeman or fireman while I was still working the company's street car line in Santa Cruz. Mr. McEwan was the section boss.

Question: Do you remember anything about the locomotives on the South End?

Answer: Usually the locomotives were assigned to the Southern Division in pairs. We started out with 4-4-0's, No. 1 and No. 2. During the time I worked on the north end one of the

engineers let No. 2 run out of water at Majors. As a result, the crown sheet blew out and the engine was useless. Later we had engines No. 3 and No. 5 on the south end and finally ceased operations with No. 4 and No. 6. Most of our engines were fairly small. Thus, we couldn't pull too much of a load. The short grade coming out of the flats at Scott Creek was very steep. Sometimes it required, although not very often, double-header operations.

Question: What was the operation like at Santa Cruz?

Answer: Our depot was between the S.P. depot and the beach. The office was up on Bay Street and the Roundhouse was on Delaware Avenue. We had a single connection with the S.P., and we got our freight and cars from them.

Question: Who were some of the other men on the South End?

Answer: O.S. Smith (Ocean Shore Smith we called him) was Senior Conductor on the south end for a long time. Archie Speaker, who used to play professional baseball for Boston, was an Engineer for many years. For a short time, I fired for him. Other

Above: About the time one morning Tom Wilson was making up the train in the Transfer Yard, a flatcar broke loose at San Vicente main camp and rambled down the Little Creek Canyon for over a mile before finally coming to rest under this Ocean Shore combine. Fearing the worst, because there had been a lady and her small son in the car bathroom at the time, he darted aboard the train only to find said travellers embarrassed rather than hurt. — Courtesy: Tom Wilson

Right: The crew with No. 5 at Swanton one late afternoon. — Courtesy: Alverda Orlando Collection

Engineers were Adolph Seigel and Dave Parsley. Fireman Billy Soria was another regular.

Question: Any lasting impressions about the Southern Division of the Ocean Shore Railroad?
Answer: The men were all good men and I have many fond memories of the good times we had. The line was a rather slow roller coaster affair. My biggest problem used to be in reading tickets in the dark on the early morning and late afternoon trains. We didn't have electricity in those days and I used to have to carry a lantern from person to person checking tickets in the dark.

For Tom Wilson, Archie Speaker, and all the rest of the Ocean Shore Railroad employees, working on the line was a gamble. Most felt that if the line were ever completed, and the railroad developed to its fullest potential, all concerned would be in an excellent position for the benefits of seniority and future financial security. That is why they clung to a sinking ship so long. Unfortunately, such was not to be their good fortune.

By 1920 the gasoline self-powered vehicles had come on the California scene. As a result, a goodly portion of the Ocean Shore's previously lucrative freight and passenger business was now being lost to trucks, auto stages (buses), and the family automobile. While a boon to many, this technological change in transportation was causing dire consequences for the Ocean Shore Railroad Company. It was already operating with an accumulated deficit of $355.000. In addition, its current indebtedness was another $77,600. As if this wasn't bad enough, $75,000 more was going to have to be spent on maintenance and upkeep of the right-of-way before 1921 just to keep the line in operation.

After reviewing all of the company's income and expense statements over the past eight years and analyzing what future possibilities might lie in store for the Ocean Shore Railroad; management decided to petition for the abandonment of its Southern Division and use the revenues from its disposal to maintain and improve the Northern Division. This did not mean the company was throwing in the towel. Rather, it was their intention to hold on to all of its real estate, and if the opportunity ever presented itself, rebuild the south end and complete the line to Santa Cruz. With this in mind, John G. Sutton, Vice President and General Manager of the Ocean Shore Railroad, on May 4th, 1920, filed application No. 5663 with the California State Railroad Commission for the abandonment of the Southern Division. In the application he stated that:

Practically all of the business of said line of railroad consists in handling logs for the San Vicente Lumber Co., which logs are delivered to the line of the Ocean Shore Railroad Co. at Swanton in cars owned by the S.V.L. Co. and hauled to the mill of the S.V.L. Co. at Rapetti near Santa Cruz.

The S.P. Co. operates a line of railroad paralleling the line of railroad of the O.S.R.R. Co. and on the same roadbed from Santa Cruz to Davenport.... which line of railroad can handle all of the freight and passenger business of the territory served by the O.S.R.R. Co.

Ocean Shore Railroad Southern Div. Statement Of Revenues & Expenses

Year	S.V.L. Co.	All Others	Passenger	Total	Expenses
1917	$18,763.47	$4,904.15	$3,892.10	$27,469.72	$27,051.65
1918	$14,725.73	$2,493,45	$3,852.75	$21,071.93	$31.292.58
1919	$17,519.00	$2,010.60	$4,421.52	$23,951.12	$33,396.43

Original Cost: $836,678.25
Reproduction Value: $879,904.80
Present Value: $828,755.45*
*Does not include Real Estate valued at $90,894.60.

Wherefore, based on our statement of Revenues & Expenses and the previous information, we ask for the abandonment of the Southern Division.

On July 8th, 1920, a public hearing by the State Railroad Commission was held in Santa Cruz to review the abandonment application. The only protestant, the San Vicente Lumber Company, declared in a written statement that were the line to close, it would pose severe hardship on the continued operation of their lumbering concern. Taking this under advisement, the Commission decided to postpone the matter until a future date.

On Tuesday, August 27th, Engineer, Dave Parsley; Fireman, Billy Soria; and Conductor, Tom Wilson; made the evening run to Swanton and back as they had done so many times in the past. After the run had been completed, the men, along with the rest of the Ocean Shore crewmen, went out on strike for the same higher wages that had already been granted to employees of other railroads. Unfortunately, the Ocean Shore was in no financial position to meet the increases demanded in wages. This would prove to be the straw that broke the camel's back. Although the crew on that August 27th evening train didn't know it at the time, they had just made the last run of the Ocean Shore Railroad.

The Company, now with its back to the wall, with no more money coming in and lots more required if they were ever again to reinstate service, petitioned for abandonment of the north end. This, in effect, meant closure of the entire line. Because of the legalities of the situation, each division was treated individually.

It's harvest time at Davenport and the brussel sprouts, artichokes and lettuce await shipment from the S.P. depot. — Courtesy: Alverda Orlando Collection

Typical of the many S.P. commuter trains which ran from Santa Cruz to Davenport and which helped bring the demise of the Ocean Shore, was this one photographed by Fireman Jimmy Walker at Santa Cruz in 1920. — Courtesy: Fred Stoes Collection

On October 25th, 1920, the California State Railroad Commission in decision No. 8278 made the following ruling:

It is evident that the revenue derived from the operation of the Southern Division of the Ocean Shore Railroad Company has not been sufficient to defray the cost of operation or to return any interest on the investment, and there is no prospect that the revenues of the Company will be increased to a point sufficient to meet the costs of operation, fixed charges and return any interest on the Capital invested. No protest appears against the proposed abandonment of service and the application should be granted.

In this decision, it stated that no protest appears. This was true. Somewhere around October 19th, the Ocean Shore agreed to lease the right-of-way to the San Vicente Lumber Co. for $100,000. On October 20th, the San Vicente Lumber Co. lifted its protest on the abandonment.

Thus, one more company had tried to build a railroad from San Francisco to Santa Cruz, and beyond, and had failed. As of this writing it has yet to be accomplished.

The San Vicente Lumber Company

For years many of the lumber companies of the Santa Cruz County had been waiting for the day when a railroad coming from Santa Cruz would open up the North Coast timber tracts. While there had been several attempts made in the past at logging the various areas, nothing had been accomplished on a scale that was possible. Finally, in 1906, the Ocean Shore came along. Immediately, several of the companies began to lay plans to, once and for all, strip the Ben Lomond Mountain Range of its first-growth pine and redwood trees. While people could see the inevitable coming, it wasn't to be as harsh as most had anticipated. Because of the fact that fate had dictated the financial policy of the Ocean Shore Railway, the line was never extended far enough out of Santa Cruz to provide easy access to the mountains. As a result, the Ocean Shore was to have little impact on the harvesting of trees in Pescadero, Butano, and Gazos Creek Canyons where over 1,500,000,000 board feet of timber stood waiting to be cut. At the same time they did, however, build far enough to open up the 615,000,000 board feet of standing trees in the San Vicente Canyon and its tributaries.

While most of the local lumber companies had had their eye on the San Vicente area, it was to be an outside firm that finally came up with the necessary capital to go after it all. On August 3rd, 1907, Frank S. Murphy of Salt Lake City, Utah, representing the firms of the Central Lumber Company of Idaho, the

Ely Lumber Company of Nevada, and the White Pine Lumber Company of California, purchased 16,000 acres of San Vicente property from the Santa Cruz Lime Company. Shortly thereafter, on May 8th, 1908, a corporate conglomerate known as the "San Vicente Lumber Company" and controlled by President, CW. Nibley; Vice President, George Stoddard; General Manager, Ed Stoddard; and Secretary, Frank Murphy; filed formal articles of incorporation with the County Clerk to harvest the San Vicente. The company's duration was set at ninety-nine years and it was to have operations in California, Oregon, Nevada, and Utah.

By the time the Spring of 1909 rolled around, the San Vicente Lumber Company was well on its way to becoming the largest lumbering concern ever to operate in Santa Cruz County. First a monstrous 70,000-board-foot capacity sawmill, complete with a Simon log turner and a steam-powered log feed, was being constructed at Moore's Gulch near downtown Santa Cruz. At the same time, 16 miles away, two large lumber camps and a broad gauge railroad were being laid out in the Little Creek Basin above Swanton. This, of course, was made possible by the completion of the Ocean Shore Railway to Scott Creek.

The San Vicente Lumber Company broad gauge railroading operation up Little Creek Canyon was to be the single biggest lumber railway layout in Santa Cruz County. The line, when completed, would extend over nine miles into the company's cuttings. Its rightof-way would use five switchbacks and grades of 6%, 7%, and even 8% to climb from 59 feet at Swanton to an elevation of 1440 feet at the Road Crossing Camp No. 3. As fills were impossible due to the rugged terrain and the heavy mountain rainfall, bridges were the name of the game. Ten degree pine piling trestles set in water, 50, 60, 70, and even 90 feet high, in one place, were the rule of thumb when it came to spanning the various gulches and gullies. To operate on this elevated corkscrew operation, two Shay locomotives were purchased. One came brand new from Lima, and the other came second-hand from a San Francisco dealer, the Pacific Car and Equipment Company. Because of the long steep grades involved and the fact that this was large first-growth timber that was going to be harvested, 36-foot steel flatcars with knuckle couplers and Westinghouse air brakes were purchased to do the job.

The San Vicente Lumber Company was to operate in the Little Creek area from the Summer of 1909 until the Summer of 1923. Altogether, it would carry on harvesting operations in six consecutive locations. Area No. 1, known as the main camp, sat at the junction of Little Creek and Chandler Gulch. Chandler Gulch was to be the only place where oxen and skid roads would be used to get the logs to the railroad. The rest of the time, Willamette steam

Above: The San Vicente Lumber Co. mill in Santa Cruz. —
Courtesy: Harold Van Gorder Collection

**Right: Mr. Frykland receives a month's pay for a six-day
work week.** — Courtesy: Anna Schaefer Collection

San Vicente Lumber Co.

PAY ENVELOPE *April 10,* 191 *8*

Frykland, Jno.

25.7² Days at $	3 ⁵⁰		$ 90	13
Cash				
Board				
Store		25		
Rent				
Wood	4	00		
Hospital	1	00		
Total Deductions			$ 5	25
Check Enclosed			$ 84	88

Left: The S.V.L. Co. train of empties off in the distance can be seen working its way up the Little Creek Canyon above Camp No. 1. —Courtesy: U.C. Berkeley, Bancroft Library

Right: Bear Trap bridge No. 1 no doubt provided some very shaky moments. —Courtesy: U.C. Berkeley, Bancroft Library

Left: A hot Sunday afternoon, congenial friends, and a free ride to the San Vicente Main Camp all make for a fine day. — Courtesy: Rita Mattei-Lena Sonognini Collection

While environmentalists would cry rape, this stunning view of cuts and fills and steep grades and trestles tells why the employees called it the Bear Trap. — Courtesy: U.C. Berkeley, Bancroft Library

Cook shacks and the Main Camp of San Vicente Lumber Co. on Little Creek. Left to right: Swanton School Teacher, Miss Esther Hussy; Mrs. Lou Dotta; Camp Boss, Mr. Lou Dotta; unknown, Lena Sonognini, unknown. — Courtesy: Rita Mattei-Lena Sonognini Collection

donkeys were used to do the yarding and gulching operations. The second area, situated about a mile beyond Stoney Point, where several chalk cliffs were found, was called Camp No. 2. Here many permanent buildings and residences were constructed. It was also from here that most of the upper Little Creek region was cut. Camp No. 3 sat on the ridge at the County Road Crossing. From this place, the West and the Middle forks of the San Vicente Creek along with the area "affectionately" known as the Bear Trap were worked. Camp No. 4, the White House Camp, was located about a mile and a half farther up the ridge beyond Camp No. 3. From this point, Deadman Gulch and the rest of the San Vicente West fork were cleared. Area No. 5, known as Camp Bonnie Doon, was established about the beginning of World War 1. From this position all of the East fork of the San Vicente Creek and the east side of the Bear Trap was harvested. Finally, toward the close of the war, the company finished its cutting operations at a point situated on a ridge overlooking the upper portion of Big Creek. For the most part, all of the different camp buildings were constructed on flatcars. Whenever a new camp was established, the buildings would simply be relocated. Also, the rail would be ripped up and relayed.

Considering all of the various railway operations that went on in Santa Cruz County, the S.V.L. Co.

railroad was probably the most dangerous. With a nine-mile 6% to 7% average grade, there were plenty of places for accidents to take place. Obviously, one of the most common accidents was runaway trains. Even though both engines had 135-lb. reservoirs and 110-pound mainlines, plus a steam jam, it wasn't always enough to slow the train down, once it got rolling. Sometimes the trains would "tip over" (go beyond the speed where the brakes would slow them down) and commence to run away. Many was the time that engineers and and firemen like Quackenbush, George Bell, Howard Gorrill, Harry Delamater, Jerry McCabe, Harry Taylor, Hank Humphrey, and Frank Cooke had to make the decision as to whether to stay with the train or "join the birds."

There was the time in 1911 when Engineer Frank Cooke aboard No. 1, the smaller of the two shays, kicked the brakes off before he cut in the air while traveling down the 6% grade toward Stoney Point. By the time he woke up to what was going on, the train was running away. To make a long story short, the train went all the way to the end of the second switchback and crashed as it ran out of track. When the dust had settled, the engine had been so badly damaged that it had to be sent to South San Francisco to be rebuilt. As for Engineer Frank Cooke, it wasn't long before he was back at the throttle once again tempting fate.

Both S.V.L. Co shays await train down the mountain as flatcars are being loaded. Shay No. 1 on left, Shay No. 2 on right — Courtesy: Rita Mattei-Lena Sonognini Collection

The strain of the cable, the heavy dust from moving saw logs, and the rail pounding of Shay No. 1 tells that it's logging time for the San Vicente Lumber Co. — Courtesy: Bob Willey Collection

Then there was the time that retired Engineer Hank Humphrey tells about when:

One time while I was firing on the way to Stoney Point, the train tipped over, and we began to run away. Both the engineer and myself finally decided it was about time to jump as we weren't going to stop and there was a sharp curve and a trestle up ahead. First the engineer jumped. I looked back out of the left side of the cab to see he had jumped right into a tree and was wrapped around same. I couldn't jump right yet as there was a cliff below. Finally, I unloaded in a cut. Having done it before, I hit the ground running in order to maintain my balance. I did not, however, have any idea as to how fast we were going. The distance between my first and second step (I later measured it) was nineteen feet. After the second step, I went upside down on my head. Luckily for me, I was able to get up sore but unbroken. Fearing the worst for the train, I went down the track to see the crash. Evidently, when the train, the engine with one flatcar ahead of it, reached the curve, the front trucks were yanked right out from underneath the flatcar. when this happened, the drawbar on the end of the flatcar dropped between the rails. For almost half a mile the train continued down the line in this fashion. The drawbar broke every tie including all those on the bridge, but it did not derail the train. By the time I got to it I found the train sitting there in perfect shape as if nothing had happened except for the wrecked flatcar.

While these were only two of the many runaways that occurred, they served to explain Jerry McCabe's statement that "many a new man rode up the hill and walked down the hill never to be seen again."

Runaway trains were not the only problem on the line. Runaway flatcars also caused many a headache. Well known among most of the S.V.L. Co. employees was a steep switch track which ran from the Bear Trap mainline down to a loading dock near the San Vicente Creek. Because of an 8% grade between points, the company's shays were only able to haul one loaded flatcar at a time up to the mainline. At the point where the branch met the mainline, there was a sharp rise in the track rail joint. Every once in a while a car would come uncoupled from the locomotive at this spot and return from whence it came. One time when the cable from a spool donkey was strung across the track, a car broke loose and began its trip down the hill. When it caught the cable, it unwound the spool donkey like a fishing reel. There was donkey bouncing down the mountain like a rubber ball tied to a string. Finally, when the car came to the end of the line, it hit two loaded flatcars and unloaded them faster than any crew could. Incidentally, no one was hurt.

Runaways were the exception rather than the rule.

The right-of-way itself was laid out in such a fashion that every so often there would be a switchback going uphill. If the train began to tip over, it was all right because the engineer knew that a short distance ahead there would be an up track on which to recover. Other safety precautions taken included no more than six flatcars at a time per train, and all loaded cars operated behind the engines on the down-hill grade. For the most part, the railroad operations ran smoothly and safely, doing the job it was designed to do, getting the massive quantity of logs to the mill.

As previously mentioned, the combined operations of the San Vicente Lumber Company made it the largest lumbering concern in the county. At any one time during the season you could expect to find as much as 9,000,000 board feet of finished timber product stacked in the Santa Cruz yard. To produce that kind of output, the company employed an average of 225 men between the woods and the mill. Its payroll, as of 1915, amounted to $80,000 a year. Individually, the average man made $20.00 a month, although he didn't get it all. The S.V.L. Co. management were all members of the Mormon Church. As a result, no matter what your personal faith, each employee contributed a portion of his pay to Salt Lake City, Utah. The pay was considered good for the times, however, and so most men didn't object.

Toward the end of 1920, the Ocean Shore Railroad ceased its Southern Division operations and the San Vicente Lumber Co. took them over. For the next three years, the company used the shays and old Ocean Shore locomotive No. 4, known to the men as the rod engine, to haul the logs into Santa Cruz. As exengineer Jerry McCabe said, "the ride aboard one of the shays at twenty miles per hour into Santa Cruz would shake your eyeteeth out." Finally, in 1923, the S.V.L. Co. operations came to an end when the company was able to purchase a large stand of sugar pine cheap from the forest service at Cromberg, California.

When all is said and done, the memories generated of the San Vicente Lumber Company for those few who are left are very precious. The best shared picture is probably that of the camp after the day's work has been completed. Situated around the fire under the stars on a warm Summer evening sits a hodgepodge of humanity. Italians, just over from the old country, Greeks, Irish, Swedes, and what management referred to as "Whites." The embers of the fire burn, casting shadows on the surrounding camp buildings, an onion is sliced, a loaf of bread is passed around, a jug of local mountain wine touches the lips and trickles into the aching body that has just put in twelve back-breaking hours in the woods, a concertina is brought out and the beautiful voice of an Italian fills the warm night air, while inwardly each man is at peace with himself and his fellow man.

It's movie time on the San Vicente and silent superstar "Charles Ray" is involved in the making of "Sudden Jim." In this scene, Engineer Jerry McCabe has just been paid $15.00 to run Shay No. 1 across an abandoned trestle with two loaded flatcars while cables attached to the bents below him are yanked one at a time, collapsing the bridge as he goes. When action commenced the first six bents accidentally went all at once, and what started out as a motion picture stunt became a race for life. Shortly after the scene was completed and nerves were calmed, Jerry McCabe returned to take this snapshot of what was left of the bridge.

Pajaro to Swanton, all coastal operations of railroads

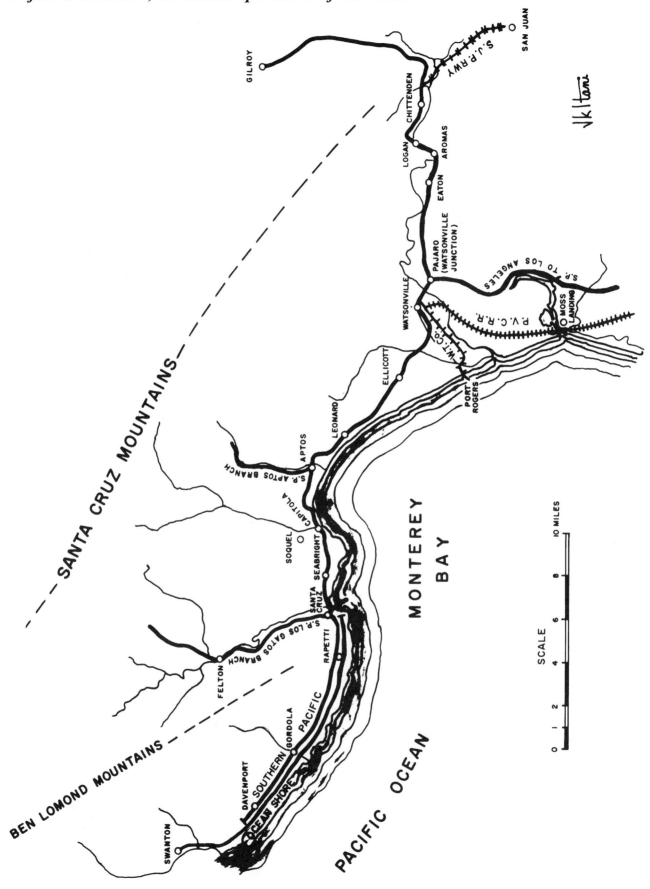

200

5

The Transition: The Contracting Reality

To everything there is a season,
and a time to every purpose under the heaven.
Chap. 3, Verse I   Ecclesiastes

The year was 1900. The dawning of a new century was about to take place. The prophecy of the early pioneer, which had foretold of the events leading up to this point in time, had come true. Civilization had moved west. The goals of linking the continent with lightning and stream had been accomplished. Cities had begun to rise, arts and industries had been established, and mankind had subdued the wilderness. The expanding dream was fast becoming a reality. For Santa Cruz County, this had meant the coming of the telegraph, the telephone, the electric light and power company, and the railroad.

By now the city of Santa Cruz had become the county's main hub for business, industry, and tourism. To that end, the newly constructed freight depot and passenger station were doing a booming business. Between the narrow gauge from Alameda and Boulder Creek via Felton and the broad gauge from San Francisco and Monterey via Pajaro, over 25 freight and passenger trains daily arrived and departed the Santa Cruz area. In support of this heavy railroad activity, machine shops and maintenance facilities had also been established. As of now, it looked like Santa Cruz had all the earmarks of a division point for the Southern Pacific.

While business was booming in Santa Cruz, events were happening 300 miles away which were making the residents in the Watsonville-Pajaro area also sit up and take notice. In 1870 the Southern Pacific had reached Watsonville (Pajaro) with the broad gauge. A short time later, the line had been extended into the rich salad bowl area of the Salinas Valley as far as Soledad. In 1873, the financial panic halted any further construction, and Soledad became the end of the line. By 1886, the country and especially the State of California was once again in an expansion cycle. It was at this time that the Southern Pacific management decided the line via Pajaro and the Salinas Valley should be extended to Los Angeles. With that in mind, construction began. By the end of 1900, the S.P. coast line to Los Angeles was less than 20 miles from completion.

Up to now, Watsonville had been just another town along the right-of-way that saw trains going to Monterey, Soledad, San Francisco, and Santa Cruz. With the completion of the coast line, rumor had it that Watsonville (Pajaro) was to become a point of prominence. From this place, all freight and passenger trains would be dispatched to the surrounding areas. And so it was that on March 31, 1901, when the first train ran from San Francisco to Los Angeles, the Watsonville residents watched the event with keen interest.

Ironically, the folks in Watsonville didn't know how close to the truth they were. At this point in history railroads were the only way you traveled from here to there. Tourism and passenger travel generated just as much revenue as did freight traffic. The Watsonville-Pajaro area just happened to be the gateway to one of the finest tourist areas in California. It was with this in mind that the Southern Pacific had laid out some very heavy plans for the immediate future. It was their intention that once the coast line had been completed and beefed up for heavy travel, many of the mainline passenger trains would be rerouted via Watsonville, Aptos, Santa Cruz, Big Trees, Los Gatos, and San Jose.

To that end, the Southern Pacific put its plans in motion. By December of 1902, the line from San Jose to Los Gatos had been broad gauged. By mid-April of 1903 the broad gauge had been extended from Los Gatos as far as Wright's in the Santa Cruz Mountains. At the same time, 62-pound rail had begun to be laid down from Pajaro to Santa Cruz to handle the larger

March 31, 1901: The first through passenger train from Los Angeles to San Francisco up the coast pauses at Pajaro for local celebrations. — Courtesy: Santa Cruz County Octagon Museum

trains. On May 2, 1903, the Hollister Advance newspaper lamented that "once the narrow gauge from San Jose to Santa Cruz is made broad gauge, all the fancy coast trains, including the Sunset Limited, will be run via Santa Cruz. The lines between San Jose and Watsonville via Gilroy will become mere "jerkwater affairs." By July of 1904, all of the new rail had been laid between Pajaro and Santa Cruz and the right-of-way and several bridges had been strengthened -and rebuilt. By January of 1905, broad gauging of the line from Santa Cruz to Wright's commenced, and it looked as if the first broad gauge train would run from San Jose to Pajaro by the Summer of 1906.

In response to the current growth, and that which was surely coming, many smaller railroad enterprises had been undertaken. The Santa Cruz, Capitola & Watsonville electric street car line (later part of the Union Traction Co.) had begun service between Santa Cruz and Capitola. Several horse car lines around Santa Cruz had now become electric lines. Over in Watsonville, several of the local citizens had incorporated under the name of the "Watsonville Railroad and Navigation Co." to build an electric line from town, three and a half miles, out to a newly constructed wharf on the ocean. This little three-foot electric line even had its own ship, the "F.A. Kilburn," named after its treasurer. At the same time, the Pajaro Valley Consolidated narrow gauge railway, which had recently been completed between Watsonville and Salinas via Moss Landing, was now running two local passenger trains a day over their three-foot track. Throughout Santa Cruz County and the Pajaro Valley areas, all was in readiness for the obvious financial benefits which were to follow.

In retrospect, this five-year period in time from 1901 to 1906 was probably the crescendo of growth for railroads in Santa Cruz County. The electric lines had obvious plans for expansion, creating a network from Santa Cruz to Hollister. The Ocean Shore was underway from Santa Cruz to San Francisco, as was the Southern Pacific's Coast Line Railway. Several electric companies had incorporated to build lines from the San Francisco Bay Area into the Big Basin. The Southern Pacific was going to expand its line from Boulder Creek to Pescadero. And of course, the coast line passenger trains would soon be running via Santa Cruz. Had fate not interjected her unyielding hand, most of this would have probably come to pass. The continuance of the expansionary dream, however, was not in the cards. As most of you already know, three separate events would happen three years in a row which would turn the expansionary dream around and send it tumbling toward the reality of today.

One, the earthquake of 1906: While the pot was only stirred for a few minutes, the resultant movement spelled catastrophe. In one instant in time, the Ocean Shore had been wiped out. The Southern Pacific coast line plans had been stopped when the 6,200-foot Summit tunnel at Wright's took a four-and-a-half-foot lateral shift. In addition, their 450-foot bridge across the Pajaro River, and unknowingly at the same point across the San Andreas fault, was decommissioned when the concrete support pillars separated three and a half feet. Also, their line from the bridge to Aromas looked like a corkscrew. As for the poor Pajaro Valley Consolidated, their bridge across the Pajaro River and their facilities at Moss Landing looked like one big junk yard. While physical damage was visible everywhere, the obvious was hidden. The earthquake meant that money earmarked for expansionary projects would now be spent on reconstruction. It also meant that some monies counted on from certain financial backers were no longer available due to their own financial ruin.

Two, the financial panic of 1907: During the Summer of 1907, President Roosevelt began to lean very heavily on big business and finance. Many large business interests and holders of securities became uncertain as to what the President had in mind for the future of big business based on what he said in the press. As a result, a sell-off occurred on the New York Stock Exchange that turned into a financial panic. A chain of banks and copper interests failed, followed by the Knickerbocker Trust Co. on October 27th, 1907. What this meant locally was that construction and expansion stopped for a time. There was a surplus of materials such as cement. This caused a slowdown at the plant at Davenport for a time and halted the construction altogether of the plant at San Juan Bautista. Also, it meant that there was no eastern capital available for western projects such as the Ocean Shore-San Juan Pacific-San Joaquin Valley Western conglomerate.

Three, the winter of 1908: The violent storms during this time caused monumental damage to much of the local railroading in the area. It completely shut down the Southern Division of the Ocean Shore and the San Juan Pacific. It forced the S.P. to spend large sums of money to shore up its right-of-way to keep it opened. It also slowed the reopening of the Summit tunnel at Wright's. While of and by itself it wasn't that disastrous, when coupled with the events of the previous two years, it leveled a death blow to all future dreams of expansion.

Thus, when the summer sun of 1908 had dried the last drop of water from the rubble once known as the expansionary dream, the contracting reality was the result. No more expansion would ever again take place in Santa Cruz County.

The Santa Cruz Beach Railroad was incorporated by Fred Swanton in 1906 to run from the Casino area to the San Lorenzo River and back. It operated under public utilities regulations with each train having an engineer and fireman. Swanton had gold embossed passes made for the S.C.B.R.R. which he sent to many of the major railroad presidents, who reciprocated the honor by sending him one of theirs. Most of them never realized the size of Swanton's operation. Swanton, however, rode all over the country for free. In 1912, the railroad and the casino went bankrupt. The train as seen above was sold to the City of San Francisco, where it continued its operation at the Zoo until 1978. Currently the little train sits in storage until a new home is found for it. — Courtesy: Bruce MacGregor Collection

The Santa Cruz Depot as it appeared in the early 1900's. — Courtesy: John D. Schmale Collection

Lumbering, lime, fruits, vegetables, and tourism were not the only money making industries in Santa Cruz as can be seen by this fish packing operation on the railroad wharf around 1906. — Courtesy: The Society of California Pioneers Collection

Monday, May 13, 1901: Engineer Charles Glass, chosen by the Southern Pacific to do the honors on this very special train, is about to leave Santa Cruz for Pajaro with President McKinley and party. — Courtesy: U.C. Santa Cruz, Special Collections

Left: It's 1905 and the community of Seabright is substantial enough to not only warrant its own railroad station but also one of the new electric lines. — Courtesy: Roy Graves Collection, U.C. Berkeley, Bancroft Library

Right: Ever since the time when the railroad first came to Pajaro (Watsonville Junction) a small two mile portion of the S.P. Coast mainline has run through the southeasternmost corner of the county. For many years the station of Chittenden served the area. Today, the depot is just a memory, as trains roll by at better than seventy miles per hour. However, this is how it appeared in 1908. — Courtesy: Pajaro Valley Historical Association

Left: Pajaro Valley Consolidated narrow gauge locomotive #7 sits on the Watsonville turntable about to pick up its train and head for Moss Landing, Salinas, and Spreckels. — Courtesy: Bill Harry Collection

The Granite Rock Co. crew poses on the Southern Pacific main near Chittenden in 1900. — Courtesy: Albert D. Snyder Collection

Eastern bound refrigerator cars line the yards at Watsonville waiting for their precious cargos of apples and other local grown produce. — Courtesy: U.C. Santa Cruz, Special Collections

Granite Rock narrow gauge locomotive No. 1, one of eight, pauses in the gravel pits at Logan just west of the Pajaro River Bridge. — Courtesy: Granite Rock Collection

Although the 1906 earthquake didn't last very long, these three views definitely show its severe consequences. Boxcars being loaded with cordwood at Chittenden lay on their sides, having been shaken right off their trucks. The Southern Pacific coast right-of-way coming off the west side of the Pajaro River Bridge has just been realigned. A Watsonville Junction bound freight train which was stopped near Aromas at the time suffered major resorting. — All photos courtesy Albert Snyder Collection

A weakened Pajaro River Bridge found its piers slightly modified as witnessed by this photograph and diagram. — Courtesy: U.S. Geological Survey, Menlo Park, California

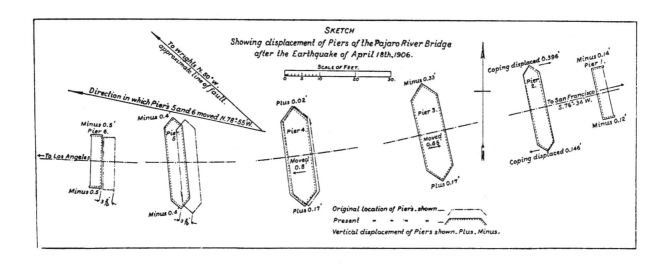

March 2, 1904: The Watsonville Transportation Co. electric line is open from town and big things are happening at Port Rogers. — Courtesy: Pajaro Valley Historical Association

As if earthquakes weren't enough, the floods of 1908 completely devastated many local areas such as the main street of downtown Watsonville, shown here. — Courtesy: Harold Soper Collection

Chittenden Area - San Juan Area Railroads

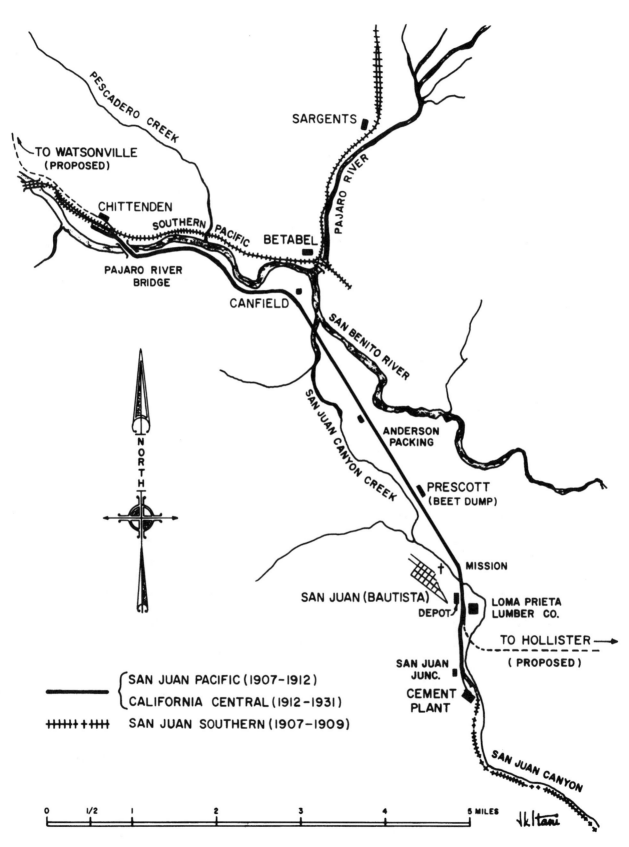

PESCADERO CREEK

SARGENTS

TO WATSONVILLE
(PROPOSED)

CHITTENDEN

SOUTHERN PACIFIC

BETABEL

PAJARO RIVER

PAJARO RIVER
BRIDGE

CANFIELD

SAN BENITO RIVER

NORTH

SAN JUAN CANYON CREEK

ANDERSON
PACKING

PRESCOTT
(BEET DUMP)

MISSION

SAN JUAN (BAUTISTA)

DEPOT

LOMA PRIETA
LUMBER CO.

TO HOLLISTER →
(PROPOSED)

SAN JUAN
JUNC.

CEMENT
PLANT

SAN JUAN CANYON

SAN JUAN PACIFIC (1907-1912)

CALIFORNIA CENTRAL (1912-1931)

++++++++++ SAN JUAN SOUTHERN (1907-1909)

0   1/2   1   2   3   4   5 MILES

JKItani

San Juan Pacific Railway
The Old Mission Route

It was early spring in the peaceful little California Mission town of San Juan Bautista. Once again, as they had done since long before man had ever set foot in the San Juan Valley, the wild flowers were beginning to bloom. The frost had subsided and the season's crops of sugar beets and various other vegetables were in the process of being planted by the local farmers. All around the town and in the valley, the rural pursuits of the local residents were being carried on as they had been for the past 110 years, ever since the founding of the Mission San Juan Bautista in 1797. But it was the Spring of 1907, and changes, which many of the local residents felt would make San Juan Bautista one of the more prosperous California communities, were about to take place.

For years it had been known that there were large lime deposits near San Juan Bautista and inexhaustible clay beds at Chittenden. Thus, when the demand for concrete and clay products started to rapidly increase because of the growth that was taking place in California, a group of businessmen came together and incorporated the San Juan Portland Cement Company to go after this vast mineral wealth. The company purchased 2,460 acres of land in two parcels; one was near San Juan Bautista in San Benito County, and the other was at Chittenden in Santa Cruz County. In addition, they had an option to buy 8,500 acres more of what was then known as the Bryan property. With the three parcels, the company felt they had enough limestone and clay to manufacture at least 2,000 barrels a day of the finest grade Portland Cement and the high-demand pottery materials for the next one hundred years.

In addition to the construction of the cement plant, there were other projects developing close by that were also causing much interest and anticipation among the local residents. The Ocean Shore Railroad was rapidly being constructed down the coast from San Francisco to Santa Cruz. Also, the Ocean Shore and Eastern Railroad had been incorporated to build a line from Santa Cruz to Watsonville. At the same time, it was being rumored by a Fresno newspaper, the *Fresno Republican,* that the San Joaquin Valley Western Railroad, a tributary and Ocean Shore promoted railroad, was about to commence construction from Fresno up the San Joaquin Valley to Hollister. Once the railroads reached Watsonville from the north and Hollister from the south, the local residents knew that it would only be a matter of time before there would be a connecting Ocean Shore rail line between the two towns. In addition, they knew that the Ocean Shore line would have to come through San Juan Bautista because such a proposed right-of-way had been surveyed accordingly many times before.

Thus, when it was announced by the local newspapers, the *San Juan Echo* and the *Hollister Free Lance,* that the San Juan Pacific Railway had been incorporated on May 4th, 1907, to build a connecting rail line between Chittenden, on the S.P. mainline, and the cement plant, and in the near future possible extensions to Watsonville and Hollister, no one was totally surprised.[8] Further, when it was announced that John B. Rogers, then Chief Engineer of the Ocean Shore Railroad, was also to be the new chief engineer on the San Juan Pacific, most of the townspeople put two and two together and came up with the conclusion that an O.S. mainline, via San Juan Bautista, was just about a virtual certainty.

By the end of May, the necessary money and manpower had been acquired to commence activities on the new Watsonville to Hollister mainline connection and so, without further delay, the work of surveying and constructing the S.J.P. was begun.

Chief Engineer Rogers brought in a crew of surveyors from the Ocean Shore Railroad to survey the 6.42 miles of right-of-way from Chittenden to San Juan Bautista and the 1.52 miles of right-of-way from there to San Juan Junction where the cement plant was being constructed. There was nothing complicated about the survey, as the natural terrain was such that no steep grades or tight radius curves were required. In addition, other than the trestle across the Pajaro River, there was also no real bridge work necessary. By the end of May, the survey was completed, and 60-pound rail and redwood ties began arriving at Chittenden.

In June, Rogers brought in a construction crew of 80 men and 150 work mules from the O.S., and the work of building the broad-gauged San Juan Pacific Railway was begun. The work had to be hurried along because 664 carloads of materials and machinery which were necessary for the construction of the cement plant were due to arrive at Chittenden shortly. In addition, the cement plant had ordered a locomotive and 20 boxcars, and they were also on the way.

Originally it had been planned that the right-of-way was to go under the Southern Pacific tracks at Chittenden such that the Ocean Shore Railroad could

---

[8]It should be pointed out for purposes of historical clarity that on the day the articles of incorporation were filed, the railroad was incorporated by a group of local businessmen and ranchers under the name of the "San Juan and Chittenden Railway." It was incorporated at a capital cost of $200,000 to run from Chittenden to San Juan Bautista with no other extensions. Shortly afterward, a group of businessmen from the San Juan Portland Cement Company, the Palmer Oil Company, and the San Joaquin Valley Western Railroad came together and organized the railroad under the name of the "San Juan Pacific Railway." In doing so, they changed the capital costs to $2,000,000 and added clauses for possible extensions to Watsonville and Hollister. One interesting sidelight was that when checking the original articles of incorporation, it was found that they had simply been typed over and added to. New articles of incorporation were never filed.

This logo off the company stock prospectus depicts a five car San Juan Pacific Railway train on double track mainline. In truth, they had only the one combine and a single track. — Courtesy: Stanford University Library

Opening day at Chittenden for the San Juan Pacific. — Courtesy: Stanford University Library

gain access across the S.P. mainline at that point. The official explanation from the San Juan Pacific ls management was that this was necessary to reach a suitable depot location and transfer point on the north side of the S.P. mainline. This did not happen, however, because of the allotted short construction time. Instead, the connecting mainline and two holding tracks were laid down "temporarily" on the south side of the S.P. mainline to allow for the arrival of incoming freight.

By mid-July, construction of the Pajaro River bridge and grading of the entire right-of-way had been completed. A locomotive was leased from the S.P. for construction purposes so that the laying of track could begin at Chittenden. From Chittenden the work was pushed south 2.2 miles across the Pajaro River to Canfield. At Canfield they spiked down a 600-foot siding to be used for the unloading of general merchandise and the loading of hay. From Canfield they constructed three miles of track to Prescott where another siding of 700 feet was built to handle sugar beets. In addition, the local farmers built a 20-foot-wide by 160-foot-long by 5-foot-high beet dumping platform to make the transfer of sugar beets from wagon to railroad car easier. By the first of August, the rails had reached San Juan Bautista[9], and a long lumber and merchandising siding was then laid down. Finally, the line was completed to San Juan Junction and a spur of about a third of a mile was run up to the gravel pits where roadbed ballast was obtained for the entire right-of-way.

An excess 4-4-0 locomotive, No. 1313, was purchased from the S.P. to do the primary work of the line. In addition, the S.J.P. purchased 17 boxcars and 8 flatcars along with a combination baggage-passenger coach to meet the needs of the cement company and the local community. The line had cost just a little over $40,000 a mile to construct with the locomotive and rolling stock costing about $45,000.

On Friday, August 30th, 1907, state and local dignitaries were invited to ride the first train from Chittenden to San Juan Bautista and to share in the local ceremonies and festivities before and afterward. After over a hundred years of sleep, the town of San Juan Bautista was awakened to the stark realities of the changing world by the shrill whistle of the San Juan Pacific's No. 208 as she steamed into town for the first time. On September 1, 1907, the S.J.P. was officially opened for any and all business.

----

[9]Originally San Juan Bautista was known as San Juan.

This rare company map shows the plans and dreams of the San Juan Pacific. — Courtesy: Stanford University Library

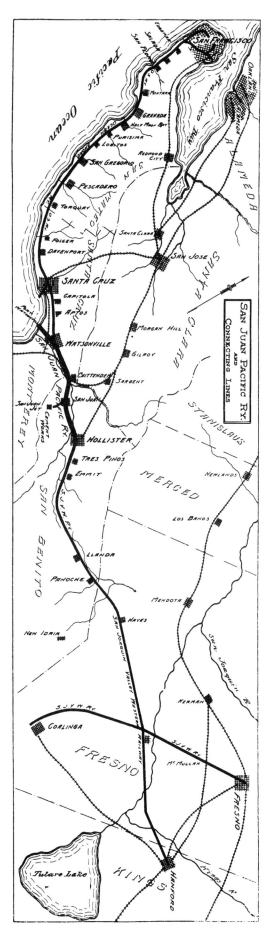

For one very brief moment in time the San Juan Pacific and the San Juan Southern took up a quarter page in the Official Guide. — Courtesy: Stanford University Library

It was anticipated that once the cement plant opened up in early 1908 the railroad's business was going to show a substantial profit. It had been estimated by management that over 400 tons of cement, 200 tons of clay, and 160 tons of oil were to be hauled over the S.J.P. daily. In addition, there was to be 8,000 to 10,000 tons of sugar beets shipped out each season. Also, the railroad was expecting to ship over 100,000 tons of lime-rock annually. Altogether, this was to produce a yearly revenue of over $97,000 and would far exceed the necessary monies needed for operating expenses and interest on bonds. All of this information looked good in a stock prospectus, but the fact of the matter was the railroad needed business.

By the end of September, the incoming freight shipments to the cement plant had been mostly completed. The farming season was over, and it would be quite a while before the cement plant would be in operation. As a result, management decided to offset the S.J.P.'s expenses by beginning passenger service between San Juan Junction and Chittenden where connections could be made with eastbound and westbound S.P. trains. It was felt that the passenger traffic on the S.J.P. would be a large item in its revenue. Besides the natural stimulus to travel resulting from the completion of the road, there would be the additional traffic to and from the cement plant, where several hundred men would be employed, many of whom, with their families, would make frequent trips over the road. Also, there would be a constantly increasing tourist travel, as aside from the scenic beauties of the San Juan Valley, the old Mission of San Juan Bautista was one of the more interesting of the California missions. Now that steps had been taken to repair and restore portions of the old mission, which needed it, so that the historic landmark could be preserved, it was felt that the mission would attract many new visitors.

Mark Regan, who had previously operated the daily stage between San Juan Bautista and the S.P. mainline at Sargents, was hired to be the S.J.P.'s head conductor, express and baggage agent. His massive passenger operations consisted of locomotive No. 208 and the S.J.P.'s baggage-passenger combine car.

Thus, on Saturday, October 19th, 1907, the S.J.P. began its passenger service over the "Old Mission Route" by running three trains a day out to Chittenden and then running three trains a day back to San Juan Junction.

By November, the San Juan Pacific Railway was well on its way to having a substantial freight and passenger business for the short line that it was. After visiting the S.J.P., A.W. Osborn, then traffic manager for the Iowa Central Railroad Company, wrote Frank L. Brown, President of the S.J.P., the following letter:

Dear Sir:

I am pleased to report the road in a most healthy and sound condition in all departments. I have given careful consideration to the construction and find it to be most substantial and economical; so thoroughly has this construction work been done that much maintenance and repair cost will be saved.

The location is well chosen for the traffic interests of the road - the beet-dumping platform and siding at Prescott being in the heart of the beet-growing district, and the San Juan freight and passenger stations being conveniently located for the public at San Juan.

The terminal at San Juan Junction is laid out with the object in view of simplifying the shipping of the San Juan Portland Cement Company, and will prove very economical in the handling of the Cement Company's freight.

The Chittenden terminal switching connection with the Southern Pacific Company's tracks is well chosen and constructed, there being room for an entire trainload of freight at a time on the switch, connecting the Southern Pacific tracks with the San Juan Pacific.

The motive power and rolling stock I find of excellent quality and in first-class condition.

Considering the road as a whole, it is remarkable for its sound construction and large earning capacity.

And so it was that in 1907 the San Juan Pacific Railway was born, grew and looked forward to a long and prosperous future. This, however, was a future which was not to happen as the financial panic of late 1907 hit the S.J.P. just about the time its operations had begun in earnest.

Joint depot and freight platform for the Southern Pacific and San Juan Pacific at Chittenden, California, 1908. — Courtesy: Pajaro Valley Historical Association

The San Juan "Mission" waits for the connecting S.P. passenger at Chittenden. — Courtesy: Francis J. Carney Collection

The S.J.P. "Mission" poses at San Juan Junction. — Courtesy: Stanford University Library

S.J.P. No. 208 gets the once over at the company's only Pajaro River Bridge crossing. — Courtesy: Francis J. Carney Collection

In this rare view California Central #2 pauses along the main with its freight train, 1915. — Courtesy: Valerie Tobitt Collection

In November of 1907, the San Juan Portland Cement Company announced that due to financial difficulties construction of the cement plant was to be halted until further notice. In addition, most of the capital needed to build the connecting Ocean Shore and Eastern Railroad and the San Joaquin Valley Western Railroad was tied up in New York banks which had been affected by the panic. As a result, they never happened. This also included the propose extensions of the S.J.P. to Hollister and Watsonville.

From early 1908 on, it was nothing but a downhill story for the S.J.P. There was just not enough freight and passenger business available to keep the railroad alive without the cement plant. By May 1909, passenger service had been suspended, and Mark Regan had gone back to driving his daily stage. Freight operations were reduced to one train a day, then three times a week, and finally when operations warranted. In February of 1910, severe rains caused landslides along the right-of-way where it followed the Pajaro River, and it was not until the following summer that the road was opened again. In March of 1911, the Pajaro River bridge washed out to sea in one of the worst rain storms ever to visit Santa Cruz County. This time the railroad was not back in operation until late July. Finally, in November of 1911, the San Juan Pacific, having spent its last operating dollar, threw in the towel and ceased operations. Shortly afterward, its operations were taken over by a new company, the "California Central Railroad," and plans were laid out to possibly begin operations once again.

Such was the fate of the San Juan Pacific Railway. What had started out as a possible connection in a great transcontinental railroad had ended as a dream being carried out to sea by the financial sands of the time.

San Juan Southern Railway

On August 3, 1907, three of the directors of the San Juan Pacific Railway and two of the area's local businessmen incorporated under the name of the "San Juan Southern Railway Company," at a cost of $300,000, to run a branch line from San Juan Junction up San Juan Canyon to some of the local farms and ranches in the area. It was scheduled to be constructed as soon as the San Juan Pacific was completed. Originally, according to the articles of incorporation, the San Juan Southern Railway was to extend six miles up San Juan Canyon to a point on Thomas Flint's ranch known as Flintsville. In addition, it was planned, although not stated as such in the articles of incorporation, to extend the line to the ranches of Pierce and Underwood in the near future.

With this in mind, a 60-foot right-of-way was purchased to the Underwood ranch, and when the San Juan Pacific was completed in September, the laying of track was commenced up San Juan Canyon. The rail had been laid approximately three miles when the Panic of 1907 befell the San Juan Southern. At this point construction was halted.

Today, 65 years later, there is some discrepancy as to whether the railroad actually was ever in operation over the three miles of track or whether they ever owned any rolling stock. One fact is certain, however, and that is that the San Juan Southern, like every other burgeoning railroad in the area, went the way of the financial winds that were blowing at the time. By 1910 the San Juan Southern took up just three words in the Standards and Poors Manual: "Ceased to Exist!"

Today all that is left is an abandoned right-of-way, which later was used by the Old Mission Cement Company for its narrow gauge operations four miles up San Juan Canyon to the cement quarry, and a few pasted-over expansionary dreams.

California Central Railroad

In January of 1912, the San Juan Portland Cement Company was put on the market in order to pay off its accumulated debts and back mortgage payments which had arisen because of the companies financial inability to complete construction of their cement plant. After a short time, it was bought out lock, stock, and unopened cement barrel by a newly formed corporation, the Old Mission Cement Company. In addition to the purchase of the San Juan Portland Cement Company, the Old Mission Cement

California Central #2 (Ex S.J.P. #208) is shown in the yards at the San Juan Cement Plant. — Courtesy: Albert D. Snyder Collection

A 17-car train works downgrade on the little narrow gauge run to the cement plant through San Juan Canyon. — Courtesy: Valerie Tobin Collection

Leased S.P. engine No. 1462 with Engineer Lee Tobin in cab poses at the plant.
— Courtesy: Valerie Tobitt Collection

On a hot summer's day in 1920 the rails split and 1462 found itself and its train on the ground. — Courtesy: Valerie Tobitt Collection

Company also purchased 95% of the San Juan Pacific's bonds such that they gained a controlling interest in the railroad.

On March l9th, 1912, in anticipation of the cement plant commencing operations in the near future, the California Central Railroad was incorporated by the new San Juan Pacific management to do basically what the previous railway had done. The same grandiose schemes and promises were made, such as possible extensions to Port Watsonville, Moss Landing, Monterey, Hollister, and the San Joaquin Valley. However, once the cement dust had settled and the cement plant finally opened up for business in 1916, the railroad, with

theexception of two miles of side tracks, was to remain 7.94 miles in length from Chittenden to San Juan Junction. No expansion was ever to take place, and passenger service was never to resume again.

From 1912 to 1915, the railroad was primarily carrying construction materials for the cement plant and sugar beets and other produce for the local farmers. During the winter of 1913-1914, the railroad again experienced slides along the Pajaro River and as a result had to cease operations for eight months. In 1915, the railroad was closed down for major rehabilitation and reorganization in preparation for the opening of the cement plant. Before the railroad was reopened, $45,141 had been spent on the rehabilitation of the eight-mile line.

During the period from 1916 to 1929, the California Central Railroad was to see its most significant operations. It had one train a day which hauled cement out to Chittenden and gypsum and oil back to the cement plant. During the harvest and sugar beet season, about 5,000 to 10,000 tons of produce were hauled annually.

While the railroad was never able to show a profit, because it was owned and operated by the Old Mission Cement Company, it never went broke, either. The railroad had no payroll to meet because it had no permanent employees. Everytime the train was run, operational personnel were supplied from the cement plant's narrow gauge crews. In addition, maintenance and storage were not costly because the railroad shared the narrow gauge facilities at the cement plant.

There is much published contradictory information as to the condition and use of the C.C.R.R.'s locomotive and rolling stock. The conclusion come to here is that locomotive No. 208 had 40 years of operation on her by 1919. She was put into storage along with her passenger coach until 1923 when she was retired and her coach was sold. From 1919 until 1927, the Southern Pacific provided a leased locomotive to service the C.C.R.R. customers. In 1927, when the Old Mission Cement Company was taken over by the Portland Cement Company, old Ocean Shore locomotive No. 5 was brought in and used until the depression forced the cement company to cease operations in 1929. In addition to locomotive No. 208, all C.C.R.R. rolling stock was also put into indefinite storage after 1919, and most of the in-and-out operations were accomplished using Southern Pacific equipment. By 1930, when the railroad ceased operations, all but three of the company's freight cars had been sold or disposed of. It wasn't long after that until they too were sold, and all that was left of the California Central Railroad was a weed-infested, rusting mainline.

Although the cement plant was to reopen in 1941, the railroad itself was never again to see operations except for one brief fleeting moment in December of 1937 when old locomotive No. 5 was

California Central Railroad No. 5 (Ex Ocean Shore No. 5) at the cement plant sometime between 1927 and 1929. — Courtesy: H.W. Fabing from the Jack Sherwood Collection

Today, all that remains of the San Juan Pacific fantasy is this small piece of curved track crossing Chittenden Road where it once approached and made connections with the S.P. mainline. — Rick Hamman

fired up and run out to Chittenden for the last time. From there she was being shipped to the Pacific Portland Cement Company's operations at Gerlach, Nevada. Shortly afterward, the tracks were ripped up. On December 2, 1944, the Public Utilities Commission signed the death certificate allowing for the abandonment of the California Central.

And so it was that the California Central was born, lived, and died in one of the most turbulent growth and depression periods in the history of the country. It never amounted to what some would call a mainline railroad, but it had a purpose and it served it well. Without it, much of the growth and development of the San Francisco Bay Area could never have happened. What had started as a continuation of the San Juan Pacific's dreams of greatness had ended as the short line that it was destined to be. Again and again in the San Juan Valley the wild flower would bloom and the crops would be planted; after a while, only a few would remember that once there was a railroad to San Juan Bautista.

Below: in the late 1970's this view of the cement plant was taken shortly after the site had been closed because the present owners, the Ideal Cement Co., had not been able to meet strict California air pollution control requirements. Under various owners the plant had operated for over sixty years. — Rick Hamman

The Contracting Reality

It was the spring of 1910. For all intents and purposes, the Southern Pacific Railroad operations to and from the City of Santa Cruz were about as substantial as they would ever be. Each day's schedule would see both freight and passenger trains operating to Felton, Boulder Creek, San Jose, San Francisco, Oakland, Davenport, and Pajaro. In addition, two through trains, No. 39 and No. 40, operated all the way to Sacramento and Bakersfield via Tracy. Also, the two San Francisco to Monterey Scenic Locals, No. 84 and No. 87, had been routed via Santa Cruz. From all outward appearances, the city was definitely the center of railroad activity in the county - so much so in fact that the Southern Pacific had classified it as a division point.

As the time clock of life continues its swing toward infinity, however, all things must change. The lumber business up the San Lorenzo and the cement business from Davenport had fallen off in recent years. As a result, freight trains were shorter and less frequent. With the broad gauging of the line from Boulder Creek and Alameda, there was no more need to provide maintenance facilities for narrow gauge equipment. Broad gauge locomotive and car maintenance could be provided just about anywhere.

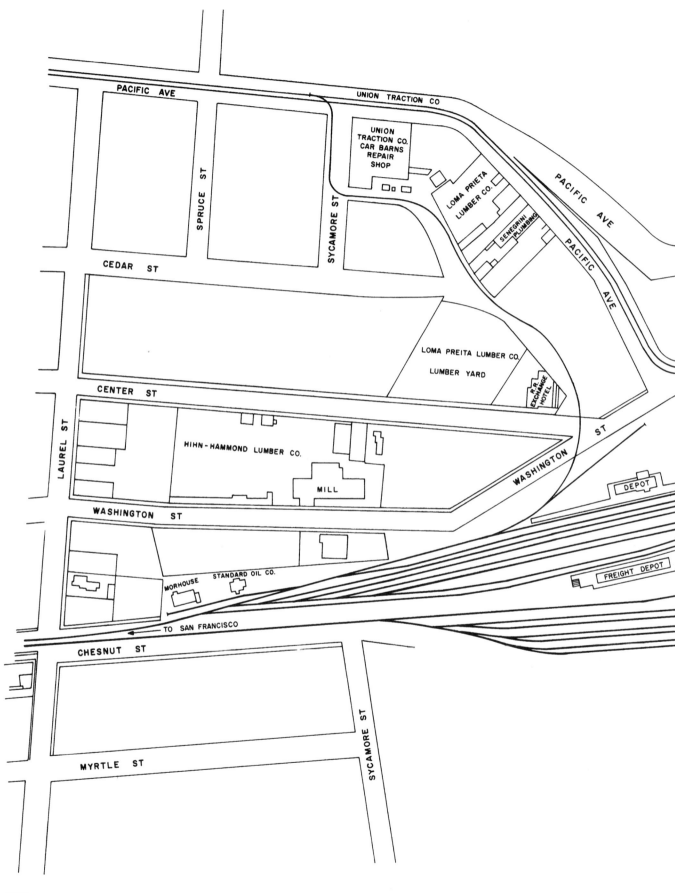

Santa Cruz Yard Map of Southern Pacific/Ocean Shore Railroads

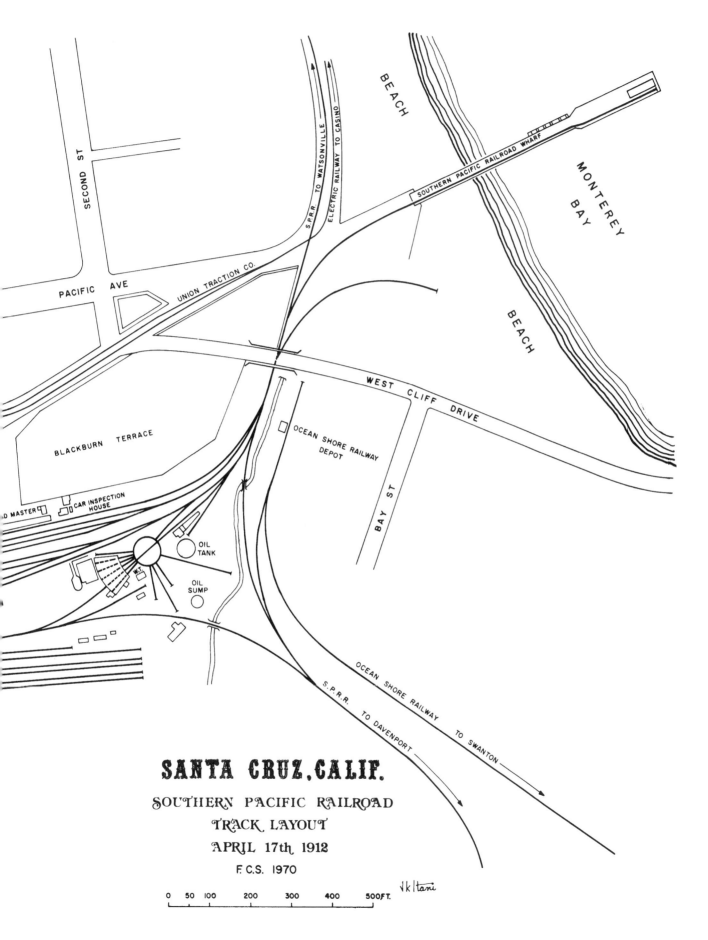

BEACH

MONTEREY BAY

SECOND ST

PACIFIC AVE

S.P.R.R. TO WATSONVILLE

ELECTRIC RAILWAY TO CASINO

SOUTHERN PACIFIC RAILROAD WHARF

BEACH

UNION TRACTION CO.

WEST CLIFF DRIVE

BLACKBURN TERRACE

OCEAN SHORE RAILWAY DEPOT

BAY ST

CAR INSPECTION HOUSE

RD MASTER

W.T.

OIL TANK

OIL SUMP

OCEAN SHORE RAILWAY TO SWANTON

S.P.R.R. TO DAVENPORT

SANTA CRUZ, CALIF.

SOUTHERN PACIFIC RAILROAD
TRACK LAYOUT
APRIL 17th 1912

F.C.S. 1970

√K Itani

0   50   100   200   300   400   500FT.

227

The long awaited broad gauge via Los Gatos and Santa Cruz to Pajaro had come. The well equipped Scenic Local bound for Monterey makes the curve leaving Santa Cruz. — Courtesy: U.C. Santa Cruz, Special Collections

of trains within the county. Where before trains had operated from Boulder Creek and Felton to Santa Cruz and from Pajaro to Santa Cruz, there would now be through trains from Boulder Creek to Pajaro with Santa Cruz merely a stop along the way. Obviously, some of the people in Santa Cruz felt slighted. For the most part, however, the change went unnoticed as the scheduling stayed basically the same, just the end points changed.

By the end of 1913, prosperity for the Southern Pacific Railroad had once again picked up in Santa Cruz County. Large amounts of lumber were being shipped from the San Vicente Mill at Santa Cruz. Increased lumber product shipments were coming over the Aptos branch from the Molino Timber Company at Loma Prieta. With the demand for cement having increased once again, the Davenport plant was running near capacity, thus providing the S.P. with greater shipping tonnage. Tourism was on the increase with F.A. Hihn's resort at Capitola and more people wanting to visit the many Santa Cruz beaches. As the trains became longer and the locomotives heavier, the decision was made to beef up the Santa Cruz branch line to mainline status. On November 15, 1913, the orders came down to rip out the ten-year-old 76-pound rail and replace it with 90 pounds to the yard. With the coming of 1914, the $89,000 job had been completed, and larger engines began to roll into Santa Cruz County.

Passenger ridership between Davenport and Santa Cruz was so light on some trains that McKeen motorcars had been substituted in place of conventional locomotives and coaches. At the same time, freight and passenger traffic on the Coast Division mainline near Pajaro was picking up. More and more, there was a continuing need for the Watsonville-Pajaro area to play a greater roll in S.P. coastal operations. Finally, the Southern Pacific management in looking at the total picture came to some obvious conclusions.

It would be more beneficial to the operations of the railroad if the division point were moved from Santa Cruz to Pajaro. Pajaro was much more centrally located to the coast mainline, the Del Monte Junction (Castroville) to Monterey branch, the Gilroy to Hollister branch, and of course the Santa Cruz branch.

Thus, with the beginning of May of 1910, all of the Santa Cruz roundhouse repair and car maintenance facilities were torn down and shipped to Pajaro. In addition, as soon as the Pajaro facilities were completed, there would be some rescheduling

During the good years of mainline railroading for Santa Cruz, many engines occupied the yard and roundhouse area. — Courtesy: Harold Van Gorder Collection

TIME TABLES

SOUTHERN PACIFIC

TIME CARD IN EFFECT JUNE 2, 1918

Leaving via Watsonville Junction
8:15 A. M.   Daily for Gilroy, San Jose and San Francisco.
9:30 A. M.—For Pacific Grove, Salinas and Los Angeles.
11:35 A. M.—For Pacific Grove, Salinas, San Luis Obispo, San Jose and San Francisco.
3:35 P. M.—For Pacific Grove, Salinas, Intermediates and Los Angeles, San Jose and San Francisco.
7:00 P. M.—Daily for San Jose and San Francisco.

Arriving via Watsonville Junction
10:18 A. M.—From Pacific Grove, Salinas and Los Angeles.
11:35 A. M.—From San Jose and San Francisco and way points.
5:45 P. M.—From Pacific Grove and San Francisco and way points.
7:30 P. M.—From San Francisco and way points.
8:50 P. M.—From Los Angeles and way points.

Leaving via Mountain Division
7:60 A. M.—For San Francisco daily except Sunday.
1:40 P. M.—For Oakland daily.
5:55 P. M.—For San Francisco daily.

Arriving via the Mountains
11:20 A. M.—From San Francisco.
12:40 P. M.—From Oakland.
6:57 P. M.—From San Francisco daily except Sunday.

NOTE—All trains stop on signal at Casino.

BOULDER CREEK LINE

Leaving	Arriving
10:25 A. M.—Daily.	
1:40 P. M.—Saturday and Sunday only.	7:55 A. M.—Daily.
	12:40 P. M.—Daily.
4:20 P. M.—Daily except Saturday and Sunday.	2:30 P. M.—Daily except Saturday and Sunday.
5:55 P. M.—Daily.	6:57 P. M.—Daily except Sunday.

DAVENPORT LINE

Leaving	Arriving
6:50 A. M.—Daily.	8:15 A. M. Daily.
3:20 P. M.—Daily.	4:50 P. M.- Daily.
10:50 P. M.—Daily.	12:15 A. M.—Daily.

JAMES DOIG, Local Agent

In effect June 2, 1918.   Telephone 169

OCEAN SHORE

Leaving for Swanton	Arriving from Swanton
8:00 A. M.—Daily.	10:10 A. M.—Daily.
3:25 P. M.—Daily.	5:35 P. M.—Daily.

Once upon a time there were 34 trains a day arriving and departing the obviously busy city of Santa Cruz. — Courtesy: Fred Stoes Collection

229

Left: It's train time at the Capitola Depot, 1920. — Courtesy: Harold Van Gorder Collection

Right: The Aptos Depot awaits the arrival of the next train. — Courtesy: U.C. Berkeley, Bancroft Librarys

Left: The morning Scenic Local crosses the San Lorenzo River Bridge at the beach. — Courtesy: U.C. Santa Cruz, Special Collection

While the ladies under the Capitola bridge were too far back for the photographer to capture a good likeness, he certainly didn't miss the late afternoon freight train bound for Santa Cruz. — Courtesy: Harold Van Gorder Collection

The period of time between 1912 and the beginning of World War One was probably Santa Cruz County railroading's finest hour. Most of the smaller concerns, such as the Molino Timber Company, the San Vicente Lumber Co., the Newell Creek Mill and the Waterman Creek Mill railroads of the California Timber Company, the Ocean Shore Railroad, the Pajaro Valley Consolidated, and the California Central, were all still in operation. The Southern Pacific was running crack trains such as the Santa Cruz Limited and The San Francisco Limited between San Francisco and Santa Cruz in under two hours and forty minutes, an unbeatable time in those days. Tourism brought in untold picnic and excursion trains. The mainline at Pajaro saw such famous prestreamlined passenger trains as the Sunset Limited, the Shore Line Limited, the Lark, and the Del Monte Express. Between freight and passenger service, the City of Santa Cruz saw the arrival and departure of over forty trains a day.

As history has already recorded, there was to come another form of vehicular conveyance that would quickly remove the railroad from its place of prominence in passenger transportation. Around the turn of the century, several companies were manufacturing a novelty for the rich called a horseless carriage. Basically it was a self-powered buggy without the horse. While a definite nuisance on city streets and country roads, it was tolerated.

It was about this time that an enterprising young man named Henry Ford concluded this luxurious plaything could be turned into a necessity. In 1903, with the financial help of some Detroit businessmen, he founded the Ford Motor Company. In 1908, after producing nine rather unsuccessful models of the horseless carriage, he hit upon the model "T" which would soon become the standardbearer of the company. It was an automobile which was capable of being used in both the city and the country. It was easy to operate, it was simple and inexpensive to maintain, and it was priced at a figure most American families could afford. By 1913 a mass-production assembly line (a new concept for U.S. manufacturing, although used by the French as early as 1776 in the making of rifles) had been completed at Highland Park, Michigan, and the first model "T"'s began to roll off that line. A short 14 years later, in 1927, over 15,000,000 model "T"'s were on the highways and roads of America. While the "T" manufactured by Ford was not the only automobile or company to come of age during this period, it represented over 50% of all the cars found on American roads in the early 1920's.

By the late 1920's, the complexion of railroading in Santa Cruz county had changed significantly. Most short-distance passenger trips were being done in an automobile or via bus. Only the longer distance passenger trains were still in operation. Lumbering in the Santa Cruz Mountains had all but come to an end. Sand and cement were now the prime freight being shipped out of Santa Cruz. Watsonville Junction — changed from "Pajaro" in 1913 because it caused much confusion among railroad people — had become the center for freight activity for the county, with three to four thousand carloads of apples and hundreds of carloads of sugar beets being shipped out annually. Also, being the division point, it was the center for daily coastline freight and passenger activity.

With the coming of the depression in 1929 also came the close of the real railroading in Santa Cruz County. By now the Aptos branch was gone. Passenger service on the Boulder branch and the Davenport branch had been replaced by Southern Pacific Transportation Co. (later Greyhound) buses. Freight trains only infrequently visited the two branches. Passenger service had been reduced to three trains a day over the hill to San Francisco and two trains a day from Watsonville Junction roundtrip to Santa Cruz. Freight service consisted of two trains a day from Watsonville to work locally within the county, and two trains a day over the hill.

As was obvious, the end of an era had come, and the golden age of passenger trains for Santa Cruz County was at hand. As with all things that must die, it happened slowly. One by one the stations were closed. Little by little the trains grew shorter. As each declining year approached, more and more buses were put on where once there had been a train. The first sign of death came when the last passenger train from Watsonville Junction to Santa Cruz operated on February 8, 1938. Shortly thereafter, in 1939, a modern two-lane road, Highway 17, was completed between San Jose and Santa Cruz thus allowing for the automobile invasion. In early 1940, the S.P. decided to abandon the mountain line. All freight was then rerouted via Watsonville Junction, buses were put on between Santa Cruz and Los Gatos over the new highway, and passenger trains were a thing of the past in Santa Cruz County.

With the end of the passenger train service, most people looked upon the railroad as a thing of the past. Oh, they were aware that an occasional freight train pulled into town or that once in a while a tourist special would come in from Watsonville Junction. But, for the most part, the railroad that the local pioneers had grown up with, and had come to love as a part of their community, was gone. No more would there be the sounds of a peanut vendor or the local drayage men arguing over a load at the depot. No more would there be the smile of the long-time friendly station agent as he asked you what was your destination. No more would their be a place for kids to hang around where there heroes could be cherished. No more would there be a train that followed the San Lorenzo River or crossed the Twin Lakes trestle. No more would the fantasy of being able to board a train to anywhere be a reality. What had started as an expanding dream had concluded as a contracting reality. It was over, finished, complete. From this time forth, only the freight trains would be left to carry on the fantasies of the past and the dreams of the future.

Ah yes!!! The fair damsels of Watsonville pose with their city's quality product about to be shipped to San Francisco. — Courtesy: U.C. Santa Cruz, Special Collections

For many years the Santa Cruz Freight Depot served the needs of an ever expanding community. — Courtesy: Fred Stoe

Typical of the 2900 twelve-wheeler locomotives which worked the Santa Cruz-Watsonville area for many years was 2921 shown here before the Santa Cruz water tank in 1936. — Courtesy: Fred Stoes

Once a very busy place, the Santa Cruz Roundhouse stands deserted in 1937. — Courtesy: Fred Stoes

Left: The afternoon freight has just crossed Twin Lakes Trestle and is headed for Watsonville Junction. — Fred Stoes

Right: The morning Santa Cruz Local rounds the curve at Rob Roy and the passengers are presented with a fine view of Manresa Beach and the Monterey Bay. — W.C. Whittaker

Left: Headed downgrade on Ellicott Hill, Watsonville Local #188 charges the track through the San Andreas Valley. — W.C. Whittaker

236

February 8, 1938: After over 62 years of continuous passenger service the last train from Watsonville has just arrived in Santa Cruz. In remembrance of same, the men who gave so much of their fives in support of such service, pose for one final photograph.
— Both pictures courtesy Harold Van Gorder Collection

Once upon a time the busy Santa Cruz Mountain mainline reverberated with the sounds of double headed freights and snake length passenger trains such as the Scenic Local shown here arriving at Glenwood in 1915. Now it is March, 1941. The station buildings are gone, the unkempt right-of-way turns rusty with disuse, plant life returns to where it hasn't been in over 60 years and in a short three months the once famous route will be abandoned forever.-
Courtesy: — Fred Stoes Collection; Photos by Bill Harry

The men who kept the S.P. running out of Watsonville Junction pose at the roundhouse, circa 1920. — Courtesy: Charles Ford Co. Collection

It is 10:25 a.m. on this particular 1921 morning. Engineer J.G. Walker has just taken a picture of the "Watsonville Junction Passenger" which he worked from San Francisco. — Courtesy: Fred Stoes Collection

Watsonville Junction, circa 1925: The Santa Cruz train has just arrived and the San Francisco train is being made up to continue on. Santa Cruz train, left side; San Francisco train in front of depot. — Courtesy: Charles Ford Company Collection

December 6, 1920: The Scenic Local #84 and the morning San Francisco Local #24 pose after having just arrived at Watsonville Junction. — Courtesy: U.C. Santa Cruz, Special Collection

Right: Santa Cruz to Watsonville Local #188 is seen leaving Capitola Depot. — Courtesy: Bill Harry Collection

Left: S.P. Superintendent J.J. Jordan's private car graces the Santa Cruz bound local as it crosses the Capitola Bridge. — Courtesy: Fred Stoes

Right: The Santa Cruz Depot poses in the afternoon sun late in the 1920's. — Courtesy: Harold Van Gorder Collection

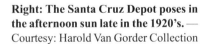

It is a bright 1921 morning in Santa Cruz and Engineer Walker is photographing the lazy crew of the local shortly before it is to leave for Watsonville Junction. Ironically, almost sixty years later and forty years after the last run of this train, the County Of Santa Cruz is actively pursuing the reinstatement of such service. — Courtesy: Fred Stoes Collection

6

Lingering Ghosts of Another Time

The Santa Cruz Branch & Watsonville Junction

While it was true that with the end of rail passenger service to Santa Cruz in 1940 most people looked upon the railway as a thing of the past, it still had a very dominant place within the county. What before had been a hodgepodge of operations was now referred to as the "Branch." Each day would see three to four freight trains making roundtrips from Watsonville Junction to Santa Cruz and back. These were heavy-duty freights of considerable consists that required double-header operation to get them over the 2.5% grade at Ellicott Hill.

The first train over early in the morning was the merchandise freight or what the railroadmen referred to as the "Little Zipper." It was a continuation of the manifest freight, the "Zipper," which stopped momentarily in the predawn hours at Watsonville Junction to cut out cars on its way to San Francisco from Los Angeles. It was reported that the cars bound for Santa Cruz would be cut off the back end of the Zipper, made up into the Little Zipper, and both trains would be underway in less than five minutes. According to many senior engineers, the express Little Zipper rarely stayed within the posted speed limits of the branch on its way to Santa Cruz. Later in the day, the second and third freights would come over the branch doing local switching along the way and finally end up at Santa Cruz to drop off and pick up freight cars. Operating out of Santa Cruz was a local freight known as the Switcher. In the morning, it would start out by making a roundtrip to Davenport to service that section; in the afternoon, it would make a second roundtrip up to Olympia to bring back sand and lime. For several years after the close of the mountain line, almost up until the time of dieselization, the freight on the branch would be handled in this manner.

By 1940, the emphasis on railroading had entirely shifted from Santa Cruz to Watsonville Junction. The Southern Pacific Coast Division had now become the main artery for most freight and passenger service between the San Francisco Bay Area and Los Angeles. On that artery, Watsonville Junction played a very important role. Here, 330 men were employed by the Southern Pacific. Forty men alone were involved in the upkeep and maintenance of the massive steam locomotives which terminated here from San Jose and Santa Margarita. Each month saw the repair of over 250 freight cars going on and over 60,000 cars a month were handled through the Junction. The payroll for this entire operation was over three-quarters of a million dollars a year at 1940 wages.

Besides providing the upkeep, maintenance, and operation facilities, Watsonville Junction was also the freight distribution center for the four surrounding counties of Monterey, Santa Cruz, San Benito, and Santa Clara. Each day, local freight trains would originate from the Junction bound for the cities of Monterey and Pacific Grove, Castroville and Salinas, Gilroy and Hollister, and of course Santa Cruz. In addition, Watsonville Junction, unlike Santa Cruz, was still very much an active passenger station.

Up until just before World War II, name trains such as the Lark, the Daylight, the Sunset Express, the Del Monte, and locals No. 72 and No. 92 made scheduled stops at the Junction. Once many of them had been streamlined with stainless steel cars and 4400 series Lima locomotives, and their schedules upgraded, they no longer stopped at the Junction. This, however, caused no consternation among the local residents, because the S.P. had added several new trains that did. Among them was the soon to be famous Noon Daylight No. 96 which was put on on March 30th, 1940. It should be added that with the new trains many riders came from outside the immediate area. Ralph Peterson, long-time ticket agent at the Junction, remembers when many was the time that more people came from Santa Cruz to ride the San Francisco-bound trains that did those from nearby Watsonville.

During the war years, the Junction moved one heck of a lot of freight up and down the coast. On weekends a special train, No. 31, would be run from Camp Roberts to the Junction to allow the soldiers a little rest and relaxation in Monterey and Santa Cruz. When manpower became scarce, many a woman took on worker's jobs in the yard and brakeman jobs on some of the freights

With the end of the war, Watsonville Junction only became bigger. The locomotives became larger, the trains handled became longer, and the passenger traffic increased. One of the trains which added to this ridership increase was the ever-popular Sunday "Suntan Special" to Santa Cruz.

October 21, 1942: As the sun rose, the South Pacific Coast-Southern Pacific Santa Cruz Roundhouse stood for its last day of existence. — Courtesy: Bob Willey

#3107 on the early morning freight to Santa Cruz crosses Capitola Bridge over Soquel Creek. This was a merchandise train known as the Little Zipper by the local railroadmen. It brought any freight left at Watsonville Junction by the mainline Zipper and also any additional freight not handled by other trains. — Courtesy: Fred Stoes

Local residents pause to watch the doubleheaded freight lumber through their community of Aptos while Engineer, Gene O'Lague casually snaps the shutter.

It's late afternoon and the doubleheaded Watsonville Junction bound freight prepares to leave the yard.—Courtesy: Bob Willey

Above: it had been almost six years since a passenger train had wandered into Santa Cruz County. Because of the war effort trains such as this were deemed unnecessary and so didn't run. Now, however it was June of 1947, and the Y.L.I. Special was the first of many to arrive. — Courtesy: Bob Willey

"Fred's out there boys so let's give him some smoke." Thus, the morning local once again puts on the show coming through Seabright for photographer, fireman and friend, Stoes.

Freight was the name and power was the game as these two heavy consolidations work the morning train across Twin Lakes Trestle. It should be noted that Photographer Stoes, being a fireman, knew everybody out of Watsonville Junction. Therefore, it didn't take much to get a dark puff of smoke out of the lead engine or a blast on the whistle to set the stage for this view.

Left: The lure of the Big Trees brought others also such as the State Bar Special shown here in Henry Cowell's Park. — Courtesy: Bob Willey

Right: That portion of the Santa Cruz Branch which led to Davenport, likewise developed its large share of the freight. Shown here freight 774 is just returning to Santa Cruz from its wanderings along the Pacific Coast. — Courtesy: Bill Harry

p248ml

Left: July 2, 1950: Even after the line over the mountains had been closed for a number of years, the lure of Big Trees and the San Lorenzo Gorge still loomed large in the minds of the tourists. Thus, for several years the S.P. operated a short local from time to time between Santa Cruz and Felton. — Courtesy: Bob Willey

Right: In another view, freight 773 is seen near Davenport on its return trip. — Courtesy: John Schmale Collection

The largest engine ever to work the Santa Cruz Branch and especially the San Lorenzo Gorge, was this 2-8-2, No. 3224 shown here at Mount Hermon on April 23, 1949. Weight: 265,000 pounds. — Courtesy: Bob Willey

The harsh winter sunlight catches the Davenport local at end of track, almost 12 miles from Santa Cruz, and the closest the Coast Line Railway ever got to San Francisco some forty-five years earlier. — Courtesy: Bob Willey

The Davenport branch like the San Lorenzo Gorge provided the railfan and tourist with breathtaking but different scenery. Here, Bob Willey captures a doubleheaded excursion train crossing Wilder Creek Trestle bound for Davenport, and likewise, its return a short time later. — Courtesy: Bill Harry Collection

It's back to Watsonville Junction time as the evening freight works a heavy drag past the roller coaster at the Santa Cruz Boardwalk. — Courtesy: Fred Stoes

The cold of a clear but wintry 6:00 a.m. Chittenden morning works on the hands of the photographer. The walk up the hill in the frost covered grass will no doubt leave stains. But so what, it's worth it. The sun is coming up in the east, the birds of the Pajaro Valley are already at work, and off in the distance a high speed thundering can be heard. Approaching from the west, past the Granite Rock Quarry and across the Pajaro River Bridge it comes, around the tall eucalyptus trees, and there it is. The Express Zipper charges the block and one of the fastest trains on the coast ever is recorded on film to be viewed on yet another day. — Courtesy: Fred Stoes

The roundhouse at Watsonville Junction awaits the incoming and outgoing locomotives for the day. — Courtesy: U.C. Berkeley, Bancroft Library, Roy Graves Collection

The oldest named train on the Southern Pacific roster, the "Del Monte," rambles through the Watsonville Junction Yard on its way to Monterey and Pacific Grove. — Courtesy: Fred Stoes

One of the many S.P. workhorses pauses in the Watsonville Junction Yard before taking on the day's assignment. — Courtesy: Fred Stoes

For a time during the 1940's, when trains entered and left the yard, the crews were required to ride on top and inspect each train. This practice called "Dressing Up" was soon stopped, however, when a few crewmen were hurt. Seen here freight 765 enters the top end of the Watsonville Junction Yard while two brakemen view their train as ordered. — Courtesy: Fred Stoes

The new pride of the railroad, the "Noon Daylight" passes through the small community of Aromas just outside of Watsonville Junction where it will be making its next stop. — Courtesy: Fred Stoes

The citizens of Watsonville, many of them employees of the S.P., were proud of the fact that the new "Noon Daylight" now made a stop at the Junction. In support of this the downtown National Dollar Store posted this display. — Courtesy: Jerry McCabe Collection

July 1938: Watsonville Junction; S.P. Daylight #99, crew picking up orders, one set for the Hoghead and one set for the Conductor. — Courtesy: Fred Stoes

Destined to be the most famous Southern Pacific locomotive ever built and most photographed steam locomotive in the U.S., GS-4 Daylight locomotive #4449 waits at Watsonville Junction to return to San Francisco with the Suntan Special. It continues to operate in motion pictures and on periodic excursions around the country. — Courtesy: Fred Stoes

2-10-2's such as 3670 leaving the bottom end of the Watsonville Junction Yard provided the main muscle on the coast between San Francisco and Los Angeles. — Courtesy: Fred Stoes

254

Strong in the minds of both the railfan and the railroadman was the Southern Pacific's "Daylight." Many considered it to be the most beautiful train in the world. Shown here, Fred Stoes captures the speed and grace of this Golden State Lady as she glides down the track through the Valley of the Birds at 79 miles per hour.

#2815 eases out of the top end of the Watsonville Junction Yard with the Hollister Local bound for Gilroy and Tres Pinos. — Courtesy: Fred Stoes

Engineers Al Page and George Irwin on train 2-763 charge the block at Eaton just east of Watsonville Junction with the local bound for San Jose. — Courtesy: Fred Stoes

The Suntan Special

In 1927 the Southern Pacific decided to capitalize on the popularity of the Santa Cruz Beach and Boardwalk and the Henry Cowell Big Trees near Felton by starting a new excursion train over the mountain from San Jose. This new train was to be known as the Suntan Special. Initially it began service on Memorial Day and operated every Sunday and holiday thereafter until the last week in September. As the S.P. management had guessed, the Suntan Special was an almost instant success. Soon, so many tourists jammed the train that it had to be run in two sections. As had been the case ever since the first South Pacific Coast excursion trains back in the 1880's, the appeal of a relaxed Sunday outing to one of the many recreational areas in Santa Cruz County by train caught the imagination of thousands of tourists.

In 1932, the Suntan Special origin point was moved from San Jose to San Francisco. As could be expected, this only increased the ridership, and soon there were at least three sections making a roundtrip over the hill every Summer Sunday and holiday. In 1934, another section of Suntan was added from Oakland. From 1935 to 1939 would be the glory years for the Santa Cruz Mountain division. While normal Fall, Winter, and Spring passenger traffic had fallen off to nothing, the Suntans were making the hill look like the once great mainline that it was. On July 4th and Labor Day, and on especially hot Sundays, there would be as many as seven double-headed sections making the roundtrip over the hill. Quite a contrast to the rest of the year.

In later years, when the mountain route had been closed, the demand for the Suntan Special had not lessened in the least. Thus, on April 28th, 1940, the first new Suntan special made the trip to Santa Cruz and Big Trees via Watsonville Junction. While the trip took 35 minutes more via the Junction, no one minded because it was an excursion train. Besides, in many ways the ride was just as interesting. Now, city folks, used to the hill, could see the lower Santa Clara Valley lush agricultural lands and the beautiful Monterey Bay on their way to Santa Cruz. Also, if they stayed aboard the train, they still saw the magnificent splendor of the San Lorenzo Gorge as the train climbed to Big Trees.

The Suntan Special would cease operations after the Summer season of 1941 because of World War II. All during the war years, the locomotives, passenger cars, equipment, and manpower were needed in other areas.

On July 4th, 1947, after almost six years, the Suntan Special was once again put on via the Junction to Santa Cruz. From that day until the end of the Summer season of 1959, the Sunday Suntan Special would run uninterrupted. As in the past, many would

be the time it took numerous sections to do the job.

In retrospect, this author was fortunate enough to have ridden the Summer Suntans many times during the late Fifties from Palo Alto to Santa Cruz. Each ride was an experience unto itself and one which my friend, Jim Garcia, and I thoroughly enjoyed. We would arrive at the Palo Alto Depot at about 8:45 a.m. The sun was well up by then and the morning air was almost always warm. Waiting for the Suntan along the platform would be several hundred people, all noisily chattering with excitement. Soon in the distance, the rumble and the air horn from a big 4-8-4 Daylight locomotive would be heard. Slowly, the Suntan Special would drop down from the steel bridge into Palo Alto in a snake-like fashion with what would seem to be an endless string of passenger cars. Already, the train was well filled with passengers from San Francisco and Burlingame. Soon it would come to a slow brakescreeching halt, the air would relax, and the big Daylight-type engine would seemingly let out a longheld breath.

Once aboard the train, the mood for the day would soon be set. It was a happy time, a good time, a time to relax and enjoy what was happening around you. People from all walks of life and of all ages were in companionship on this train. Some would be wearing suits and be very well dressed, while others would be clad only in their swimming attire with an accompanying paper bag holding their towels and beach paraphernalia. Up and down the cars would come peanut vendors hawking donuts, rolls, milk, and sandwiches to those people who didn't quite get up early enough for breakfast. For those wishing to walk a little, there was a combination lounge/snack car in the middle of the train where one could get something a little more substantial. Up near the locomotive, there would sometimes be an empty baggage car with 2"x4" railings placed across open door spaces. From here you could lean out the side, although you weren't supposed to, and watch the locomotive as it sped down the track or watch the 20-car train behind you as it snaked around curves. Always on the rear of the Suntan special would be an open-ended observation car where you could step out and watch the world go by.

The ride from Palo Alto to Santa Cruz, with stops at San Jose and Watsonville Junction, would take about two and a half hours. The big 4400 series steam locomotive would turn it on after leaving San Jose, and soon we would be charging down the track at 79 miles per hour. It was always fun to watch the people as we passed their slower automobiles where the railroad paralleled Highway 101. For some strange reason, there was always that urge to wave and shout at these slowpoke motorists who obviously couldn't compete with the speed of the train. Soon after leaving Gilroy, the train would slow to 25 miles per hour while it threaded its way through the narrow pass along the Pajaro River. Normally, the Suntan arrived at Watsonville Junction at about 10:30 in the morning. Here, the high speed GS-4 locomotive would be cut off the train, and two smaller 2800 series consolidated engines would be put on for the twisting, turning, roller-coaster ride over the branch into Santa Cruz. It was this portion of the trip which always drew the oh's and ah's from the passengers as we snaked along the seashore on high bluffs and long trestles above Monterey Bay. Finally, at 11:30 a.m., the Suntan would arrive at the Seaside Amusement Company station point called Casino. As the people alighted from the train for their summer fun, they would usually be greeted by a big band playing up tempo tunes to welcome them to Santa Cruz. For the next six hours, it would be a lie and play day at the beach. For those who stayed on the train, it would continue on to Big Trees for a day of picnicking and solitude.

At 5:00 p.m., the train would return to the Casino, and all the day's travelers and excursionists would reboard for the ride home. The return trip always went faster than the trip over. For some reason, the combination of the salt air, the exercise, the new suntan, and the warmth and gentle swaying of the train all seemed to come together to dull the senses. It didn't take long before much of the train was asleep. In our case, we seemingly arrived in Palo Alto in almost no time at all.

In 1959, unlike most passenger trains, the Suntan Special was still a very popular item. While running in the black, the train, due to current S.P. philosophy, was one big pain in the neck to management. As a result, the decision was made in early 1960 that it would not run during the coming summer season. Because it was not a scheduled train and because it saw only seasonal operations, there was no legality requiring its continuance. As a result, the last passenger train to operate in Santa Cruz County had been on Labor Day of 1959. From that day to this, freight service has been the only railroading in the county.

During the period from 1955 to 1957 the Southern Pacific Coast Division and the Santa Cruz Branch in particular would take part in a technological change. For years the steam engine had dominated the motive power requirements of the Southern Pacific. Now, they were being phased out by a new concept called a diesel. While the diesel had been around for a number of years, no one really thought it would replace the mighty steam locomotive. Yet it had come.

Unlike its steam predecessor, the diesel offered greater distance between stops because it didn't require water every so often. Also, it offered a more even distribution of pulling effort on the rails. In addition, it offered greater standardization of interchangeable parts. Likewise, it offered greater periods of time between maintenance checks, and, most obviously, it offered a tremendous cost savings.

By 1958, the diesel had become the S.P.'s prime motive power, and the steam locomotive was just another antique of the past. With the demise of the steam engine would also go the need for Watsonville Junction to remain a Coast Division point. Due to the extended range of the diesels, most trains were now routed through the Junction and crew changes ceased to take place. Also, the need for a large maintenance facility for steam power was no longer necessary. For the most part, any diesels assigned out of the Junction came from San Jose. From this time to the present, the primary function of the Junction would now be to serve as a focal point for local operations.

Another change took place during and after the dieselization period. Due to the gradual decline in freight business on the branch and the extended capability of the diesel, the Switcher at Santa Cruz was done away with. Instead, one train a day made the freight run into Santa Cruz. Upon its arrival, it would spend the rest of the day doing the Davenport and Olympia work and then finally return to the Junction late in the evening. This practice would continue from then until the present.

The last change to take place most recently, and one which has yet to be completed, was the abandonment of the passenger train in favor of the airplane. As the airplane became more popular and more used during the 1950's and 1960's, ridership on the coast passenger trains seriously declined. One by one the trains were taken off, and by 1971 the only streamliners left on the coast were the Daylight, the Lark, and the Del Monte. On May 1st, 1971, a government-funded rail passenger corporation nicknamed "Amtrak" took over most passenger trains in the country. This included all Southern Pacific trains, especially on the coast. Unfortunately, the Del Monte, which was the only train that stopped at the Junction, was not continued. Thus, on April 30th, 1971, just six months shy of the anniversary date of one hundred years ago when the first broad gauge passenger train made its run, the oldest name train in the country, the Del Monte, made its last stop at the Junction. From then until now, Watsonville Junction has been a freight station only.

Above: #4356 with its mail train graces the Santa Cruz foothills as it follows the Pajaro River around the Granite Rock Quarry. — Courtesy: Fred Stoes

Right: Two motion picture stars of the 1940's pose on the platform of the Southern Pacific's "Suntan Special." — Courtesy: Southern Pacific Company

The Suntan Special arrives along the Beach Front after just coming over the mountain from Los Gatos and San Francisco. — Courtesy: Fred Stoes

A Sunday Suntan Special works its way across the concrete arch and down the San Lorenzo Canyon toward Santa Cruz. — Courtesy: Fred Stoes

July 6, 1941: The last section of the Suntan Special departs the Santa Cruz Yard after another busy day by the beach-loving tourists. — Courtesy: Bill Harry

Four sections of the Suntan Special sit ready at Santa Cruz for the return trip home. — Courtesy: Malcolm Gaddis

Two 2300 series S.P. locomotives with Suntan Special in tow charge the steep San Lorenzo Canyon upgrade just outside of Santa Cruz. — Courtesy: Fred Stoes

The war is over and the first Suntan Special arrives at the beach in over six years. — Courtesy: Fred Stoes

Hundreds of well wishers greet the arrival of the Suntan Special at the official S.P. location known as Casino. — Courtesy: Skip Littlefield Collection, Seaside Company

Left: Railfan Bob Willey talks to the Suntan Special Engineer while waiting to pick up passengers at the Casino. — Courtesy: Bill Harry

Right: Two Alco diesels are seen on the head of the Suntan as it approaches Capitola shortly before the train was to run no more. — Courtesy: Gene O'Lague

Left: The first Suntan Special via Watsonville Junction poses before the lens of W.C. Whittaker on April 28, 1940.

Southern Pacific GS-6 4-8-4 #4460 has just arrived at Pajaro on the point of the Suntan Special from San Francisco. It uncouples and heads for the refueling and water tanks near the roundhouse. Soon, two new SD-9 diesel locomotives hook up to the train to take it to the Beach Boardwalk. Thus, the transition from steam to diesel motive power in Santa Cruz County has happened. This last run of a steam locomotive into Watsonville Junction and the Central Coast region drew a crowd. #4460 would go on also to be the last steam engine ever to operate on the Southern Pacific, November 19, 1958. As of 2002, it resides in the St. Louis Transportation Museum. — Both photos: Gene (Jr.) O'Lague, 46 years with the SP as fireman and engineer.

Early evening approaches and the useable fight for a photograph is fading fast in the forest. Then, in the clearing at Shady Gulch, Fred Stoes luckily finds a partially lighted opening. Shortly thereafter, this view of two consolidations working the Suntan Special up the cumbersome San Lorenzo grade is recorded.

The Suntan Special, bound for Santa Cruz, crosses Aptos Creek under full power. — Courtesy: Alfred Brumit Collection

The Present

The Santa Cruz Branch as of 1979 is both a modern and, in many ways, an antiquated system. Six days a week, three General Motors GP-9 diesels bring the morning freight over from the Junction. Once in Santa Cruz, two of the engines do the local freight work in the area. On Tuesdays, Thursdays, and Saturdays the run is made up to Davenport to serve the cement plant which is still very active. On Mondays, Wednesdays, and Fridays, the diesels travel the old route of the Santa Cruz and Felton up to Olympia to drop off an occasional car at the Santa Cruz Lumber Company yard at Felton and to take up empties and bring back loaded gondolas and hoppers from the two sand plants.

Recently, over four and a half million dollars have been spent by the S.P. to upgrade the branch. New concrete bridges are routinely replacing old wooden trestles, the Santa Cruz yard has been reworked, the two remaining tunnels on the Olympia leg have been retimbered, new quarter-mile welded rail is being laid down in place of the old steel, much of the right-of-way has been reballasted, and several thousand ties have been replaced. From all outward appearances, the Southern Pacific Transportation Company plans to be a continuing force in the economic growth of Santa Cruz County. While the passenger trains are long gone, the freight business, which up until recently had declined, is now once again on the increase. As of the present, it looks like the Southern Pacific is here to stay.

Even as this aerial photo was being taken, the last sign of the steam era, the old Watsonville Junction roundhouse was coming down. No doubt, by the time this photo sees the printed page the roundhouse will be gone. — Courtesy: Joe Faust

267

In the back yard of W.H. "Bill" Connell, long time resident of La Selva Beach, hangs the original station sign for "Rob Roy." In addition to Rob Roy, it is also the original sign for "Manresa." Previous to 1922, when the Rob Roy real estate development took place, the station point and sign was known as and read "Manresa." The sign with the advent of the development was repainted Rob Roy. In 1935 the development changed hands and became "La Selva Beach" as it is known today. The sign, however, was never repainted for a third time, instead, it somehow disappeared. — Rick Hamman

While the Aptos Depot is long gone and the days of horses being used for transportation with it, this little girl and her pony are standing next to the original station sign less than 200 feet from where it used to stand. — Rick Hamman

It is 8:00 am. and the Santa Cruz morning local is leaving the Watsonville Junction Yard. — Courtesy: Bruce MacGregor

The current S.P. Railroad Yards and the Santa Cruz Municipal Pier are seen from the air. —
Courtesy: Joe Faust

Shortly after Ted Benson took this antique view, the depot was torn down and once again the sign vanished. The branch, however, remains very active.

The early morning Santa Cruz Local passes the Aptos-Seascape Golf Course on its way west. — Rick Hamman

The 582 ft. long, 50 ft. high Capitola Bridge still dissects the town much as it did when it was first built. — Courtesy: Joe Faust

Many an inner tear was shed on that day when the first diesel locomotive arrived for work at Watsonville Junction. Sad but true; the railroadmen all knew that the monster they had grown up with that belched forth clouds of fury, that breathed thundering fire, that shook the ground with each hissing cylinder blast, was soon going to be entirely replaced by a nondescript piece of machinery that went whirrrr!!! — Albert D. Snyder

Two GP-9 diesel units pick up loaded hoppers at the Davenport-Lone Star Industries cement plant. —Rick Hamman

The view from the cab of a locomotive along the Davenport branch can often be awe inspiring. So it must have been during this particular day's sunset. — Rick Hamman

The sun sets on the lead GP-9 at Santa Cruz as Senior Engineer on the branch, Blair Kough, sets his evening train up for the trip back to Watsonville Junction. — Rick Hamman

The Lone Star Industries Cement Plant and the community of Davenport as seen from the air. The old depot used to sit at the switch in the lower right. Also, a portion of the original Ocean Shore right-of-way, now a dirt road, can be seen. — Courtesy: Joe Faust

The sand train from Olympia approaches the curve through which used to be Summit Tunnel, No. 7, at Rincon. — Rick Hamman

The face of the San Lorenzo Gorge walls have been, and will continue to be in transition. On this day, December 30, 1977, the sand train came only this far. — Rick Hamman

There are no passenger trains which stop at Chittenden anymore, or Watsonville Junction either for that matter; still, Amtrack's very successful Coast Starlight pictured here crossing the Pajaro River gives rise to the hope that someday, soon, there will be. — Rick Hamman

While no longer used, this 1929 date head nail reveals when this particular tie was first installed in the San Lorenzo Canyon. — Rick Hamman

Above: 360 tons of diesel muscle drags a loaded 22-car sand train across the Zayante Creek Trestle at Mt. Hermon on its return from Olympia. —Rick Hamman

Left: Wednesday, October 18, 1978: The steel bridge at Henry Cowell Park; a warm, shadowy, fall afternoon sees a lazy San Lorenzo River, a young girl, a passing train, and a friendly wave, likewise returned. —Rick Hamman

Although it is now the 1970's, the original Freight and Ticket sign of the 1930's still hangs over the entrance to the Santa Cruz Depot. Shortly after this photo was taken the depot became a first class restaurant and the sign vanished. — Rick Hamman

"Big Trees" is probably the only place on the entire S.P. Railroad where side clearance regulations exist for trains because of thousand year old giant redwoods which are found near the right-of-way. While by most standards the redwood on the right at 22-ft around and approximately 175 ft. tall is a big tree, at Big Trees it's not even average. — Courtesy: Bruce MacGregor

Track crews at Rio Del Mar repair a wrecked right-of-way while fellow riggers set ten wayward cars back in place. Although the possibility of derailment has always loomed large for the S.P. within the county, most such disasters have been minor in nature. — Rick Hamman

It's midnight among the sleeping monarchs. With the camera lens open for one hour the moon beautifully silhouettes the redwoods all along the right-of-way at Big Trees. — Rick Hamman

276

Roaring Camp & Big Trees
Narrow Gauge Railroad

I lie on my back in the short green grass of the Felton Meadow and watch the quiet Boeing 707 jetliner ten thousand feet above me as it makes its final approach for the San Francisco Airport 60 miles away. There is a very gentle breeze pushing the warm summer afternoon air around through the redwood trees. The wild ducks can be heard on the pond near the Covered Bridge. In the distance, a banjo and a fiddle are being played on the stage at the Oak picnic grounds. Close by, the smell of baked beans and steak lingers light in the atmosphere. Glancing at my watch, I note that it is just about time for the 2:00 p.m. train from Bear Mountain to arrive.

In a moment a faint offbeat rhythm is heard coming from the direction of McSkunk Junction. Soon, out of the dense Big Trees Forest, into the bright sunshine, appears the Dixiana Shay with its narrow gauge train just down from the mountain. The engine pauses while the brakeman throws the switch for the left track into town. Two short blasts come from the whistle, and then the train moves slowly down the track to the millpond. Here it stops again. Passengers gasp as the air is suddenly filled with a continuous jet of noisy hot steam while the Shay blows off the buildup and cleans out the sediment accumulated during the previous run. The noise stops. Two more short blasts from the whistle are heard, the train lurches forward, and the next stop will be Roaring Camp Depot. With the approach of the train, the down home country music of the Red Mountain Boys heralds its arrival, and people gather trackside for their first glimpse of a genuine, 100%, narrow gauge steam locomotive. As the Dixiana Shay appears from around the curve, its whistle blasting, I watch the unbelieving faces. There's the old man with a slight held-back tear of joy in his eyes as he momentarily dreams of yesteryear when such a sight was a common everyday occurrence. There's the young child clutching her mother's neck and at the same time trying to cover her ears so as to gain some protection from this obvious monster that will soon consume her. And then, there's the rail buff with camera and tape recorder in hand trying to catch a passing glimpse of history that except in places such as this doesn't exist anymore. Finally, the train comes to a gear-clattering halt at the Roaring Camp Depot. The passengers become spectators, the spectators become passengers, and the train once again departs for the five-mile journey to Bear Mountain.

The Roaring Camp & Big Trees Narrow Gauge Railroad, started in 1964 under the careful guidance of its founder Norman Clark, is a company dedicated to preserving the historical past. The original concept behind Roaring Camp was to share the Southern Pacific's right-of-way from Santa Cruz to Olympia for old-time steam-powered passenger train excursions and tri- weekly freight service. Ideally, the railroad would have been a broad gauge duplicate of the original Santa Cruz and Felton route as it followed the winding forest right-of-way, crossing large trestles and passing through several tunnels, on its way to Big Trees and Felton. After several meetings, the concept was abandoned, however, when both companies decided that the stiff insurance requirements and strict state regulations made the venture almost impossible.

As an alternate plan, Roaring Camp instead leased a large tract of property which extended from the Felton Meadow next to Big Trees all the way to the top of Graham Hill Summit. Here, over a two-year period, they were able to lay out and construct a narrow gauge railroad right-of-way from the original Felton Depot to a point on the top of the San Lorenzo Valley Ridge known as Bear Mountain.

In building this railroad, several things had to be taken into consideration during its planning stages. First and foremost, it was management's intention that everything possible would be done to maintain the integrity of the forest. As a result, the right-of-way in many places was laid out so as to avoid large stands of trees. Secondly, the roadbed where possible was to follow the contours of the land. This would eliminate the need for extensive cuts. Thirdly, the difference in elevation between the low point and the high point on the railroad was over 500 feet. Thus, while this was an excursion line, some very heavy engineering would have to be accomplished. The resultant of the foregoing is that the Roaring Camp right-of-way has the sharpest curves and the steepest grades of any railroad operating in the United States today.

Sharp curves and steep grades, however, were not the only things required to get the railroad up the hill. In many places, large trestles were necessary to span small gulches and canyons and to gain elevation. Two of the most impressive of these were those built in Spring Canyon at a place known as Cork Screw Loop. Here, the track crosses Spring Canyon on trestle No. I and does a full-circle turnabout on a second trestle coming back to the same point, only higher. While the first trestle is good sized, the second trestle is almost 500 feet in length and over 80 feet tall at its high point.

To provide the motive power for Roaring Camp's steep grades and sharp curves, two used logging-type steam locomotives were initially purchased. Engine No. I was the Dixiana Shay. It had just completed 24 years of service on the Coal Processing Corporation's railroad near Dixiana, Virginia. Engine No. 2 was the Tuolumne Heistler which had recently seen numerous years of operation on the famed West Side Lumber Company railroad out of Sonora. Together, they were selected to try to preserve a piece of the past while their counterparts fell prey to the cutting torch.

For over 12 years, up until the Summer of 1976, the railroad had been able to successfully operate to intermediate points such as Big Trees, Indian Creek, Grizzle Flats, Deer Valley and West Side Junction without a serious mishap. Then, late one hot afternoon, the trestles at Cork Screw Loop somehow caught fire. By the time the California State Forestry Service and hundreds of local volunteers had the fire under control five hours later, the two trestles were a total loss. The trestles were not insured, and the cost of rebuilding them was put at $250,000. While Roaring Camp did not have that kind of money lying around, they vowed that they would be rebuilt.

In the meantime, Roaring Camp, seeing a very unprofitable future until such time as the line could be reopened, set out to use some old time engineering to solve a very current problem. In almost no time at all, track workers and graders were hard at it cutting out a series of switchbacks up the side of Spring Canyon around the ruined trestles. By the end of 1976, the switchbacks were completed and service was once again reinstated from Roaring Camp to Bear Mountain.

While Roaring Camp is obviously a haven for the rail buff, it is also a good spot to get in touch with the past. The Depot at Roaring Camp is authentic in every detail and shares its roots with that of the original Felton Depot. The General Store is also an exact replica of early Americana and one can spend much time here reminiscing with goods purchasable during earlier times. The site of Roaring Camp itself lies within 30 feet of the original South Pacific Coast Railroad right-of-way built in 1879 and is also within walking distance of the Henry Cowell Big Trees. There are many hiking trails which honeycomb the property, and the original Graham Hill to Big Trees stagecoach road is visible in many places. The views from close-by vantage points of the San Lorenzo Valley can not be duplicated. Finally, there are many first-growth redwood trees filling out the surrounding forest that are only slightly bigger than they were over a hundred years ago when Cowell, Davis, Graham, and Hihn first walked the very same property.

Today, Roaring Camp continues. Daily steam train service is available throughout the year with at least one scheduled train a day except during bad weather. It takes only one hour for this trip through yesteryear. After you've done it, you truly come away with the feeling that steam-powered narrow gauge railroading is alive and well in the Santa Cruz Mountains, and it will continue to be in the future.

The train from Bear Mountain arrives. — Rick Hamman

Above: Down home country music makes the day at Roaring Camp. — Rick Hamman

Below: Nestled deep in the redwoods, the Heisler works the train down from Bear Mountain. — Rick Hamman

The "Dixianna" Shay crosses Cork Screw Loop. — Rick Hamman

The "Dixianna" Shay roams the lands of the San Lorenzo redwoods darting in and out of the shadows caused by mammoth trees which block the sun's rays from striking the ground. — Rick Hamman

California Division of Forestry firefighters along with volunteers stand helplessly by while Roaring Camp trestles No. 2 & 3 burn at Spring Canyon. — Ron Rohrer, Courtesy: Valley Press

The old pot belly stove warms the inside of the Roaring Camp Depot shortly after a light winter snow had dusted the Felton Meadow. — Rick Hamman

Roaring Camp's President, Norman Clark, strikes a dapper pose while coupling up No. 3 to the company's covered coach. — Courtesy: Bruce MacGregor

The 70-ton, three-truck Shay "Sonora" off the famed Westside Lumber Company is Roaring Camp's latest addition to its roster of classic operating steam locomotives. — Photo by Phil Reader

Ex D & RGW switcher No. 50, now used in helper service, relaxes at the enginehouse after a hard day's work. — Rick Hamman

The Kahuku and diesel #50 head a train into Roaring Camp after just making the switch at McSkunk Junction. — Rick Hamman

A put on? No! The Little Green School at Roaring Camp is an ongoing private institution that combines the best of the old with that of the new to provide quality education. Shown here the school's principal and teacher, Rich Mills, and his student body take time out to pose for the camera. — Rick Hamman

The Heisler just down from Bear Mountain pauses in the bright sunlight while the conductor runs to set the McSkunk Junction switch for the left track into Roaring Camp. — Rick Hamman

The Future

On Sunday, December l9th, 1971, the following editorial appeared in the Santa Cruz Sentinel newspaper:

Out Of The Past ...

Editor: Who is this that calls me from my vanished past? For what purpose do you disturb my slumber? Why do you again beckon my service after such a long demise? How can 1, who was superseded by your asphalt and concrete paths of privacy and convenience, ever again hope to be your servant? After all, there are but a few of you who know me well. Who knows that my primary purpose for existence is to improve the economic and physical condition of the environment in which you live? Who knows that I do not take up unnecessary recreational space that could be used by you for enjoyment rather than a place to park your tinware? Who knows that the air I breathe, both in and out, is free from defilement? Who knows that I can run and hum in relative silence? Who knows that my feet are capable of traveling the route of the iron compass at velocities far exceeding those of my precedessors? And, who knows that my interior can be clean, comfortable, and inviting; inviting to the point that you might be willing to give up your privacy and convenience and come join me in mood of tranquility and relaxation while I once again convey you through the awe inspiring Santa Cruz Mountains to the Pacific Ocean and the beach at Santa Cruz?

Ah, yes, it is well that you dream of me once more, but I doubt very seriously if I will ever again see the day when I replace that Tin God you call the automobile as an alternative to your transportation needs.

So let me sleep in my vanished past and disturb me not lest ye come to your senses and realize your responsibility for, rather than reign over, your environment.

"The Ghost of the Suntan Special" as told to; William H. Anderson.

Recently, a group of citizens from all walks of life had become concerned about the future transportation policies of Santa Cruz and Santa Clara Counties. They saw the dwindling fuel supplies over the next 20 years; they saw the increasing pressure that heavier traffic on Highway 17 was bringing for a new freeway, and thus, increased and unwanted growth; they saw the air they were breathing becoming more foul; they saw more and more of their valued open space being given up to asphalt and concrete; and finally, they saw the need for an integrated transportation system that would encompass all forms of transportation, not just the automobile. To that end, the Modern Transit Society, as they called themselves, set out to turn things around. Almost immediately a plan was set forth to start looking at alternatives.

One alternative which drew immediate attention was the idea of rebuilding the old mountain route for modern electrified light rail transit service between San Jose and Santa Cruz. To make a long story short, this idea was kicked around for almost two years before it finally caught the public's attention. All of a sudden in 1973, the country fell into a gas crisis and getting from here to there became more complicated. People going back and forth over the hill began to say, "Hey, maybe these folks pushing this Suntan revival proposal have something." Push came to shove, and within a year local officials had jumped into action. Shortly thereafter, the California Legislature had passed and the Governor had signed a bill authorizing that a $75,000 feasibility study be conducted as to reopening the hill.

By the time the study had been completed a year later in December of 1976, many of the Santa Cruz County public officials had become disenchanted with the proposition. While they mostly agreed with its concept, they disagreed as to whether it would be more of a detriment rather than a betterment for the county. The contention was that their primary concern was to protect the over-all quality of life within the county. If a rail line were re- established over the hill, it would induce a greater influx of people and thereby increase growth and decrease the quality of life. This was something they didn't want, and it certainly was something they didn't need. As a result, the proposal was shelved. For the time being anyway, the County government has assumed the posture that no expansion of existing transportation corridors or development of alternate transit along Highway 17 will best serve to slow growth.

Probably in the long term of things to come, the future energy and environmental problems will far outweigh the worries over growth. For after all, by shelving the proposal, they did not solve the very problems that caused its inception in the first place, they only deferred their solution until a later date. Someday, the railroad in some form or another will no doubt return. Two interesting possibilities have already arisen which give testimony to this.

Included in the over the hill feasibility study for comparison was the route of the post-1940 Suntan Special via Watsonville Junction. While the Santa Cruz County government had expressed no interest in reopening the mountain route, the idea of reinstating the Suntan was greeted with great enthusiasm. It was felt that starting up the Suntan on Saturdays and Sundays might relieve some of the traffic on Highway 17 and solve some of the automobile congestion at the beach. Also, because of the time involved and because of the fact it would only be run on weekends, it would in no way affect population growth. As of this writing, steps have been taken to pursue such a possibility.

Due to current social and community pressures involving local transportation, Amtrak had been requested to reinstate the Del Monte just as soon as details and financing can be worked out among the cities and counties involved. Santa Cruz County, being one of them, has asked if the train might be split at Watsonville Junction on a daily basis and brought into Santa Cruz. While only in the talking stages, it definitely shows that people have not forgotten what a valuable resource the railroad is.

Rail passenger traffic however is not the only future possibility for Santa Cruz County. Already underway is the complete modernization of the coast leg of the branch from Santa Cruz to Davenport. The Lone Star Davenport cement plant, due to dwindling supplies of natural gas, is converting over to a coal fired system. As a result, 80 to 100 additional carloads of coal per week will be coming up the Coast from Santa Cruz. At the same time, the Granite Rock quarry at Wilder has started to ship more sand. Also, more light manufacturing facilities are developing all along

the branch and this is leading to increased carloads. It is predicted that in the near future the Southern Pacific may have to go back to operating a switcher out of Santa Cruz as there is too much work to be done by the one lone train crew each day. Already, train lengths of 35 to 40 cars with total weights of 4,000 tons are moving back and forth between Santa Cruz and Watsonville. Finally, Pacific Gas & Electric Company has proposed a new coal fired power plant on the coast above Davenport. While there are many environmental issues to be considered concerning the proposal, if it ever came to pass no doubt the S.P. line up the coast would be extended several miles further. And so, Santa Cruz, which had originally been a large lumber shipping point, would then become a coal center.

Only time and the tide of events will determine what the future really holds. Obviously, the Southern Pacific will have a great deal to say about whatever happens as much of it could and would involve their right-of-way and operations.

An empty Los Gatos-Santa Cruz railroad right-of-way perhaps could offer a possible solution to the Highway #17 automobile congestion. — Courtesy: Bruce MacGregor

286

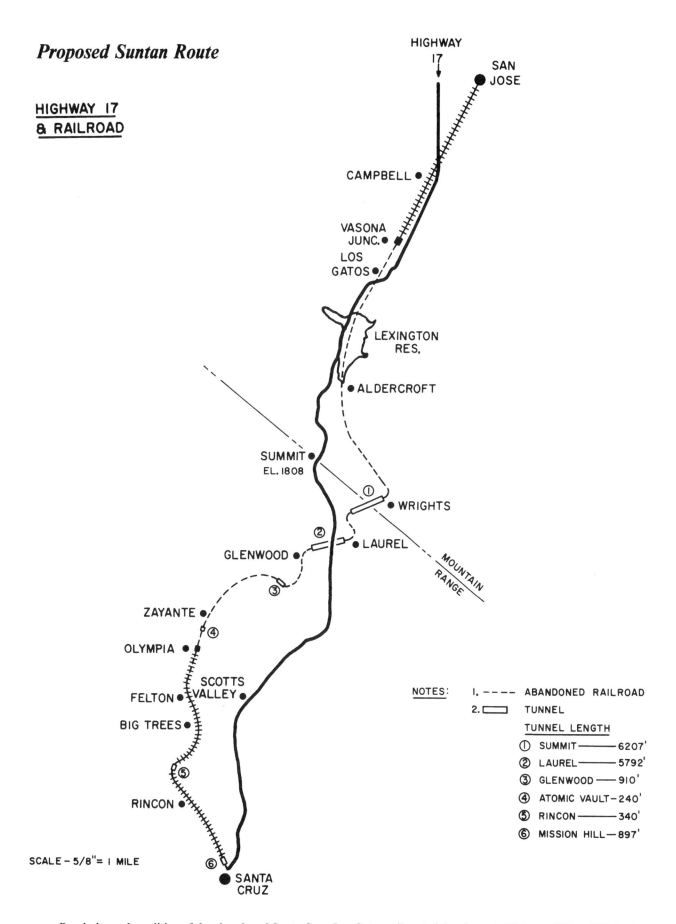

Proposed Suntan Route

HIGHWAY 17
& RAILROAD

HIGHWAY
17

SAN JOSE

CAMPBELL

VASONA
JUNC.

LOS
GATOS

LEXINGTON
RES.

ALDERCROFT

SUMMIT
EL. 1808

① WRIGHTS

② LAUREL

GLENWOOD

③

ZAYANTE

④

OLYMPIA

FELTON

SCOTTS
VALLEY

BIG TREES

⑤

RINCON

⑥

SANTA
CRUZ

MOUNTAIN
RANGE

SCALE – 5/8" = 1 MILE

NOTES: 1. - - - - ABANDONED RAILROAD
2. ▭ TUNNEL

TUNNEL LENGTH
① SUMMIT————6207'
② LAUREL————5792'
③ GLENWOOD——910'
④ ATOMIC VAULT–240'
⑤ RINCON————340'
⑥ MISSION HILL—897'

Proximity and condition of the abandoned Santa Cruz-Los Gatos railroad right-of-way to Highway #17. — V.K. Itani

Left: Boeing-Vertol sketch of a light rail electric Suntan Special which could be used over the mountain. — Courtesy: Glen Hughes

Right: Perhaps again someday these 70-year-old Summit Tunnel walls will echo to the sounds of a Los Gatos or Santa Cruz bound electric train. — Courtesy: Bruce MacGregor.

Left: Out of the past, into the future: approximately 400 highway miles from the Santa Cruz Mountains, on the eastern side of the Sierras, sits the nearly abandoned town of Keeler, California. For over half a century it served as the southern terminus for the very active S.P. Owens Valley narrow gauge operations. The day is Monday, November 7, 1977. The last of the narrow gauge cabooses aboard a Biggie truck is making a brief stop in front of the Keeler Depot. For the last 55 years this relic has been sitting on the Owens Valley floor collecting age and antiquity. Previous to that time it spent 18 years in local service. Previous to this period, it spent 23 years in service on the South Pacific Cost between Alameda and Santa Cruz, Boulder Creek and Felton. In order that future generations can keep in touch with the life and times of days gone by, the caboose is returning after 102 years to its original construction site, the Carter Brothers car shops in Newark, California. Hopefully, ex-South Pacific Coast-Southern Pacific caboose #47 will be restored to its 1875 condition. — Rick Hamman

This Seaboard Coastline experimental diesel rides the highiron along the Santa Cruz-Davenport branch in preparation for the coal trains which are to come. — Courtesy: Joe Faust

2:00 p.m., Wednesday, April 27, 1977: After 22 years of absence a proud Golden State Lady, No. 4449, returns from a triumphant tour on the head end of the American Freedom Train to the Pajaro Valley and the place through which she used to pass known as Chittenden. — Rick Hamman

The Centennial

Friday, May 7th, 1976 ...

It was still rather cool at 6:15 a.m. when my daughter Laurel and I started to drive the old convertible, top down, from Boulder Creek to the Southern Pacific Watsonville Junction yards at Pajaro. The thick fog, which had hung so close to the ground over most of the County for the last three days, had now dissipated into the atmosphere. As a result, the air was clear and fresh and the day was perfect for the events which were to follow.

Upon reaching the railroad yard at 7:15 a.m., we parked the car and walked over to the Trainmaster's office. It was a small two story S.P. yellow and brown building which had obviously seen much history in its prime. As we walked up the long flight of well worn wooden stairs I stopped to ponder how many hundreds of railroadmen over the years had trod these steps before me. When we reached the top of the staircase we were met by a well informed secretary who escorted us into a comfortable office overlooking the railroad yard. Here, we were greeted by Trainmaster Harold Fulkerson and others. Obviously a very busy man with a lot on his mind, we quickly passed through the social amenities and were introduced to Engineer Blair Kough who would be at the throttle of the days events. After a brief farewell Engineer Kough led us out of the building and into the holding yard where several freight engines of various sizes, shapes, and classifications were sitting at the ready.

As we walked along the oil saturated path between the many parked diesel locomotives we began to anticipate the beginning of a special day. At last, we came to the three locomotives which were to be on the first train in the second hundred years of railroading in Santa Cruz County. There they stood, three freshly painted red and gray General Motors GP-9 diesels which would represent the original Santa Cruz Railroad engines, the Pacific, the Jupiter, and the Betsy Jane, in the day's events. Their quiet rumblings seemed to signal another time just one hundred years ago when a new Baldwin engine, "The Pacific," sat in approximately the same location about to go through similar circumstances. Locomotive number 3820 would be the lead engine with numbers 3396 and 3834 to follow. Engineer Kough informed us that he had asked those involved to furnish him with the best locomotives available. Judging from the results, they had done just that.

It was now 7:45 a.m. With flags, banners, bunting and signs Engineer Kough, my daughter, and myself decorated locomotive No. 3820. As a final historical touch we clipped two signs on the front and side hand irons which appropriately read "Pacific & Jupiter."

At 8:30 a.m., the engines moved out of the holding area and into the yard where they were coupled up to the twenty-seven car consist which made up the day's train. Shortly thereafter, the rest of the crew, Conductor Robert Dickie; Brakeman Jerry Cordoza; and Brakeman John Collins, joined the train. At 8:45 a.m., the Southern Pacific-Santa Cruz County Railroad Centennial Train signaled goodbye to Pajaro and began to inch its way out of the yard and on to its first destination.

By the time my daughter and I reached the Pajaro River Bridge at the county line near the end of Walker Street in Watsonville, about one hundred people had gathered. The Watsonville Wildcat band was playing up tempo tunes. People, for the most part, were standing around reminiscing about the past. Among others, Mr. Dickie, who had himself put in an untold number of years in the service of the Southern Pacific, was there to see the train. I couldn't help but notice a small sense of tearful pride in his elderly eyes as he told me that his son, Conductor Dickie on today's train, had twenty-five years of service in, and that his grandson had seven. Other people present included parents and their smaller children, many retired railroad employees, curious onlookers, and local officials.

At 9:00 a.m. Al Schadel and Derek Reynen of the County Historical Museum, and organizers of the event, strung a red, white, and blue ceremonial ribbon across the S.P. Pajaro River railroad bridge. A moment later Engineer Kough began blowing the air horn on the lead S.P. diesel as it rounded the curve and approached the bridge from the opposite side of the river. Foot by foot the Centennial Train creeped across the bridge until it came to a stop just short of the ribbon. After a brief ceremony was held, Santa Cruz County Supervisor Cecil Smith and Watsonville Vice Mayor Rex Clark cut the ribbon, and the first train of the second hundred years proceeded on its journey into Santa Cruz County. From Watsonville the next stop would be Aptos.

The town had been decorated in every imaginable manner of red, white, and blue. Hundreds of school children and their older counterparts had gathered trackside to witness the commemoration of one hundred years of railroading in Santa Cruz County. The local high school band was present stomping out rousing marches and other current festive music. Everywhere one looked one saw signs that people such as Chamber of Commerce President Chuck Holcomb and Secretary Terry Streller had put lots of time and energy into making this a special occasion that would long be remembered. Hundreds of colorful balloons had been furnished to the children. Several of the Town's local citizens had dressed up in costumes befitting the ceremonies which were held here on May 7th, 1876.

Earlier, some people had scoffed at the idea of getting excited about a dumb old freight train with a few flags on it. They, unfortunately, did not understand the message behind it. The train was simply a conveyance that allowed people in the Bicentennial year a way to re-establish their roots in the community and country.

The time had come. It was a small boy standing trackside who first shouted, "I heard the whistle." Far off in the distance Engineer Blair Kough began to let people know the train was coming. Little by little the rumbling of the three diesels filled the air as they approached closer and closer. The air horn, with each blast, grew louder and louder. All eyes were cast toward the Valencia Creek bridge. All at once, there it was. Out of the redwood trees came engine 3820, with its thirteen star flag on one side and the Bicentennial flag on the other, rounding the curve onto the Valencia Creek bridge. People began to shout with excitement. Just as the first engine hit the bridge the sun spotlighted its bright red Bicentennial front. Slowly, Engineer Kough inched his way into the enthusiastic crowd which had gathered all along the right-of-way in downtown Aptos. Finally, as he brought the big freight to a brake screeching halt in front of the old Bay View Hotel, he was greeted with the applause of everyone.

As has always been the case, it was the engines the children were interested in. Realizing this, Conductor Dickie and Engineer Kough opened up the cab of the lead engine and allowed many of the school children (and adults posing as school children) to pass through and inspect the locomotive. At the same time many older citizens posed in front of the engine for that special photograph that would say I was there back in "76" when ...

Eventually, all the speeches had been given and the ceremonies attended to. Engineer Kough gave a long blast on the air horn and the train crew commenced to get on with the business of moving down the line toward Santa Cruz. Just as the train was about to move, Lucille Aldrich, a local resident in costume, layed down in the middle of the track as she had done some years previous while protesting a road closure by the Southern Pacific. This time, however, it was in jest. Conductor Dickie and Brakemen Collins and Cordoza, caught up in the frivolity of the whole affair, went through the animated motions of being angry. Finally, the lady was helped to her feet by courteous S.P. officials and the train proceeded on its way.

As the train moved on to Santa Cruz several people were waiting along its route to take a photograph, get a glimpse of a rare railroad special in the County, or just break the monotony of a Friday. Near 17th Avenue in Santa Cruz the train stopped to cut out some cars on a siding. By the time it had

started up again teacher Gerald Boudreaux and 380 students from nearby Del Mar School had gathered trackside to observe this red, white, and blue centennial recreation. As the train crossed the San Lorenzo River bridge into Santa Cruz several photographers had positioned themselves on the rooftops of nearby buildings and along the track to record the arrival for posterity.

Finally, at about 10:30 a.m. the nose of 3820 poked around the curve at Blackburn Terrace and the train came to a stop in front of the 83 year old Santa Cruz Depot. Thus, the first train in the second Century of railroading in Santa Cruz County had completed its run from Watsonville Junction (Pajaro) to Santa Cruz. The date; May 7th, 1976 ...

While the first run had now been completed there still was something missing from this historic commemorative occasion. At about the same time the Santa Cruz Railroad had originally built their line, the Santa Cruz and Felton Railroad had also built a connecting branch from Santa Cruz to Felton. It was this line in connection with the Santa Cruz Railroad that opened up all the lumbering and lime operations in the San Lorenzo Valley. Therefore, it was only fitting that the Santa Cruz and Felton Railroad should also be acknowledged.

And so it was that at 11:30 a.m. Conductor Dickie began to make up the regular freight train for Felton. Ironically, engine No. 3, 3834, was cut off the rear end and placed on a siding. Today there would be just two diesel locomotives pulling the train up the San Lorenzo Canyon, one carrying the sign "Santa Cruz" and one carrying the sign "Felton."

By 11:45 a.m. the completed train sat in front of the Santa Cruz Depot where many people had gathered to witness this second leg of the ceremonies. A local high school band was on hand to play. Different people were posing for photographs in front of the centennially decorated engine. Once again many elderly citizens were reminiscing about the "good" old days. Mr. Macy, who had previously been in the drayage business, summed up the feelings of most of those who were present when he said; "For thirty-five years this station and the railroading connected with it helped provide my family with a good portion of our livelihood. I have many fond memories of the events which took place here over the years and this special day only serves to bring them to mind."

At 12:15 p.m. local dignitaries, S.P. officials, and retired railroad personnel, along with many Santa Cruz residents gathered for a brief salute to one hundred years of railroading in Santa Cruz County. A short history was given along with several anecdotes from retired Engineer Harold Soper as to the life and times involved. Finally, a few words were said as to the future of railroading in the County and the ceremonies

The Southern Pacific-Santa Cruz County Centennial train sits poised on the Pajaro River Bridge about to enter the County for the first time in the second one hundred years of railroading. — Rick Hamman

were over. The crew boarded the train bound for Felton and the final event of the day was about to take place.

Nothing could be more fitting for the conclusion of the days events, and this book, than to involve a steam locomotive in the celebrations. Fortunately, such was a possibility. As previously mentioned, the original S.P. Felton Depot was now owned by the Roaring Camp and Big Trees Narrow Gauge Railroad Company. By coincidence, a spur coming off the S.P. mainline near the depot ran into a section of three rail track that was both broad gauge and narrow gauge. Thus, the stage would soon be set. The old would be joined with the new to commemorate the span of time from May 7th, 1876 to May 7th, 1976.

At about 1:15 p.m. people began to gather at the Felton Depot. All were waiting for the first sounds of the S.P. freight train as it worked its way up the San Lorenzo Canyon. As with all the previous stops along the way, people were again reminiscing about the times when ... There was Mrs. Ley who had lived in Felton most of her life. She told of the many times she had boarded the train at Felton bound for San Francisco or Santa Cruz. She also talked about the spur which used to go over to Old Felton and the lime kilns where many of her relatives had worked. Also present was Doug Sarmento, a long time resident of Boulder Creek. He reminisced about the many times he had stood in the exact same spot fifty years previous waiting for the train to Boulder Creek and about the activities that went on around the Felton Depot. Likewise, there was Ed Paulsen, now a mechanic for Roaring Camp, who used to be the mechanic on the Shay at the Santa Cruz Lumber Co. mill in Pescadero Canyon. In addition, there was Art Albach, President of the Santa Cruz County chapter of the National Association of Retired Railroad Employees, who himself had put in twenty-nine years working in and around Watsonville Junction. Finally, there was Bruce MacGregor, author of two books on the South Pacific Coast, and his son Haig who were there to photograph this special occasion.

And then, off in the distance, the faint echoes of the S.P. sand train, working its way up the 3.54 percent San Lorenzo Canyon grade, were first heard. In a matter of minutes Engineer Kough was laying on the air horn as the two unit freight crossed the San Lorenzo River bridge and entered the Henry Cowell Big Tree grove. When the two big GP-9 diesels emerged from the grove and approached the Roaring Camp Depot, Fireman Tom Shreve aboard the little 0-4-0 narrow gauge "Kahuku," which had just come down the mountain, began to blow its whistle in return. Soon, the atmosphere was filled with the sounds of pulsating air and hot steam. As the two EMD locomotives slowly passed by Roaring Camp and moved through the Felton Meadow, the brakes were ever so gently applied. Carefully, the Centennial train approached the three rail spur at Felton. Brakemen Collins and Cordoza jumped down from the diesels and set the two switches necessary for the train to enter the area. Inch by inch the big 56 foot long diesels entered the spur testing the well rusted rail until they came to within three feet of the derailer. They paused. Next, the "Kahuku whistled and steamed into the depot area from Roaring Camp. As it stopped, Roaring Camp Conductor Ed Stollery jumped down from the engine and through the switch onto the adjoining three rail track. Then, the little Kahuka inched its way forward to the end of the narrow gauge portion of the three rail spur, about two feet short of the S.P. GP-9. Engineer Kough climbed back into the cab; with the guidance of the two train crews, S.P. officials, the crowd, and a little luck, he inched the 120 ton engines two feet further until the two locomotives touched noses with each other. Thus, the old had joined hands with the new to celebrate one hundred years of railroading in Santa Cruz County. On the left sat the "Kahuku," which was about the same size as the original "Betsy Jane;" on the right sat the modern General Motors Diesel of Today.

At 1:45 p.m. an area was cleared in front of the two locomotives so that all could get a final picture of the event. Shortly thereafter, all the participants were introduced, a few short speeches were given, and the ceremony was concluded. The big General Motors GP-9 diesels backed off the spur onto the main line and proceeded up the branch to Mt. Hermon, Olympia and, perhaps again someday, to Los Gatos.

Santa Cruz County Supervisor, Cecil Smith, on the left holds the ribbon while the Vice Mayor of Watsonville, Rex Clark, cuts same to celebrate the beginning of the day's events. — Rick Hamman

The crew of the Centennial train looks on while S.P. officials remove Lucille Aldrich from in front of the engine. — Rick Hamman

The "Kahuku" sits on 3-rail track about to touch noses with its modern diesel counterpart at Roaring Camp. — Courtesy: Bruce MacGregor

Past and present S.P. employees pose in front of the Centennial Train at Santa Cruz. Left to right: Engineer, Fred Hinman; Carman, Eldridge Dickie; Station Agent, Syb Berdhal; Engineer, Jerry McCabe; Fireman and Photographer, Fred Stoes; Engineer, Harold Soper; Conductor, Robert Dickie, Brakeman, Jerry Cordoza; Brakeman, John Collins. — Rick Hamman

Eldridge Dickie poses with son Robert Dickie and the profession of railroadman continues through the family. — Courtesy: Bruce MacGregor

The crews of the old and the new pose for a final photo at Roaring Camp. Left to right: Engineer, Tom Shreve; Conductor, Ed Stollery; Conductor, Robert Dickie; Brakeman, Jerry Cordoza; Brakeman, John Collins; Engineer, Blair Kough. — Courtesy: Bruce MacGregor

7

THE SANTA CRUZ BRANCH RECENTLY

Santa Cruz, Big Trees & Pacific Railway

During the 1981 heavy-sand-shipping season for the quarries at Olympia, the Southern Pacific raised their freight rates by one-third. The reported reason was to recover increased maintenance costs on the branch from Olympia to Santa Cruz. At the same time, they left the rates unchanged to the quarry operator at Wilder on the Davenport Branch. As the highly competitive sand market was dependent on the best freight rates, the Olympia quarries soon went to shipping by truck at a cost near the former rate. With no customers remaining on the Olympia Branch, its future need was questionable.

Some say that because of an older hopper car fleet on which they did not want to spend money to replace, because sand produced a lower commodity dollar, and because its heavy weight and slow transportation speed impacted maintenance and operation of its coast main line, the Southern Pacific developed the higher freight rate to drive customers away and allow eventual branch abandonment.

Like so many times before in the history of Santa Cruz County railroading, the winter rains of 1981-82 would cause substantial damage to the Olympia Branch. Because of this, the line was temporarily embargoed from future use. As there was no traffic, rather than repair the line the Southern Pacific petitioned the Interstate Commerce Commission for its abandonment.

Enter F. Norman Clark, founder of Roaring Camp. Back in the early 1960's when Mr. Clark first proposed acquiring the line for tourist purposes, the Southern Pacific was not interested. Now, some twenty years later, however, the opposite was the case. After three years of fruitful negotiation, on August 12, 1985, the Santa Cruz, Big Trees & Pacific Railway, under the leadership of Mr. Clark, became the fourth owner of the 110-year-old line. Purchased for $800,000, the 8.8-mile line stretched from Taylor St. (elevation 10 ft.) in Santa Cruz to the former site of Eccles (north of Felton; elevation 425 ft.). Included in the purchase were trackage rights into the Santa Cruz Southern Pacific Yard for interchange purposes and access to the Boardwalk.

On October 12, 1985, the first makeshift flatcar passenger train, pulled by the old Olympia Quarry Whitcomb diesel (No. 20), made an inaugural run along the San Lorenzo River from Roaring Camp to Rincon. Clark, with much effort, hoped to have the line reopened all the way to Santa Cruz for tourist and freight service by the following summer.

By early December, Clark and his stalwart crew were hard at it in the San Lorenzo River Canyon, repairing the storm damaged railroad. The canyon this time of year was dark, cold and wet. In general, it was a place where dampness, mud and muck was the day to day working environment. After many such work days Norman Clark was to catch a cold. The cold would unfortunately turn into pneumonia from which he would not recover.

Over the last 25 years F. Norman Clark's dream of bringing to life early railroading history in the form of actual operation had inspired many friends. With Norman's death, they continued in his spirit. His wife, Georgiana, assumed the leadership role and has remained the company's Chief Executive Officer from then to the present.

By July 4th, 1986 the SCBT&P was in active tourist operation to the old Union Depot in Santa Cruz. With the 1987 season the Boardwalk was reached.

Left: Long time SCBT&P and former SP engineer "Junior" O'Lague, in the baseball cap, talks to a Boardwalk patron while the train waits for the return of passengers for the early evening trip to Roaring Camp. — Rick Hamman

Below: Karl Koenig leans out the cab window on the first freight load and mixed train as it passes through Rincon. — Rick Hamman

On August 4, 1989 the first test boxcar was run from Santa Cruz to Felton and back with success. The following August 16th the first freight load was carried in mixed train service. Destined for the San Lorenzo Lumber Company at Felton, the 95,000-pound flatcar load from Molalla Quad/Band Mill near Eugene, Oregon made the trip without incident.

During the winter of 1993, strengthening of the 367-foot tunnel #6 just south of Felton was being accomplished. On January 21st, a fire started from an unknown origin and the timber in the tunnel started to burn. By the time the fire department got there a goodly blaze from both ends was in process. The fire chief in charge, however, thought they would be able to save it. Little did they know that the water heavy soil above the tunnel was about to move. All at once a tall pine tree, butt first, started sliding down the mountain from 100 feet above the ground over the top of tunnel. It stopped over the tunnel, fell straight down through its roof and created a hole that acted like a chimney. The tunnel literally exploded when the extra oxygen hit the fuel already in flames.

With the tunnel destroyed, the line was closed. In short order, it was decided to reuse the original Santa Cruz & Felton narrow gauge cut around the tunnel. By March 21, 1993 the cut had been cleaned and realigned for standard gauge service. With a tight 21 degree curve required in one particular 140 foot section and two 20 degree curves of over 50 ft., the line was reopened much as it had been in the late 1870's and has functioned ever since. The tunnel was filled and abandoned after 113 years of continuous use.

Left: Track workers align the rail and force it in place around the 21 degree curve in the old Santa Cruz & Felton cut. — Rick Hamman

Right: Fresh ties and 110 pound rail go together as workers attach track bolts to rail joints. — Rick Hamman

297

The afternoon Redwood Express crosses the concrete arch at Inspiration Point northbound to Roaring Camp. — Rick Hamman

In 1995 tourist passenger service was extended to special trains from Mount Hermon a mile above Roaring Camp. In 1996 periodic Mount Hermon service to Santa Cruz was begun.

During the first ten years of SCBT&P service they went from a short 2.5 mile operation with antiquated flatcars and a small switching diesel to an excellently running short line. For motive power the company acquired two strong running CF7, 1,500 horsepower, General Motors diesel locomotives from the Santa Fe (2600 & 2641). Four period passenger cars — two steel 1927 Jersey Central commute coaches, a 1902 wooden combine and coach, originally off the Boston & Maine — were acquired from the East Coast. Eight additional flatcars were acquired for maintenance service and open vista coach conversion from the Spreckels Sugar Company at Salinas. Recently, four more steel flatcars were purchased from the McCloud Railroad for more open-vista cars.

Primary service during the summer season sees two passenger round trips a day from Roaring Camp, and selected service from Mount Hermon, to the Santa Cruz Boardwalk. Likewise, special trains like the annual "Concert in the Park" at Big Trees, the Christmas season trains, and private group excursions round out the passenger service. Periodic freight service, usually about twice a week, continues to be provided for the lumber Company.

Roaring Camp & Big Trees Narrow Gauge Railroad

As of 2002 the RC&BTNGRR was celebrating its 39th year of successful operation. Although F.

Norman Clark probably did not consider the possibility when he first began operations in 1963, the railroad is now the longest running narrow gauge ever to operate in the Central Coast area. Oftentimes during the summer season, weekend and weekday operations ridership exceeds 1,000 daily riders. With its steam locomotive roster now at six engines, the ASME (American Society of Mechanical Engineers) has designated Roaring Camp as a historic mechanical site.

No matter how you view Roaring Camp (some say it is just another amusement park), one thing is certain: on the property can be found several older men teaching younger men the time-honored technologies involved in the maintenance and operation of original eighty-year-old and older steam locomotives. Those locomotives continue to pull their historic trains over one of the last narrow gauge railroads left in the west to the delight of all who ride them. Thank you F. Norman Clark, and to Georgiana for continuing to pursue Norman's dream!

The Eccles & Eastern Railroad

On June 22, 1988, Karl Koenig (then superintendent of the SCBT&P), his wife Burneda, my wife Carol Hamman, and myself incorporated the Eccles & Eastern Railroad. Our first stock holder and long time Roaring Camp maintenance and operation associate, Jack Hanson, was elected Vice President of Maintenance. Also included were James Garcia, Jon Sirrine and Bob Gelini. The purpose of the E&ERR was to reopen the line between the current end of track at Eccles (north of Felton) and

The bell and headlight of the Eccles & Eastern #2706 adorn Jack Hanson's old Ford pickup truck parked in front of a new Amtrak streamliner. On this day Jack was maning the California Central Coast Transportation Museum information booth. — Rick Hamman

299

Los Gatos to relieve local highway congestion, provide alternative passenger service, return at least 50% of the sand and aggregate haul back to train transport and away from slow moving trucks, improve air quality, and lesson natural resource use

For the next four years we worked diligently examining all of the possible routings, the many engineering changes that would be required, all of the environmental constraints, the political realities, and the actual costing of the project. There were many obstacles, the primary being people's attitudes: "You people are dreamers. You will never be able to do this."

We determined that as of 1992 it was possible to re-lay track to complete the line using abandoned right-of-way and four miles of realignment near Los Gatos without having to displace a single person. Most of the culverts were still in place and working 50 years after abandonment. Many of the concrete bridge supports still standing could be reused. For the most part, the two large tunnels were still useable, requiring only cleanup of 1989 earthquake damage and shotcreting. Less than 10% of the former right-of-way would require substantial rework. It was estimated the line could be reopened from Eccles to the south end of Lexington Reservoir, 16-miles, for from $12,000,000 to 20,000,000 depending on engineering choices. The real money, not included in the above estimate, was in the realignment around the reservoir, through a 2,500 ft. tunnel and then along Highway 17 to end of track in Los Gatos.

In 1976 a Caltrans Study had estimated the entire project could be done for from $35,000,000 to 85,000,000, depending primarily on operating equipment choice. Using an excellent railroad engineering company for reference, our 1992 estimates came in at from $110,000,000 to $150,000,000. Using those Capital numbers with projected long term debt, operating expenses and freight and passenger revenues, the project was considered doable with a conservative estimate of a consistent 8% to 12% annual profit. What all this meant, and still means, is that a private corporation could entirely fund this public utility with private money at potentially no cost to the taxpayer.

As the company continued and more stock holders came on board, it was becoming obvious to others that "maybe this could happen!" Wanting to get started, we concluded that by using trucks to bring the product to train and then routing that train around through Watsonville to the San Francisco Bay Area on the currently operating tracks, sufficient revenue could be made to make even this interim service work. The Southern Pacific indicated that now that we were responsible for the San Lorenzo right-of-way, the freight rate could be readjusted downward.

In June of 1994 we signed a trackage rights agreement with the SCBT&P to use their upper track for sand loading purposes and their right-of-way to Santa Cruz for our trains to haul to the Southern Pacific interchange yard. We next began improving the SCBT&P to carry the heavier freight loads. During the following three months we arranged such interchange with the Southern Pacific, we developed a customer base, initially in San Francisco, and we began to line up rollingstock. By September of 1994 we were ready to ship the first 10,000 test tons using leased Southern Pacific hopper cars. Four days before the trains were to begin E&ERR had to cancel the operation because Santa Cruz County informed us we would have to have a "Level Four Permit" to load sand from truck to train. Acquiring it would take two public hearings and probably a year to at a cost of about $20,000, even though nowhere else in California was such a permit required. Further, they informed the quarries that if they now considered shipping directly by train or truck to train, their mining permits would have to be reviewed.

In parallel to what the E&ERR was trying to accomplish, although not connected in any way, a joint $100,000 federally funded study was going on by Santa Clara and Santa Cruz counties. They were updating the 1976 Caltrans study by looking at using the same and a couple of new adjacent corridors for passenger service to Santa Cruz. A few people who objected to what we wanted to do because of the close proximity of our track to their houses began opposing our plan. Further, a group in Aptos did not want any increase in freight traffic through their neighborhood on the Southern Pacific line from Santa Cruz to Watsonville. The study and E&ERR's plans completely collapsed at a public hearing when a few vociferous opponents were able to stymie the study group.

Unwilling to fight the long fight, the E&ERR changed its name to the Sierra Pacific Coast Railway, invested its capital in the Sierra Railroad, and ended its hope of a Santa Clara — Santa Cruz counties rail operation. Only a determined and focussed public will can someday reactivate that rail line.

The 2-8-0 Southern Pacific #2706

On the positive side, one project of the E&ERR continues to go forward preserving a little local history. It had been hoped to run an old steam-powered excursion train through the mountains, much along the lines of the Suntan Special. To that end, in 1989 the Company acquired a 1904 ex-Southern Pacific Consolidated steam locomotive, No. 2706, from Ramsey Park in Watsonville. It was like many of its class that had historically run from Santa Cruz to San Jose over the mountain route. The engine was inspected and deemed rebuildable, although it had been clambered over on the playground for over 30 years. After working on it for four months to get it ready to move, October 17, 1989 was chosen as the transport date.

Perhaps our previous experiences should have warned the E&ERR to be careful before tempting fate. On that day the locomotive was successfully transported aboard a 12-independent-axled, 48-tire trailer from the park to a rail line a mile away. From there it was to go to its final destination at the E&E yard in Santa Cruz. Unluckily, at 5:04 that afternoon while 2706 sat waiting on the trailer, the 6.9 Loma Prieta Earthquake struck, the largest in California since 1906 and centered near Aptos. While everyone expected the worst, the locomotive rode it out with no serious effects. Some say it was the fact that it was on the trailer with all the independent axles that saved it. The ground where it had been at Ramsey Park was criss-crossed with cracks and had sunk over three feet by the time the earth had stopped shaking.

After finally getting the engine loaded on a flatcar, moved the 20 miles from Watsonville to Santa Cruz, and put back on a track in the Santa Cruz E&E yard, restoration was begun. From 1989 to 1996, under the careful leadership of Jack Hanson and the efforts of Darren Henley, Phil Reader, and others, the engine was brought back to a point where its full restoration was a certainty. While the Company moved on and had to give up the engine, a new group has renewed the effort and are looking forward to its full operastion perhaps as soon as 2004, 100 years after it was first built.

Future Passenger Service

When California propositions #108 and #111 were passed, they provided funding to all state counties for rail type service. For Santa Cruz County it amounted to about $11,000,000. This was both matching and grant type money depending on whether the service considered was intra or inter-county. As a result, in 1994 the county proceeded with a $297,000 study to determine how this money could best be spent, if at all, and what rail service could be accomplished.

Because the only existing rail lines within the county belonged to the Southern Pacific and the SCBT&P, the county used them for its basis. Also, because there was a public demand for extension of service to the University of California at Santa Cruz Campus, such service was included in the study. While there was much initial local uproar over some very expensive proposals, polls have indicated that a 65% or better support for some kind of service exists.

Southern Pacific Consolidated steam locomotive #2706 poses in the bright sunlight, September 14, 1951, 6 years before it would be retired to Watsonvilles's Ramsey Park for playground duty. In 1989, Eccles & Eastern RR moved it on a flatcar back to Santa Cruz and began the many thousands of hours of restoration work to return #2706 to active duty. — Photo by Stan Kistler

At the time Santa Cruz County was conducting its study, Monterey County was also doing one. The City of Watsonville, located at the midpoint for a potential service around the bay between the cities of Monterey and Santa Cruz, took its own look. Local Railfairs were held to gain public support and interest, several test trains have been run to gain data and the process continues as of this writing. The primary point of contention involving the Central Coast is that Monterey County and the City of Watsonville lean toward conventional train operation using existing equipment and technology. Santa Cruz County is taking a more futuristic viewpoint by supporting self-powered rail vehicles, light-rail, and developing transportation technologies.

In an effort to preserve the railroad transportation corridor for future transit use, the County proposed to the Southern Pacific that they sell them the line from Watsonville Junction to Davenport. The Southern Pacific plant rationalization department responded with a potential yes if details and price could be successfully negotiated. That process continues. It will probably entail the acquisition by the County and then the lease back of the right-of-way via trackage rights for continued Southern Pacific freight service.

The Suntan Special

As has been the case ever since the early 1880's, the Santa Cruz Beach and Boardwalk has long been a tourist draw for the San Francisco Bay area. From the time of the first rail connection into the county until the last Suntan Special in 1961, the railroad was a part of the transportation of those tourists. Because of long-standing highway congestion, the reinstatement of tourist rail service has since been proposed many times.

With the support of Caltrans, the County, the Seaside Company and several other cities and civic groups, talk was put into action in 1996. In preparation for potential 1997 service, a test Suntan Special and joint Amtrak tour train were run from San Jose to Santa Cruz on June 10th. On board the Saturday Suntan were over 1,000 round trip riders. On board the Amtrak special, which came over on Saturday and returned on Sunday, were another 300. Both trains were sold out several weeks before they ran.

Of historical significance: the Suntan Special was the first scheduled passenger train from San Jose to Santa Cruz in 35 years. The Amtrak Special was the first revenue streamline passenger train to ever enter the County. Because the Santa Cruz Big Trees and Pacific offered connecting service from the Boardwalk, several through passengers rode all they way from San Jose to the Henry Cowell Big Trees. That last happened in the early 1950's.

Only time will dictate the future for the Suntan Special. In 1927 George B. Hansen, District Passenger Agent at San Jose for the Southern Pacific, had made a proposal to San Francisco management. He told them that all the Peninsula commute cars were sitting idle in San Jose on Saturdays and Sundays. Why not put them to good use by running a special tourist train to the Big Trees and the Santa Cruz Beach Boardwalk on those days. Thus began the original Suntan Specials. Today the weekend traffic to Santa Cruz is impossible. The Peninsula commute cars remain idle on Saturdays and Sundays in San Jose. What if?

The End of an Era

For 127 years the Southern Pacific Transportation Company had an active presence in Santa Cruz County. Many local residents can trace their heritage back to previous company employees who made their living as a railroader. Many County residents are former Southern Pacific railroaders. Likewise, the expansion of the west, the direct political history of California and the historical development of local economics can all be tied to the success and failure of the Southern Pacific.

Because of the economics of the time, an ever more competitive transportation market, and just bad luck, the Daylight flag has fallen. On September 12, 1996 the once great Southern Pacific Lines was sold to the Union Pacific Railroad to avoid a continuing downward spiral. It is no more! No more Sunset logo, no more ladies in black, no more long standing heritage, no more track-side wisdom from the men and women who loved their railroad, no more emotional rail-fan entanglement. Good by old friend!

The Union Pacific Railroad is a well run company with a rich history all its own and an eye to the future. They have the talent, the resources and the skill necessary for the 21st Century. We look forward to the bright yellow, red, gray and silver diesel locomotives which will pull the trains that will bring the breath of new life to railroading in Santa Cruz County and the California Central Coast.

Left: The first streamline passenger train ever to grace Santa Cruz County is seen coming around the curve in Aptos, June 10, 1996. — Rick Hamman

Right: The modern Caltrans Suntan Special has arrived at the Boardwalk and patiently waits for the passengers enjoying the beach to return for the trip back to San Jose. — Rick Hamman

Appendix "A": Locomotive Rosters For Santa Cruz County Railroads

F.A. Hihn Company, 36-Inch Narrow Gauge

No.	Type	Builder	
1	0-4-2	Porter	purchased new sometime after 1886

No. 1 was first used at the Valencia Creek Mill until 1892. Transferred to Gold Gulch Mill at Felton where it saw service until 1898. Transferred next to the mill at Laurel. Dates and disposition hereafter unknown. Believed could have seen service at King's Creek Mill above Boulder Creek in 1906 as Hihn had a narrow gauge railroad there. This engine was also known as the "Betsy Jane" although it was not the same engine which served on the Santa Cruz Railroad.

Loma Prieta Railroad-S.P., 56 ½" Broad Gauge

No.	Type	Builder	Date Built	In Service
1	0-4-0	- - -	1874	late 1883
72	2-4-2T	S. P.	1883	1883-1885
80	2-4-2T	Baldwin	1884	1885-1898
382	2-4-2T	Baldwin	1884	early 1890's
384	2-4-2T	Baldwin	1884	early 1890's

No. 1   Engine No. 1, the Betsy Jane, served on the Loma Prieta R.R. during its construction. While a narrow gauge locomotive, it was used to construct a broad gauge right-of-way.

No. 72   This was the first broad gauge engine used on the Loma Prieta R.R. It was built by Stevens of the Southern Pacific in Sacramento from parts of three other engines. In 1891 it was renumbered 1157. In 1904 it was changed to 1004. Scrapped in 1905.

No. 80   Locomotive No. 80 was purchased new specifically for the Loma Prieta Railroad. In 1891 it was renumbered 1010. In 1906 it was transferred to the Sacramento Shops and became engine No. 1. In 1916 it was renumbered to MWV568 and was scrapped as such in 1929.

Loma Prieta Lumber Company Railroad, 30-inch Narrow Gauge

No.	Type	Builder	Cons. #	Date Built	Weight	Cyls.	Drivers	Cost
1	2-Trk. Shay	Lima	2590	10/4/12	22,000 lbs.	5"x8"	20"	$2,750
2	2-Trk Shay	Lima	1786	9/21/06	28,000 lbs.	6"x10"	22"	$4,000
3	0-4-0	Hall-Scott	(gas pwrd)		——	——	——	——

Notes:

No. 1   Owners: Molino Timber Company No. 1. Sold 1918 to Loma Prieta Lumber Company as No. 1. Leased to Santa Cruz Beach Railroad (Amusement Line). sold 1927 to unknown lumber operation at Bass Lake, California.

No. 2   Owners: Union Construction Company as No. 2, Jamestown, California. Sold to Empire City railway as No. 2, Strawberry, California. Sold 1918 to Loma Prieta Lumber Company as No. 2, Aptos, California. Sold 1927 to unknown lumber operation at Bass Lake, California.

There is some question regarding the actual disposition of these two shay's. Both the caretaker of the L.P.L. Co. property, after the mill closed down, and two former employees firmly state the engines went to Bass lake in 1927. There is no record, however, of these engines ever operating there. To further confuse the issue, a former scrapper claims to have torched one or both of them in the late 1920's. Also just recently, several people while hiking in the area have reported sighting such an engine rusting away in one of the remote gulches up Aptos Creek. No photograph of same has appeared, however. Could one still be in the canyon some place?

Molino Timber Company, 30" narrow gauge

No. 1: See Loma Prieta Lumber Company No. 1.

Ocean Shore Railway/Railroad: Southern Division, 56" Broad Gauge

No.	Type	Builder	Cons. #	Date Built	Weight	Cyls.	Drivers
1	4-4-0	Baldwin	5511	1880	——	16"x24"	——
2	4-4-0	Hinkley	1465	1881	——	16"x24"	——
3	4-6-0	Schenectady	1308	1881	89,000 lbs.	18"x24"	57"
4	2-6-0	Baldwin	23256	1903	91,000 lbs.	18"x24"	54"
5	2-6-0	Baldwin	32627	1908	124,000 lbs.	18"x24"	48"
6	2-6-0	Baldwin	32646	1908	124,000 lbs.	18"x24"	48"

Notes:

No. 1 Arrived in September of 1905 from the O.R. & N. as No. 15. Scrapped 1915.
No. 2 Arrived in November of 1905 from the O.R. & N. as No. 18. Scrapped sometime previous to 1910 when the crown sheet blew out at Majors.
No. 3 Arrived April of 1906 from the Southern Pacific. Scrapped 1915.
No. 4 Arrived November 1907 from the Quakestown & Eastern as No. 1. Sold 1922 to San Vicente Lumber Co. Operated at Cromberg, California from 1923 to 1928 for Nibley-Stoddard Lumber Co. Sold 1928 to Fruit Growers Supply Co. as No. 34. Renumbered to 3, scrapped 1942.
No. 5 Purchased new. Sold to Pacific Portland Cement Company as No. 2 in 1920. Operated at Pacific Portland Cement plant, San Juan Bautista, 1927-1929, as No. 5; operated at P.P.C. Co. plant Gerlach, Nevada as No. 5.
No. 6 Purchased new. Leased by San Vicinte Lumber Co., Swanton, California 1920-1922. Sold 1922 to Sierra Railway as No. 26. Sold to Davis Johnson Lumber Company as 26. Scrapped 1939.

Roaring Camp & Big Trees Narrow Gauge Railroad, 36-inch

No.	Type	Builder	Cons. #	Yr Built	Name	Cyls.	Drivers
1	2-Trk. Shay	Lima	2593	1912	Dixiana	10"x12"	29½"
2	2-Trk. Heisler	Stearns	1041	1899	Toulumne	15"x12"	36"
3	0-4-2T	Baldwin		1890	Kahuku		25½"
4	0-6-2T	Baidwin			— —		
"5"	2-Trk. Clmx.	Climax		1928	— —		
50	0-4-0 Diesel	Caterpillar	5132275		— —	— —	
7	3-Trk. Shay	Lima	2465	1911	Sonora	11"x12"	32"

Notes:

No.1 Built as a standard gauge, 56 1/2", locomotive. Owners: Alaculsy Lumber Co. as No. 3, Conasauga, Tenn. Sold 1917 to Tennessee Lumber Co. as No. 3. Sold 1919 to Southern Iron and Equipment Co. as No. 1466, Atlanta, Georgia. Resold same year to W.M. Ritter Lumber Co. as No. 3 (Smokey Mountain R.R. No. 3), Proctor, North Carolina. Converted to narrow gauge, 36", when transferred to company operations at McClure, Virginia. Sold 1938 to Coal Processing Corp. as No. 3, Dixiana, Virginia. Sold 1962 to Roaring Camp and Big Trees Narrow Gauge Railroad as No. 1, Felton, California.

No. 2 Built new as narrow gauge, 36", locomotive. Owners: Hetch-Hetchy & Yosemite Valley Railway No. 3, the "Thomas Bullock," Toulumne, California. Sold 1923 to Pickering Lumber Co. as No. 3. Sold 1934 to Westside Lumber Co. as No. 3. Converted by Westside to standard gauge locomotive in 1947. Sold 1958 to Pickering Lumber Co. as No. 3. Sold 1963 to Roaring Camp & Big Trees Narrow Gauge Railroad, Felton, California, where it was converted back to narrow gauge upon its arrival.

No. 3 Owners: New as No. 1, Kahuku Plantation Co., Oahu, Hawaii. Sold 1966 to Roaring Camp & Big Trees Narrow Gauge Railroad, Felton, California.

No. 4 This Baldwin saddletank engine is being stored and occasionally operated at Roaring Camp by a private owner. No information available as of this writing other than it was reboiled in 1940 under Baldwin extra order No. 104.

No. 5 Unofficially No. 5, this recent addition to the Roaring Camp roster, Sept. 1977, carries much historic value. It was the last Climax locomotive ever built. Although unrunnable since its last service in 1972 for the Pennsylvania company, the Carroll Park & Northwestern as No. 3, it promises a healthy future when rebuilt.

No. 50 This rare narrow gauge diesel comes to Roaring Camp from the famed Denver & Rio Grande Western.

No. 7 Altogether the Sonora has had seven owners since 1911 with the Westside Lumber Company being the longest. Roaring Camp acquired it in January, 1986 and it has been mostly active ever since.

San Juan Pacific Railway/California Central Railroad, 56 $^1/_2$" Broad Gauge

No.	Type	Builder	Date Built	In Service
208	4-4-0	Schenectady	1879	1907-1920
1462	4-4-0	Rogers	1887	1920-1927
5	2-6-0	Baldwin	1908	1927-1929

Notes:

208 Originally No. 2 on the S.P. of Arizona, 1885 became No. 82. In 1891 became S.P. No. 1313. Acquired by San Juan Pacific in 1907 as No. 208. Sold 1912 to California Central R.R. as No. 2. Scrapped in 1921.

1462 Originally Union Pacific No. 770, became U.P. No. 840 in 1892. Sold to Southern Pacific in 1901. Leased to California Central 1920-1927. Scrapped 1935.

5 Ex-Ocean Shore No. 5

In addition to the above, the California Central also maintained five narrow gauge locomotives for the cement plant at San Juan. They were a climax, two 0-4-OT Porters, and two Plymouth diesels.

Santa Clara Valley Mill & Lumber Co./California Timber Co., 36-inch

No.	Type	Name	Builder	Con. #	Date	Weight	Cylinders	Drivers
1	0-6-0	Dinkey	Porter	201	1874	20,000 lbs.	9½"x14"	30
2	0-4-OT	Kitty	Porter	3565	1906	37,000 lbs.	10"x16"	

Notes:

No. 1 The "Dinkey," formally the "Felton," served on both the line out of Boulder Creek and at Newell Creek. Altogether, it saw over 40 years of service in Santa Cruz County.

No. 2 Bought new, disposition unknown. Last saw service in 1913 at Newell Creek Operation.

In addition to the above locomotives, the S.C.V.M. & L. Co. also had two other locomotives that were buried in a slide in 1884 somewhere in Zayante Creek Canyon and are still there today. Their type and kind are unknown.

Santa Cruz & Felton Railroad, 36-inch

No.	Type	Name	Builder	Con. #	Date	Weight	Cylinders	Drivers
1	0-6-0	Santa Cruz	Porter	218	1875	20,000lbs.	9½"x14"	28"
2	0-6-0	Felton	Porter	201	1874	20,000lbs.	9 /2"x14"	30"

Notes:

No. 1 Bought New. Later construction engine for South Pacific Coast. Sold 1881 to Nevada & Oregon Railroad as No. 1. sold 1885 to Lake Valley R.R. as No. 4. to Lake Tahoe R.R. as No. 4. Sold 1890 to Nevada County Narrow Gauge as No. 4. Became stationary boiler 1916.

No. 2 Bought new. Later construction engine for the South Pacific Coast. Sold 1887 to the Santa Clara Valley Mill & Lumber Company as No. 1, Boulder Creek, California. 1904 it became No. 1 on the California Timber Co. Last known operation at Boulder Creek in 1914.

Santa Cruz Lumber Company, 56 1/2-inch Broad Gauge

No.	Type	Builder	Con. #	Date	Weight	Cylinders	Drivers
1	2-Trk.Shay	Lima	2461	1911	84,000 lbs.	10"x12"	29½"

Notes:

Original owner: Fresno Flume & Lumber Co. as No. 2, (Shaver Lake R.R. No. 2) Clovis, Calif. Sold 1919 to Shaver Lake Lumber Co. No. 2, and then leased to Southern California Edison until 1926. Sold then to San Joaquin & Eastern R.R. as No. 2, Cascade, Calif. Sold to Santa Cruz Lumber Co. as No. 1, 1930. Scrapped 1954.

Santa Cruz Portland Cement Co.

No.	Type	Builder	Con. #	Date	Weight	Guage
1	0-4-OT	Porter		1906	70,000 lbs.	56½"
2	0-4-OT	Porter	4390	1908	90,000 lbs.	56½"
(1) sec.	0-4-0 Elect.	Baldwin	41328	1914	36,000 lbs	36"
(2) sec.	0-4-0 Elect.	Baldwin	41329	1914	36,000 lbs.	36"

Notes:

1&2   Both Porter standard gauge locomotives, originally purchased new, were sold to the Henry J. Kaiser Co. at Oroville in 1922. No. 2 was resold to a private owner in Sacramento, Calif. in 1967.

1&2 sec.   Second No.'s 1 & 2 were purchased from the Gastinau Gold Mining Co. at Thane, Alaska in 1922. Each had two Westinghouse 90 horsepower electric motors. Both engines operated until August 27, 1970, when the line was abandoned.

In addition, the cement company operated four Porter 36" narrow gauge dinkies at the quarry from 1909 until 1922. Also, the company operated three storage-battery electric locomotives, two 6-ton and one 5-ton at the quarry in later years.

Santa Cruz Railroad, 36-inch Narrow Gauge

No.	Type	Name	Builder	Con. #	Date	Weight	Cylinders	Drivers
1	0-4-0	Betsy Jane	——		1874	10,000 lbs.	——	——
2	——	Neptune	——	——	——	——	——	——
3	4-4-0	Jupiter	Baldwin	3972	1876	44,000 lbs.	12"x 18"	42"
4	4-4-0	Pacific	Baldwin	3774	1875	40,300 lbs.	12"x 16"	42"

Notes:

1   The "Betsy Jane" was designed and built in San Francisco. It was believed listed on the company records as a donkey engine. Cost, $1,073,18. Disposition unknown other than it was shipped out of Watsonville Junction (Pajaro) in January of 1884 to either be scrapped or used in Central America on one of C.P. Huntington's railroads.

2   Not much is known about the "Neptune" except that it appears by name twice in local newspapers of the time and that according to S.C.R.R. records it cost about the same as did the "Jupiter" and the "Pacific," $7,000. could have been a third Baldwin 4-4-0 purchased second-hand. Baldwin has no record of it. Some claim it was only another name for the "Pacific."

3   Although labeled No. 3 from Baldwin, the "Jupiter" did not arrive until seven months after No. 4 the Pacific. Sold 1885 to Guatemala Railroads as No. 3. Renumbered No. 61 in 1904. Sold 1928 International Railways of Central America as No. 84. sold 1967 to Kennedy

Park, Washington, D.C. On display until 1975 when transferred to Smithsonian Institute for restoration and Bicentennial display in Philadelphia, 1976.

4   Disposition of the "Pacific" from the Santa Cruz Railroad is not known, however, according to Baldwin records, it was reboiled in 1904 for subsequent owner.

San Vicente Lumber Co., 56 1/2" Broad Gauge

No.	Type	Builder	Con. #	Date	Cylinders	Drivers
1	2-Trk. Shay	Lima	2058	6/13/08	11"x12"	35"
2	2-Trk. Shay	Lima	1745	8/31/06	11"x12"	32"
4	Ocean Shore No. 4					
6	Ocean Shore No. 6					

Notes:

1   Purchased new. Transferred to Nibley-Stoddard Lumber Co. as No. 1, Cromberg, California in 1923. (Same management and ownership as San Vicente Lumber Co.)

2   Acquired from Standard Lumber & Shingle Co. as No. 1, Clipper, Washington, in 1908. Transferred in 1923 to Nibley-Stoddard Lumber Co. same as No. 1.

4   Leased from Ocean Shore 1920-1922. Purchased from Ocean Shore 1922. Transferred to Cromberg operation in 1923.

6   Leased from Ocean Shore 1920-1922. Both Ocean Shore engines, No. 4 & No. 6, operated only between the transfer yard and the sawmill in Santa Cruz. Never were they on the hill.

Other Railroads Which Operated in Santa Cruz County but Not Mentioned:

South Pacific Coast Railroad: 25 locomotives, all 36" narrow gauge steam.

Pajaro Valley Consolidated Railroad: 12 locomotives, all 36" narrow gauge steam.

Granite Rock Quarry near Chittenden: 10 locomotives; eight 36" narrow gauge steam, two 56 1/2" broad gauge steam, and one diesel currently in operation.

Opposite page: Three Southern Pacific GP's work the morning inbound to Santa Cruz on the Schoolhouse Grade near Ellicott. — Courtesy: Bruce MacGregor

Bibliography

Newspapers:

The *Boulder Creek Log (1975)*, the *Boulder Creek Mountain Echo (1897-1916)*, the *Oakland Evening Tribune (1874- 1876)*, the *Palo Alto Times*, the *San Jose Daily Mercury*, the *San Jose News*, the *San Jose Weekly Mercury*, the *Santa Cruz Courier Item*, the *Santa Cruz Daily Surf* the *Santa Cruz Evening News*, the *Santa Cruz Sentinel (1861-1876)*, the *Santa Cruz Weekly Courier (1880-1890)*, *The Valley Press*, the *Watsonville Register-Pajaronian*.

Magazine Articles:

Rudolph Brandt, "The Ocean Shore Railroad," issue 151, *Western Railroader*, 1965.

Fabing, H.W., "The Watsonville Transportation Company," November, 1966, *Western Railroader*.

Fabing, H. W., "The San Juan Pacific Railway/The California Central Railroad," September, 1964, *Western Railroader*.

Alverda Orlando, "From Steam to Electric," March, 1975, *Rail Classics*.

Shelburne, D.J., "The Molino Timber Company," August, 1971, *Pacific News*.

Periodicals:

California Highways and Public Works Journals (July, 1934; October, 1934; April, 1937; November, 1937; October, 1938), the Inland Monthly (November, 1872), California Reports (1873-1874, Davis & Cowell vs. the San Lorenzo Railroad).

Public Records:

California Railroad Commission Applications; No. 1006 (the South Pacific Coast Railroad, March 23, 1914), No. 5663 (Ocean Shore abandonment, Santa Cruz to Swanton, May 6, 1920), No. 6070 (Ocean Shore abandonment, San Mateo County to San Francisco, August 27, 1920). California Railroad Commission Decisions; No. 3991, January, 1917; No. 4564, August 21, 1917; No. 8276 October 25, 1920; No. 14873, April 30, 1925; No. 15381, September 11, 1925; No. 15365, September 3, 1925; No. 17017, June 26, 1926; No. 18026, February 24, 1927; No.'s 21643 & 21644, October 3, 1929; No.'s 14641 & 15642, October

3, 1929; No. 24737, May 2, 1932; No. 24098, July 21, 1932; No. 25212, August 26, 1932; No. 26107, June 26, 1933; No. 32025, May 23, 1939; No. 33168, June 4, 1940. Public Utilities Commission Reports (1920 & 1921, 1925-1940).

Stock Holders Annual Reports:

Atlantic and Pacific Railroad (December 31, 1874 & 1880)

Ocean Shore Railroad Company (December 31, 1915)

San Juan Pacific Railway (1908)

Southern Pacific (1873-1942)

Miscellaneous Pamphlets, Notes, Reports, and Unpublished Theses:

Congressional Act incorporating the Atlantic and Pacific Railroad, Boston, 1870.

The Route for a Railroad to the Pacific Ocean, Boston, 1870.

San Francisco Citizens Report by the Committee of 100, June 16, 1872.

Regas, Juile, Santa Cruz Casino and Wharf Ancestory, De Anza Historical Museum, August 17, 1970.

Thomas L. & Alice M. Reedy, In the Beginning - A History of the Paradise Park Site, published by Paradise Park Masonic Club.

The Life Story of George L. Colegrove, Pioneer California Stage Driver and Railroadman, as told by himself.

Watsonville - The First Hundred Years, published by the Watsonville Chamber of Commerce, Watsonville 1952.

Melendy, H.B., One Hundred Years of the Redwood Lumber Industry (1850-1950), doctorial dissertation, Stanford University.

Southern Pacific Station List (1905), official Southern Pacific systems publication. Southern Pacific Historical Outline (1931), published by the Southern Pacific.

Aram, Joseph H., Ex-Boulder Creek Station Agent (1885-1924), Notes on the History of the South Pacific Coast Railroad, Santa Cruz, 1928.

Engineering Feasibility Study for Providing Railway Service across the Santa Cruz Mountains, Senate Bill 283, section 13, Caltrans District 4, December, 1976.

Southern Pacific Company Coast Division Employees Time Tables; September 12, 1921; March 30, 1940; May 26, 1974.

Wood, John A., Local resident since 1906, Historic Scrapbook on the Summit Area of the Santa Cruz Mountains.

Poor's Railroad Manuals of the United States, 1875-1881.

The Official Guide of the Railways, 1908, 1915, 1927, 1929, and 1933; published by the National Railway Publications Company.

California Powder Works Catalog, circa 1890 by the Company, Santa Cruz.

Books:

Abdill, George B., Pacific *Slope Railroads,* published by Superior Publishing Company,1959.

Adams, Kramer, A., *Logging Railroads of the West,* published by Superior Publishing Company, 1961.

Andrews, Ralph W., *Railroad Classic,* published by Superior Publishing Company, 1958.

Bradley, Glen D., *The Story of the Santa Fe,* published by Richard G. Badger-The Gorham Press, Boston 1920.

Dreusbach, Robert H., *Handbook of the San Francisco Region,* 1969.

Duke, Donald and Kistler, Stan, *Santa Fe-Steel Rails through California,* published by Golden West Books, 1963.

Dumscomb, Guy L., *A Century of Southern Pacific Steam Locomotives,* published by the Author.

Elliot and Moore, *History of Monterey County,* 1881.

Fleming, Howard, *Narrow Gauge Railways,* published by Inquirer Publishing Company,1876.

Fraser, J.P. and Munro, *History of Santa Clara County,* published by Alley, Bowen & Company, 1881.

Guinn, James Miller, *Santa Cruz County Biography-Central Coast California,* published by the Chapman Publishing Company, Chicago 1904.

Harrison, E.S., *History of Santa Cruz County,* published by Pacific Press Company, San Francisco, 1892.

Harrison, E.S., *Santa Cruz County — A Report for the Board of Supervisors,* published by Pacific Press Company, San Francisco, 1890.

Koch, Margaret, *Santa Cruz County — Parade of the Past,* published by Valley Publishers, Fresno, 1973.

Koch, Michael, *The Shay Locomotive — Titan of the Timber,* published by World Press   Incorporated,   1971.

Labbe, John T., and Goe, Vernon, *Railroads in the Woods,* published by Howell North, Berkeley, 1961.

Lewis, Oscar, *The Big Four,* republished by Ballantine books, 1974.

MacGregor, Bruce, *Narrow Gauge Portrait — South Pacific Coast,* published by Glenwood Press, Felton, 1975.

MacGregor, Bruce, *South Pacific Coast,* published by Howell-North, Berkeley, 1968.

Meyrick, Henry, *Santa Cruz and Monterey Illustrated Handbook,* published by San Francisco News Publishing Company, San Francisco, 1880.

314

Morison, Samuel Eliot, *The Oxford History of the American People,* published by Oxford University Press, 1965.

Myrick, David F., *Railroads of Nevada,* Volumes 1 & 2, published by Howell-North, Berkeley, 1962.

Narrow Gauge Locomotives, Baldwin Locomotive Works, republished by the University of Oklahoma Press, 1967.

Polk, R.L., and Company, *County Directory for San Mateo, Santa Clara, Santa Cruz, San Benito and Monterey Counties,* 1876

Rowland, Loen, *Annals of Santa Cruz,* printed privately, 1947.
Sawyer, Eugene Taylor, *Santa Clara County, California,* pre-1900.

Stanger, Frank M., *Sawmills in the Redwoods,* published by San Mateo County Historical Association.

Wagner, Jack, *The Last Whistle — Ocean Shore Railroad,* published by Howell-North, Berkeley, 1974.

Index

Rick Hamman has worked many jobs over the years — ranch hand, kid's ranch counselor, carnival roustabout, busboy, strawberry picker, sailor, electronic component specialist at the Stanford Linear Accelerator — but his main love has always been railroads. *California Central Coast Railways* was his first book, and he later collaborated with Horace Fabing to author *Steinbeck Country Narrow Guage*, a history of the railroads of Monterey County. He also co-authored *Restless Paradise — A Santa Cruz County Illustrated History*, has contributed to several other books, and has written numerous transportation-related articles. Rick lived for many years in Ben Lomond, in the mountains north of Santa Cruz, and even got involved in several start-up railroads in the 1990s. He currently lives in Waco, Texas, where he runs a business selling original and digitized images on the internet.

Topics in
Monterey Bay Area History

A series of works that explore specific themes in and around Santa Cruz and Monterey Counties.

Published by **OTTER B BOOKS**:

Lighthouse Point: Illuminating Santa Cruz; Frank Perry
Forever Facing South: The Story of the S.S. Palo Alto, The Old Cement Ship of Seacliff Beach; David W. Heron
Santa Cruz County, Parade of the Past; Margaret Koch
Californians: Searching for the Golden State; James D. Houston
Holy City: Riker's Roadside Attraction; Betty Lewis
Santa Cat: Behind the Lace Curtains: 1856-1926; Margaret Koch
The History of Pigeon Point Lighthouse; Frank Perry

Distributed by **OTTER B BOOKS**:

Coast Redwoods: Natural and Cultural History; Sandy Lydon et al.
Chinese Gold: Chinese in the Monterey Bay Region; Sandy Lydon
Japanese in the Monterey Bay Region; Sandy Lydon
Santa Cruz County Place Names; Donald T. Clark
Highway 17; Richard Beal
Santa Cruz is in the Heart; Geoffrey Dunn
Surf, Sand, and Streetcars; Charles McCaleb
The Santa Cruz County History Journal, Vols. 2, 3, 4, 5
Santa Cruz Mountains Trail Book; Tom Taber
Animals of the Santa Cruz Mountains; Mountain Parks Foundation
Sempervirens Story: Preserving California's Redwoods; Yaryan, Verardo
Monterey County Place Names; Donald T. Clark
Monterey County: A Dramatic Story; Augusta Fink
Above Carmel, Monterey, and Big Sur; Cameron & Gilliam
Lighthouse: Point Pinos, Pacific Grove, California; Jerry McCaffery
Creating Carmel; Harold Gilliam